378.75727
DALHOUSE

D0687532

AWN

An Island
in the Lake of Fire

An Island
in the Lake of Fire

BOB JONES UNIVERSITY,
FUNDAMENTALISM, AND
THE SEPARATIST MOVEMENT

Mark Taylor Dalhouse

The University of Georgia Press

ATHENS AND LONDON

© 1996 by the University of Georgia Press
Athens, Georgia 30602
All rights reserved
Designed by Betty P. McDaniel
Set in 10/13 Galliard
by Books International, Inc.
Printed and bound by Thomson-Shore, Inc.
The paper in this book meets the guidelines for
permanence and durability of the Committee on
Production Guidelines for Book Longevity of the
Council on Library Resources.

Printed in the United States of America

00   99   98   97   96   C   5   4   3   2   1

Library of Congress Cataloging in Publication Data

Dalhouse, Mark Taylor.
An island in the lake of fire: Bob Jones University,
fundamentalism, and the separatist movement /
Mark Taylor Dalhouse.
p.   cm.
Includes bibliographical references and index.
ISBN 0-8203-1815-9 (alk. paper)
1. Bob Jones University—History.   2. Jones, Bob, 1883–1968.
3. Evangelists—United States—Biography.
4. Fundamentalism—United States—History.   I. Title.
LD457.D45   1996
378.757'27—dc20   95-41978

British Library Cataloging in Publication Data available

Contents

Acknowledgments

Completing a book is never a one-person task. Numerous individuals, many more than I can name here, enabled me to finish this project. I wish to thank first my mentor, Dr. Jack Temple Kirby, for the moral support, encouragement, and constructive criticism that he has provided over the last four years. His office door was always open to me, and his patience with my questions seemingly inexhaustible. I also wish to thank Dr. Allan M. Winkler, Dr. Mary Kupiec Cayton, and Dr. Peter Williams. Their helpful comments and suggestions steered me through many difficult passages in the book.

Thanks must also go to the staff of the Miami University libraries, especially Dr. Richard Pettitt, Janet Stuckey, and Sarah Barr. Dr. Pettitt and Mrs. Stuckey provided an endless supply of encouragement, and Mrs. Barr, with her talents as the Interlibrary Loan librarian, secured some rather obscure papers that I needed to finish writing. I also want to thank Dr. Bob Jones Jr. and Dr. Bob Jones III for the interviews they granted and for their hospitality when I was in Greenville. They truly are the epitome of "Southern gentlemen." The staff of Mack Library at Bob Jones University were unfailingly polite and helpful during my research, as was Dr. Dan Turner of the BJU Music Department.

I must thank also the many friends and members of my family who supported me. Special thanks must go to my parents, Rodney and Margaret Dalhouse, and to my grandparents, Albert and Irene Taylor, whose love and prayers sustained me more than they will ever know. To my friends, especially Bennett Bess, Jennifer Bosch, Dann Brown, Amy Cantor, Kimberly Cooper, Howard Nicholson, Julie Phillips, Susie Urbank, Mary Ellen Delsing, Peggy Orchard, and Danny Watkins, I owe you all an eternal debt of gratitude for the friendship and support you gave to me. Finally, I want to dedicate this to the memory of my grandmother, Gay Nell Dalhouse, whose character and perseverance encouraged all who knew her and whose love of history inspired my own. Grandmother, this is for you.

*An Island
in the Lake of Fire*

The Bob Joneses—Family and Fundamentalism in Greenville

Traveling on Interstate 85 between Charlotte and Atlanta, one passes through the city of Greenville, South Carolina. The town is home to several large textile firms and to several well-known educational institutions, including Furman University and nearby Clemson University. Greenville is also home to a less well known school, but one that has played a significant role in the fundamentalist-evangelical subculture in the United States: Bob Jones University (BJU). Administered by an educational dynasty that has spanned grandfather to grandson, Bob Jones University has trained thousands of ministers, teachers, and laypeople not only in the liberal arts, business, and education but also in the mores of religious fundamentalism.

In 1989 the president of Bob Jones University, Dr. Bob Jones III, wrote that his institution "is proud to be known as fundamentalist . . . we oppose all atheistic, agnostic, and humanistic attacks upon the Scripture."[1] To the secular mind the term "fundamentalist" evokes an era in which Bible-thumping preachers tried to "win souls" and ban the teaching of evolution, yet "fundamentalist" is a badge that Bob Jones University has worn proudly for more than sixty years. The flourishing status of an institution committed to a militant theological and cultural conservatism marks Bob Jones University as worthy of note for observers of American religion.

This book seeks to understand just what makes Bob Jones University "fundamentalist." The Joneses are, of course, products of and heirs to the fundamentalist-modernist controversy that raged in the American church in the 1920s. That battle, waged by conservatives against the onslaught of modernism, gave Protestants like the Bob Joneses not only an absolutist theological worldview but an abiding taste for battle as well. In 1992, nearly seventy years after the tumultuous twenties, the eighty-one-year-old chancellor of BJU, Bob Jones Jr., could write that "Bob Jones University always does what the conditions demand—attack infidelity when infidelity lifts its head up, go after that which is unscriptural when that is being promulgated and promoted."[2]

In the 1950s, when fundamentalists such as Billy Graham, Harold Ockenga, and Carl Henry began to call themselves "new evangelicals" in an effort to shed the negativity associated with the term "fundamentalist," the Bob Joneses emerged as key leaders in opposing them. As Graham especially began to practice inclusive evangelism by working with theologically liberal Protestants and Roman Catholics, Bob Jones Jr. told a fundamentalist gathering in Chicago that the greatest religious danger was no longer modernism; it was "compromise with modernism on the part of Bible-believing Christians."[3] Shortly thereafter the university began running ads in various religious periodicals labeling themselves "ultrafundamentalist."[4] As we shall see, there were many internal as well as external factors that led the Joneses to break with the burgeoning new evangelical movement, but their critical role in this division certainly helped to give shape to a post–1920s definition of "fundamentalist." It also without question helped solidify their self-proclaimed reputation as the "world's most unusual university."

The break with Graham and the new evangelicals exacerbated a Jones penchant, manifest since BJU's founding in 1927, for separation from the mainstream, whether it was in the secular world or even among their own fundamentalist ranks. In quick succession, following the Graham controversy, the Bob Joneses severed ties with Youth for Christ, Child Evangelism Fellowship, Moody Bible Institute, and even with the editor of the militantly fundamentalist periodical *Sword of the Lord,* John R. Rice. In all these cases, the Joneses charged that the individuals and institutions involved were somehow insufficiently separatist. Then, in 1980, as Jerry Falwell launched his Moral Majority effort to mobilize fundamentalist political power, the Joneses labeled Falwell as the "most dangerous man in America."[5] Falwell's transgression, which in the Jones worldview eclipsed even the evil influences of liberalism, was his political alliance with conservative Catholics, Jews, and Mormons.

Simultaneous with their ardent pursuit of theological purity, the Bob Joneses were also actively constructing a separatist subculture for their students on the Greenville campus, one they hoped would filter out the corrosive influences of society. Billy Graham, who before his new evangelical transformation had been a student at BJU for one undoubtedly long semester, remarked later that he "just couldn't believe the rules there."[6] No movie attendance, no rock music, on-campus dating done with a faculty or staff chaperon along, no interracial dating, six days a week required chapel attendance and required Sunday church attendance, and "no griping tolerated" signs on residence hall doors—all attest to BJU's desire to provide a safe haven for students. On a campus where even in the 1990s one stolen kiss could bring a week's loss of social privileges, it is clear that the Joneses have been successful in preserving Bob Jones Sr.'s original intentions, which were, as he wrote in 1927, the creation of a place where "parents can send their children and go to sleep at night knowing their children are safe physically, mentally, and spiritually."[7]

Closely allied to the Bob Joneses' quest for pure theological associations and clean student living is also a firm, unambiguous sense of their educational mission. "We're unusual," Bob Jones III once told an interviewer, "in our objective to teach the student what he believes. . . . we wouldn't tolerate any teaching in this school that was contrary to the biblical position."[8] As we shall see,

BJU in this regard resembles the nineteenth-century denominational colleges, institutions in which the transmission of facts and
cultural values were the chief objectives. Not only does BJU adhere
to a nineteenth-century educational ideology, it has also defied
one of the mainstays of modern American higher education, accreditation. Asserting that "Bob Jones University is 'land' made up
of God's people," Bob Jones III charged that "accrediting associations will not approve our educational process if it does not include the worship of their gods. All education is brainwashing. We
wash with the pure water of God's Word, and they wash with the
polluted waters of the New Age."[9]

Looking at the Joneses' attitude toward other fundamentalists,
the student culture on their campus, and their unyielding educational philosophy, it becomes unmistakably clear that when Bob
Jones III wrote that his institution is "proud to be known as fundamentalist," he was proud of far more than just fidelity to a set of
doctrinal principles. Doctrinally, the Joneses started from the same
place as Billy Graham, John R. Rice, and Jerry Falwell. All were heir
to traditions of revivalism, holiness, premillennialism, and separatism, traditions that fused together in the early twentieth century to
produce fundamentalism.[10] Yet for the Joneses, separatism emerged
from this plethora of traditions as their defining ideology, per-
meating their worldview. So when one reads Bob Jones III's statement that BJU is "proud to be fundamentalist," one can easily
substitute "separatist" for "fundamentalist."

With the resurrected rhetoric of the seventeenth-century separatists, the Bob Joneses have carved out for themselves a distinctive
niche in conservative American Protestantism. This book is an ex-
ploration of why this separatist theme overshadowed all others in
the history of BJU. The theology of separatism, coupled with the
colorful personalities of the three Joneses and the internal dynamics of BJU, does much to explain why the break with Billy Graham
occurred, why Jerry Falwell was labeled the "most dangerous man
in America," and why BJU, despite its modern curriculum and campus, is in many respects a return to the old-time church college.
But merely explaining the theological, educational, and social rami-
fications of BJU's separatism is not enough.

We are faced with more basic questions. Why did separatism become for the Joneses the pervasive ideology that it did? Are there factors among the Joneses themselves, in the internal workings of the University, that pushed separatism to the fore? Why did this doctrine, rather than premillennialism or holiness or revivalism, come to be the Joneses' litmus test of true fundamentalism?

To pose these questions is to pull back the veil on a fascinating family and on an equally fascinating subculture in American religion. In their zeal to "come out and be separate," the Bob Joneses not only developed a critique of American religion and society, they also attracted a national constituency who shared in their alienation. Beginning with the evangelistic contacts of Bob Jones Sr. and continuing through the work of his son and grandson, the spreading of alumni throughout churches, Christian day schools, and the business world, the outreach efforts of traveling student teams and a publishing house, the Bob Joneses have created a national network that supports and publicizes their school. The existence of this constituency and the Joneses' efforts to create and sustain it throughout the nearly seventy years of BJU's existence allow us to frame more questions.

One of the most intriguing questions we can ask is how the son of a Confederate army officer could begin a school in the South that regarded racial segregation as a biblical mandate and yet, almost since its inception and continuing into the 1990s, draws its largest pool of students from Michigan, Pennsylvania, and Ohio. We might also ask why these people choose to come to a school as theologically rigid and personally restrictive as BJU, and unaccredited to boot. Yet every year three thousand or more flock from across the nation to the Greenville campus to experience "the world's most unusual university." Clearly, despite extreme rhetoric and rules that most find anachronistic, BJU is offering a product that sells. Bob Jones Sr. described the phenomenon vividly when he remarked that after tasting the "heavenly manna [of BJU]," the garlic and onions [of the world] can never taste good anymore."[11]

And yet, as we explore BJU, its commitment to theological and lifestyle separatism, and the constituency that continues to support it, we will find that the school is not a monastery and its supporters can hardly be considered separatist pilgrims. Instead, we will discover that, while this school does not allow its students to attend movie theaters, it has produced films that won awards at the Cannes film festival and represented the United States at an international film conference. We will find a school that refuses accreditation in the name of separatism yet whose graduates are regularly admitted every year to leading graduate schools around the nation. We will find a school begun by a southern revivalist whose top majors are accounting and finance and whose graduates can be found working for Merrill Lynch, IBM, Dow Chemical, Delta Air Lines, and Arthur Anderson. We will also find a school whose founder once remarked that "every time we hire a Ph.D. we need a week of revival," yet which boasts an internationally acclaimed art gallery, regularly hosts international opera companies, and whose president once regularly took faculty members to spend summers studying at Stratford-upon-Avon. We will find a school whose president, Bob Jones III, once exclaimed that the United States, thanks to the Supreme Court, was fast becoming a nation "that I can't be loyal to anymore," but who also told an interviewer that, "because they were conquered by Christ at Calvary," his students do not rebel.[12]

Bob Jones University, its founding family, and its passionate supporters, are an eclectic mix of hard-and-fast convictions and ambiguous actions. They insist they are in the world but not of it, and yet they are a bastion of nationalistic and cultural, as well as theological, orthodoxy. We will explore the separatist path trod by the Bob Joneses throughout the history of their school. We will see how, for them, "separatist" became synonymous with "fundamentalist." We will see how and why the Jones family contributed to this mindset as they set out to establish a school that would always run counter to many of the prevailing winds of twentieth-century society and religion.

To begin understanding BJU, it must first be grasped that the school is quite literally a family affair. Bob Jones Sr., Bob Jones Jr., and Bob Jones III have over a sixty-six-year period left an indelible impression upon the school that bears their name. This trio of remarkable, paradoxical, and charismatic men have built an institution where fundamentalist theology and personal loyalty to them were and are the prerequisites to success for all who work and study there. Understanding their distinct and colorful personalities is a significant step toward grasping what it is that makes this, to borrow the Joneses' own phrase, the "world's most unusual university."

Bob Jones Sr. (1883–1968), affectionately referred to as "the founder," once stood in a chapel service and asked, "So you want to know where a man stands with God? You have only to ask him one question: what do you think of this university?"[13] While such a statement was obviously self-serving, it nonetheless expressed the patriarch's firm conviction that he had established a school true to the Bible. Bob Jones Sr. was a revivalist in the mold of Billy Sunday and Sam Jones. Converted to evangelical Christianity at an early age, Jones Sr. also discovered that he had a talent for public speaking. His faith and his talent propelled him into an evangelistic career that, until he began the school in 1926, took Jones all over the United States as a revival speaker. Jones Sr. never lost his love for preaching, and until his death always referred to the ministerial students at BJU as his "preacher boys."

Jones Sr. was a man who, according to his grandson's 1992 recollection, could "preach the devil out of people" yet who was also warm and approachable in his dealings with others. Bob Jones III recalled his grandfather as a "people person," who often wandered the BJU campus with candy in one pocket and nickels and quarters in the other. Years later, Jones III encountered BJU graduates who still carried the quarter or nickel "Dr. Bob" had given them long before. The patriarch also incessantly teased others, particularly young couples he encountered on his campus wanderings, and he enjoyed shocking visitors and new students by imitating a drunk with slurred speech and disheveled clothing. Once he got the desired shocked reaction, he immediately introduced himself as Bob Jones.[14] The elder Jones saw his college through the Depression (when he was forced to declare bankruptcy), through dramatic growth in the post–World War II years, and through its move from Panama City, Florida, to Cleveland, Tennessee, to its final home in Greenville, South Carolina. When he died in 1968, he was buried on campus on a small island in the middle of a huge fountain. Every year, on the anniversary of his birth, the university celebrates "Founders Day," complete with a chapel service, featuring a recounting of Jones Sr.'s life, and an evening banquet.

Besides conceiving the school and giving it his name, Jones Sr. bequeathed other, long-lasting characteristics to his college. Bob Jones Sr. was an absolutist. In the mental world he inhabited, no ambiguity existed. The nineteenth-century Protestant values that Jones Sr. held were, as far as he was concerned, timeless. The Bible was a ready reference book of answers. It not only told humanity the correct way to heaven, it also clearly delineated such matters as the proper roles of men and women and segregation between races.

While Bob Jones Sr. may not have tolerated ambiguity, the world around him in the late nineteenth and early twentieth centuries increasingly did so. As he traversed the nation on the revival circuit, the United States was becoming increasingly urban, Roman Catholic immigrants were pouring into the cities, and both scientific and biblical scholarship was beginning to call many of the old verities into question. Bob Jones Sr., with thousands like him, was caught in the cultural transition of that period. He could not, or would not, leave that less complicated world behind. His college became a place where the old values could be resurrected.

Perhaps the most colorful member of the Jones family, and certainly the dominant figure in blazing the trail of separatism for BJU, was Bob Jones Jr. (b. 1911). He emerges from the history of the school as a man whom even his son described as "harsh, unyielding, and inflexible" when it came to defending the fundamentals of the faith and monitoring the associations of other fundamentalists.[15] This staunch commitment to ideological purity, echoing the battle cries of the seventeenth-century Puritans, led Bob Jones Jr. over the years to sever ties with Billy Graham, Youth for Christ, the Moody Bible Institute, and even other separatist fundamentalists such as John R. Rice. Jones Jr. also consistently demonstrated a distinct flair for the dramatic. In the wake of the 1970 Kent State shootings, for example, Jones stated that the antiwar movement "has stirred the wrath of God." Later he publicly called for God to "smite" a government official who displeased him.[16]

Yet, ironically, for a man so ironclad in his convictions, Bob Jones Jr. also emerges as perhaps the most paradoxical figure in the history of BJU. Raised in a home headed by a revivalist preacher, Jones Jr. grew into a man whose renditions of Shakespeare won him an offer of a screen test from Warner Brothers in the 1930s (which he refused). Like his father, Bob Jones Jr. became a preacher of the "old-time religion," but he spent his summers traveling through Europe collecting Baroque art. His love for the fine arts gave BJU a character not often found in a school run by self-proclaimed fundamentalists. This enigmatic man lent the same qualities to the school he led from 1948 to 1971, and his personality is inextricably tied to the ardently separatist, but also ambiguous, course charted by BJU over the years.

The current president of BJU, Bob Jones III (b. 1939), assumed office in 1971. Like his grandfather, he preaches old-time revivalism and, like his father, regularly performs in the college's Shakespearean dramas. Yet these were not roles he initially sought. Reminiscing in the summer of 1992, Jones III recalled his life at BJU, a life where as a boy nearly all family meals were taken in the dining common with the students, and a life where "I always had to share my father with someone else." Most of the people demanding his father's time were preachers, and Jones III remembers becoming resentful of them. "I didn't want to be a preacher," he asserted. Yet he began speaking to youth groups as early as age fourteen, and he spent two summers working with Ernest Reveal, founder of the Evansville, Indiana, Rescue Mission. In his senior year at BJU, young Jones had, as he put it, "settled with the Lord" that he would return to the college.[17] He did indeed return, serving as a residence hall supervisor, speech teacher, and assistant to his father before becoming president.

Under Jones III's leadership, BJU has gone from calling itself the "world's most unusual university" to "God's Opportunity Place." The strident separatism practiced by his father has decreased under Jones III but, as we shall see, this may be more a shift in rhetoric than in actual policy. The younger Jones led the charge against fellow fundamentalist Jerry Falwell in 1980 for aligning himself with Catholics and Mormons in the Moral Majority. He also led the school through its tumultuous conflict with the Internal Revenue Service over BJU's racially discriminatory dating policies. But now that those conflicts are past, Bob III's administration has steered the school away from advertising its "minority status" to one emphasizing the personal and academic opportunities available at BJU.

Together these three men, grandfather to grandson, have built and maintained an institution that bears their imprimatur. Under their guidance, BJU has produced scores of alumni who pastor churches, administer Christian day schools, span the globe as missionaries, teach in seminaries, and populate the business world. As we study the Joneses further, we shall see more fully how their individual personalities and style contributed to the character of this unique institution.

In addition to family, the other vital ingredient in understanding the Bob Joneses and their school is American fundamentalism. That movement, or perhaps more correctly that collection of movements, coalesced around opposition to theological liberalism, or in the parlance of the time, "modernism." Dividing individual churches and whole denominations, fundamentalists went into battle confident that the defense of the very Word of God and of civilization as they knew it rested with them. That apocalyptic worldview, coupled with the unshakable conviction that they possessed ultimate truth, are fundamentalist characteristics still present on the BJU campus. While the theological quest for doctrinal purity has been relegated to the history books for many, for the Bob Joneses the battle continues. We must now look briefly at the movement that gave life and identity to the phenomenon in Greenville.

"Heave an egg out of a Pullman window," H. L. Mencken wrote in 1925, "and you will hit a fundamentalist anywhere in the United States." Mencken's sarcasm may have overestimated the number of fundamentalists in the United States in 1925, but it signaled the addition of the word "fundamentalist" to the national vocabulary as a pejorative term. Writing in a somewhat more serious vein two years later, Maynard Shipley stated that with the advent of fundamentalism in the 1920s, "organized ignorance has come into conflict with organized knowledge."[18] For many Americans, by 1925 religious fundamentalism was the last gasp of a dying worldview overtaken by modernity. Following the rhetorical excesses of some ministers during World War I, the participation of some fundamentalists in the new Ku Klux Klan, and the disastrous Scopes Trial of 1925, the word "fundamentalist" became synonymous with uncritical patriotism, racism, and anti-intellectualism. In the cultural upheavals of the 1920s, the theological complexity and history of the term "fundamentalist" were effectively lost.

The fundamentalist controversy occurred in the 1920s, a particularly unsettled time both for the nation and for the American Protestant community. The United States was in a period of self-redefinition as the nation became more urban and as modern theories began to call old certainties into doubt. A microcosm of this transitional period could be found in the religious community. Denominations such as the Baptists and the Presbyterians experienced a series of internal convulsions that graphically portrayed the clash between the old and the new. The battle revolved around whether or not conservative Christianity, given its reliance upon the historicity and reliability of the Scriptures, offered relevant answers for the more secular age the nation had entered.

Many Protestants, calling themselves modernists, felt that the old orthodoxy was anachronistic and championed the recasting of orthodoxy by incorporating the ideas of more critical scholarship, especially the higher criticism and evolutionary theory. Other Protestants held that this new approach, in stripping away many of the supernatural elements of conservative Christianity, in effect created another religion. Most importantly, it questioned the integrity of what was for them the very Word of God. For these antimodernist Protestants, then, the stakes were the highest. The resulting clash not only changed the religious landscape by splitting churches, seminaries, and colleges, it also contributed a new word to the lexicon of American religion: fundamentalism.

The fundamentalist-modernist controversy from which Bob Jones University emerged was a battle with roots over two hundred years old. During the Enlightenment, a series of intellectual and theological developments began which, when they came to fruition, would wrack the American Church in the late nineteenth and early twentieth centuries. Enlightenment currents dealt the first severe blows to the orthodox, God-centered worldview by replacing a transcendent, personal God with an immanent, impersonal one and replacing miracles with natural processes.[19] In *What is Enlightenment?* Immanuel Kant asserted that humans were now mature and could think for themselves. Christianity, seen as superstitious and paternalistic, was no longer the authority for explanations of the world or for moral values. Instead, human reason replaced revelation. The western worldview ceased to revolve around religion.[20]

Secular rationalism influenced Christianity in a number of ways. An attitude of skepticism, encouraged by the rise in historical and literary criticism, meant that the Scriptures must be subjected to the same critical scrutiny given to other ancient documents and concepts. Historical events recorded in the Bible were particularly suspect until corroborated by some outside evidence. The biblical concept of depraved humanity also gave way to a more optimistic view of mortals that posited progress through the exercise of reason. In theology, the secular mindset helped give rise to Deism, the belief that God, rather than being transcendent with a personal interest in humans, was more of a benevolent force, which created the world but did not actively intervene in it. The most significant consequence of the Enlightenment for Christianity was that it established an atmosphere of inquiry in which religion became another topic for study rather than something to be venerated.

Closely connected to the new Enlightenment worldview was the rise of critical biblical scholarship, particularly in Germany, in the eighteenth and nineteenth centuries. One of the motivations of the early German scholars was to salvage Christianity from the onslaught of the Enlightenment. Out of this effort came theological liberalism. It is one of the ironies of fundamentalism that its greatest enemy, liberalism, began as an effort to rescue Christianity. Friedrich Schleiermacher (1768–1834), a pioneer in the field, hoped to reinterpret traditional Christianity within the new parameters established by the Enlightenment. Religion, he asserted, is based on feeling, an intuitive feeling, inside one's own consciousness, of dependence upon God. God, in other words, "was an experience."[21] Humans experienced salvation as they grew in this awareness and acted in accordance with it. The ultimate example of this and of the "God-consciousness" in each person was Jesus. A Christian was one who emulated Jesus' example. By making Christianity an experiential religion rather than a speculative one, Schleiermacher felt that he had reduced the importance of such matters as the authority of the Bible or the historicity of miracles. The "inner person" became the criterion for judging Christianity.[22]

One of the most influential German scholars was Albrecht Ritschl (1822–1889). Viewing the church as a spiritual and ethical community, Ritschl opposed the individualism which he felt accompanied orthodoxy. Christianity was not primarily a rescue from personal sin, it was rather an effort to transform society into the kingdom of God. Christians could accomplish this by living ethically, by emulating the greatest example of all, Jesus Christ. Ritschl radically reinterpreted major doctrines of Christianity: he denied the incarnation and resurrection of Christ and asserted that Christ's death on the cross was not payment for sin but functioned rather as a "moral influence" on man. Ritschl was important to the fundamentalist controversy of the next century by deeply influencing the liberals of the next generation. Adolph Harnack (1851–1930) and Walter Rauschenbusch (1861–1918) were Ritschl disciples who disseminated his ideas. Perhaps most notably, Ritschl's theology of the church striving to bring in the kingdom of God was instrumental in forming the Social Gospel theology of the late nineteenth and early twentieth centuries.[23]

The emergence of the higher criticism among German scholars would also ultimately prove damaging to conservative Christianity. Higher criticism was an effort to "read between the lines" in the biblical text.[24] It posed such questions as who wrote the text, when it was written, why and to whom it was written. "Lower criticism," conversely, dealt with more mechanical/textual problems.

It is important to emphasize that conservatives did not oppose the methods of higher criticism. Orthodox scholars regularly utilized them in their research. In the 1870s, J. B. Lightfoot of Cambridge, for example, used higher criticism to attack and eventually disprove the findings of F. C. Bauer, who in the early nineteenth century had attempted to dispute the Pauline authorship of much of the New Testament. Moreover, conservatives benefited from the rise in historical research. The discovery of the *Codex Sinaiticus* in a monastery on Mount Sinai in 1844 helped confirm the accuracy of available biblical texts. Still, without the benefit of archaeological evidence to conclusively answer all questions, many of the speculations of the German critics seemed quite damaging.[25]

Julius Wellhausen (1844–1910), for example, found different Hebrew names for God throughout the first five books of the Bible, the Pentateuch. In his *Komposition des Hexateuches* (1885), Wellhausen speculated that the use of different names meant multiple authors of the Pentateuch instead of only one, Moses. This was called the documentary hypothesis. Other scholars concluded that "Isaiah penned only half the book that bears his name, many so-called prophesies were actually written after the events they predicted, and large parts of both testaments contained myths, legends, and gross historical and even theological errors."[26]

The emergence of Darwinism in the mid-nineteenth century also had a revisionist effect upon orthodox Christianity.[27] Darwin's theories, explicated in his *The Origin of Species* (1859) and *The Descent of Man* (1871), inaugurated a scientific revolution that eventually spilled over into theology. Darwin's theory of natural selection challenged the idea of a divinely ordered world. If Darwinism were accepted, then the universe would be in effect a closed system where everything could be explained in terms of "natural" processes. The implications for a worldview holding that God had created and entered the world by supernatural means, performed miracles, died and physically rose again, were devastating. If Darwinism were true, then the biblical account of Creation, the fall of humans into sin and their need for a redeemer would all have to be reinterpreted. As one writer aptly noted, now "God's power was locked into nature's laws."[28]

Darwinism influenced theology in a number of ways. If human origins could be explained in evolutionary terms, so could the development of religious ideas. Combined with the higher criticism, Darwinism put orthodoxy on the defensive. The Bible, for example, was the record of a particular people's religious evolution, from the wrathful God of the Old Testament to the gentle ethics of the New. The Scriptures acted as a progressive discovery of God through human experience, not as a static body of theological truth. This view was reinforced as the discipline of comparative religions grew, showing how biblical episodes, such as a universal flood, appeared in other religious texts. The Bible was losing its authority and with it Christianity its distinctiveness.[29]

In 1870s and 1880s America, Darwinism and the higher criticism found a hospitable climate, helped by academic professionalization and the rise of graduate study on the German model. Numerous Protestant clergymen were taking their graduate study in German seminaries and returning home determined to incorporate the findings of higher criticism into traditional Christianity. The stage was set for conflict, as many ministers and seminary professors moved to incorporate the new findings into traditional Christianity. They were anxious not to discard Christianity, but to make it relevant for modern man, to adjust it to the new world emerging in the startling changes brought by urbanization and industrialization. These changes, and the accompanying human suffering, lent credence to the idea that God's kingdom was something to strive for now through social reform. Liberal theology appeared to accommodate this desire.[30]

The conflict was not long in coming. The new theology, positing Christianity as a product of natural historical forces, had already appeared in New England in the Unitarian and later the Congregational churches. By the early 1880s other denominations, more committed to orthodoxy, began to experience the influence of liberalism. Generally speaking, the Baptists and the Presbyterians were the denominations most influenced in the growing controversy.[31]

Crawford Toy, theology professor at Southern Baptist Seminary in Greenville, South Carolina, was dismissed in 1879 for advancing his progressive views on the origins of the Scriptures. Charles Briggs, professor at the Presbyterian Union Seminary in New York, provoked a controversy over his liberal views on the inspiration of Scripture. His opponents in the struggle, Alexander Hodge and Benjamin Warfield of Princeton, stated their "unshaken certainty that we possess a Bible written by the hands of man indeed, but also graven with the finger of God."[32] Briggs was eventually tried on charges of heresy and his case polarized the Presbyterian Church in the 1890s. Both he and Union Seminary eventually severed their ties with that denomination.[33]

Controversy among the Baptists was hastened by the activities of such men as Walter Rauschenbusch at Rochester Seminary and William Newton Clarke at Colgate Theological Seminary. Clarke's influence was particularly widespread because he authored a textbook, *An Outline of Christian Theology* (1898), that became a classic. The most notable location of Baptist liberalism was the University of Chicago Divinity School. In 1907 the Illinois Baptist Convention divided over the issue of continuing support for the Divinity School. The Northern Baptist Seminary, established in Chicago in 1913, became the conservative counterpart to the University of Chicago. Another sign of the gathering storm included the formation in 1903 of the Bible League of North America, dedicated to defending orthodox views of the Bible. In 1910 the Presbyterian General Assembly adopted a five-point doctrinal statement to which all Presbyterian ministers were required to pledge fidelity.[34]

The most significant response to liberalism, however, came from the publication between 1910 and 1915 of a series of pamphlets entitled *The Fundamentals: A Testimony to the Truth*. Written by conservative Bible scholars, *The Fundamentals* attacked Darwinism and the higher criticism and defended the essential doctrines of conservative Christianity, including the deity of Christ, his virgin birth and substitutionary death. Ultimately a total of three million copies were distributed to pastors, missionaries, college professors, and students.[35]

The First World War was a watershed in the conflict between theological conservatives and liberals. Having battled for so long the higher criticism, which emanated from German universities, many conservatives opportunistically connected the theology with German militarism. Speaking to the Bible Institute of Los Angeles in 1917, one minister warned the students that evolution inspired the idea in German minds that "might makes right" and now "it is a monster plotting world domination, the wreck of civilization and the destruction of Christianity itself."[36] This hysterical rhetoric accompanied the creation of such conservative organizations as the World's Christian Fundamentals Association (WCFA) founded in 1919. Among WCFA supporters was the Reverend Bob Jones, Senior.

Conservative alarm was heightened by the emergence of an even more aggressive liberalism after the war. An ambitious postwar plan, the interdenominational New World Movement, was also launched in 1919. This was an effort to unite the major American denominations in an attempt to combat social ills. Each participating denomination was to raise money for a collective effort to create "a civilization Christian in spirit and in passion."[37] For the conservatives, the sponsorship of the New World Movement and its goal of social reform to the exclusion of evangelism was the ultimate expression of liberal theology. They were alarmed at the prospect of subordinating their differences in order to work with liberals. To work in a joint religious venture with someone who, for example, did not believe in the virgin birth was tantamount to heresy.

The Northern Baptist Convention was particularly hard hit with the controversy. Since the 1890s, a growing rift between liberals and conservatives was evident as they clashed over control of their seminaries, colleges, mission boards, and now participation in the New World Movement. At the 1919 Baptist Convention in Denver, the denomination voted to join the ecumenical effort. Curtis L. Laws, editor of the Baptist *Watchman-Examiner,* expressed conservative dismay: "Having fought valiantly for the truth . . . are we now to compromise with error in the name of tolerance, fraternity, and Christian charity?"[38]

The battle lines were clearly drawn. At the 1920 Baptist Convention held in Buffalo, Curtis Laws used the term "fundamentalist" for the first time to describe the conservative faction. Writing in the convention issue of the *Watchman-Examiner,* Laws suggested "that a new word be adopted to describe the men among us . . . we suggest that those who still cling to the great fundamentals of the faith . . . be called 'Fundamentalists.'" The term, in its original use, was simply another designation for theological conservatives, those who believed the Bible to be the error-free Word of God, who accepted the historicity of miracles and the status of Jesus Christ as God incarnate.[39]

Theological liberals had begun to identify themselves as "modernists." From their perspective, fundamentalism denoted not only a doctrinal stance but also an attitude of hostility toward theological research and science. Shailer Mathews, Dean of the Divinity School at the University of Chicago, defined modernism as the "use of scientific, historical, social method in . . . applying evangelical Christianity to the needs of living persons. . . . Modernism is the evangelicalism of the scientific mind."[40]

Coexistence between these two factions increasingly proved impossible. At first, fundamentalists elected to stay within their denominations to fight modernism. Within the Northern Baptist Convention, for example, first the Fundamentalist Fellowship and then the Baptist Bible Union formed to contest the liberals for the control of missions boards and seminary trustee boards. Repeatedly they suffered defeats at the annual national conventions. The more militant members of the Baptist Bible Union favored a complete schism from the Baptist Convention.[41]

One of the leaders of the schismatic Baptists was Robert Ketcham, a pastor from Niles, Ohio, who maintained that "modernism is so thoroughly entrenched in the machinery of the Northern Baptist Convention that it can never be eliminated."[42] One of his Presbyterian counterparts, J. Gresham Machen of Princeton, agreed completely. Asserting that "liberalism is not Christianity," Machen advised that "a separation between the two parties in the church is the crying need of the hour."[43] Both Ketcham and Machen eventually led conservatives out of their respective denominations and formed their own, the General Association of Regular Baptist Churches (1932) and the Presbyterian Church of America (1929). Thus fundamentalists erected a bulwark against the onslaught of what they considered quite literally the forces of darkness. For these conservatives the issue was ultimately one of separating from what they regarded as religious error, error that would send souls to hell.

From the 1920s to the present, fundamentalism has been characterized, first, by an unshakable fidelity to doctrinal purity and, second, by a penchant for separating from anything or anyone that might compromise that purity. Defeated in their efforts to stem the tide of modernism within their denominations, the target of national laughter after the Scopes Trial, some fundamentalists responded by withdrawing. Yet they did not stop with mere separation. Almost immediately, a fundamentalist subculture was erected. One of the supports of that subculture, and from the fundamentalist perspective one of the most effective ways to continue countering liberalism, was the building of seminaries and colleges. Such efforts ensured both a "safe" environment for orthodox young people and the continuation of fundamentalist beliefs. It was out of this milieu of consternation at apostate denominations and a positive desire to provide young people with an alternative that Bob Jones College emerged in 1926.

The fundamentalism that gave life to BJU is alive and well on the Greenville campus today. Elements of the various strands of nineteenth-century Protestant belief—revivalism, premillennialism, the optimistic idea that God's kingdom could somehow be ushered in on earth, holiness, and separatism—which merged together in the twentieth-century fundamentalist movement, can all be found at BJU in their theology, educational philosophy, and in their view of culture and society. Separatism emerged from this plethora of sometimes incompatible traditions to give coherence and shape to the fundamentalism practiced at BJU. As we shall see, the reasons for the triumph of separatism at BJU lie in large part with the Jones family and their response to a rapidly changing world and to events within their institution. Their success in articulating a separatist worldview appealed to many fundamentalists across the nation, who in turn gave the Bob Joneses their fervent support both in students and money. Like the fundamentalist movement that produced them, the Bob Joneses and their constituency travel a controversial and sometimes paradoxical path. For the Jones family, that journey began not in a theological seminary or at a denominational convention, but on a small farm in the Wiregrass region of southeastern Alabama.

CHAPTER ONE

The Patriarch and the Foundation

The counties of Covington, Geneva, Coffee, and Dale in southeastern Alabama comprise an area called the Wiregrass region. The name comes from the long, tenacious, mostly underground grass that thrives in the sandy soil of the area and makes the land poor for crops but good for grazing livestock. Following the devastation of the Civil War, the Wiregrass area, like much of the South, was plunged into economic chaos. Prices for farm goods plummeted, tenancy and debt rose, and the region struggled to make the transition to a successful commercial economy. Trying to adapt to these changes, farmers in southeastern Alabama attempted to produce cotton, but the soil was too poor; so many reverted to raising livestock and subsistence farming.[1] It was into these times, on October 30, 1883, that Bob Jones was born to a Dale County yeoman farmer, William "Alex" Jones, and his wife, Georgia Creel Jones.[2]

The southern world that young Robert Reynolds Jones came to know in the 1880s and 1890s was a place where sentimentality for the defeated Confederacy reigned, where indebted farmers struggled for existence against forces they did not understand, where a man's "honor" was his most prized possession, and where revivalist religion provided solace and meaning.[3] Through his parents young Jones came into contact with each of these elements, and the values they forged in the young man would permeate his evangelistic career and later, his life as an educator.

Bob Jones was named after Robert Reynolds, a soldier in the Confederate Army who had saved the wounded Alex Jones in the battle of Chickamauga. Alex Jones's service in Company H, 37th Alabama Regiment, formed a compelling memory the elder Jones passed on to his son. Bob Jones later remembered that as long as his father lived, "he would talk about the Yankee who shot him."[4] His service in the Confederate Army was not the only memory Alex Jones shared with his son. Writing nearly forty years later, Bob Jones reflected, "I came along at the ragged end of the Reconstruction days, and I heard the story of the reign of the carpetbaggers and the scalawags."[5] His father's memories imparted to young Jones a sense of heritage at once proud and tragic. Bob Jones, once he became a father, would take his own son to the Confederate Memorial Day festivities in Montgomery, pervaded, as Bob Jones Jr. later recalled, by the clear feeling of regret "that the South had not won the Civil War."[6]

For Alex Jones, as for so many other Confederate veterans who returned to farming after the war, economic life was complicated by changes that seemed out of control. Like many others in southeastern Alabama, Alex Jones returned to semisubsistence farming. Unable to afford the cost of hiring laborers, Jones used his sons as plowhands, and young Bob took the crops to nearby Dothan.[7] By the 1880s and 1890s, farmers like Alex Jones felt great frustration at a system that appeared to cater to large landowners and merchants. Their frustration eventually took the form of political activism, and Alex Jones served as a secretary for the local chapter of the Farmers Alliance.[8]

A forerunner of the Populist Party, the Alliance felt, as one writer noted, "that a conspiracy was afoot to deprive them of what should be rightfully theirs."[9] The Alliancemen had definite ideas about who might be involved in such a conspiracy. They railed against trusts and monopolies and against the rise of industrial towns in Alabama. The growth of the cities particularly frightened them.

The Alliancemen, who steadfastly believed in the moral superiority of the rural way of life, felt that both their economic status and their traditional values were threatened by the cities.[10] Alex Jones's participation in the Alliance made an impact upon his son. Years later evangelist Bob Jones castigated the cities as a corrosive influence upon the nation's morals and pointed to the "country" as more pure.[11]

The South Bob Jones knew in the 1880s and 1890s was still in many respects, to employ one observer's phrase, a "culture of honor." In such a setting individuals were "ready to take matters into their own hands when revenge for familial loss was required."[12] Jones family lore contained a story of Alex Jones avenging an insult upon his grandfather. According to Bob Jones, when Alex found the offending party, they physically "fought for two hours. . . . That is the way they settled their differences in the old days."[13] Another aspect of "honor" emphasized the importance of character formation and self-discipline. This influence appeared later, when as a college president Bob Jones tossed "more potential life mottoes at his students than the average gift shop would sell in year." These aphorisms included "you can do anything you ought to do," "do right until the stars fall," and "the test of your character is what it takes to stop you."[14]

Evangelical Christianity, a powerful tradition throughout the South, was the single most important formative influence upon Bob Jones. A series of revivals in the early nineteenth century had introduced camp-meeting style revivalism to the region.[15] Spread by Baptist missionaries and Methodist circuit riders, it seemed, in religion historian Samuel Hill's words, "to penetrate every hollow, valley and plain."[16] The message the revivalists preached was an intensely individualistic one. Presented with their sinful state before God, individuals were urged to repent and accept God's provision through Christ's sacrificial death upon the cross, or else face the fires of hell for eternity.[17]

This personal decision for Christ was the most important event in one's life. Since eternal destinies were at stake, evangelizing lost sinners was the first priority for evangelical/revivalist Christianity.

Systematic theology and formal worship were reduced in importance. Ethics were presented in a personal rather than a social context. Thus, after being "saved," one was to concentrate upon personal reformation. Evangelistic preaching tended toward persuasion and exhortation rather than instruction.[18] It was also intensely emotional.[19]

In the postbellum decades evangelical Christianity in the South experienced tremendous growth. Among the Southern Methodists, the denomination in which Bob Jones was reared, membership in the churches doubled in the fifteen years following the Civil War.[20] The Southern Methodists illustrated many revivalist traits.[21] John Wesley, the founder of Methodism, had emphasized "inward experience and personal holiness" in his evangelistic travels.[22] His heirs, the circuit-riding preachers of the nineteenth century, continued in that tradition. Many if not most of these preachers were not formally ordained. Formal schooling was not required, only familiarity with the Bible and Wesley's sermons and an ability to articulate the evangelistic message. Even after he became president of a college, Bob Jones reflected on his Southern Methodist background when he observed that "the deader preachers get the more they seem to emphasize ordination."[23] Also, since so much emphasis was placed upon evangelism and the individual's relationship to God, "the prevalence of the social order," as Samuel Hill observed, "was simply taken for granted" among revivalist preachers.[24] It was this kind of revivalist heritage that Bob Jones knew as a youngster in his father's house.

In the Alex Jones household, the Bible was read every evening and family prayer offered. Attendance at Sunday services and revival services was a regular part of life. It was at a revival meeting, at age eleven, that Bob Jones had his conversion experience. The evangelist preached on the cripple in the gospels, who in his effort to get to Jesus had his friends lower him through the roof of the house where Jesus was staying. For Jones, "I got the idea that night that the fellow got to Jesus and got alright [sic]; so I went up front and kneeled down and got to Jesus."[25]

It was also in church that Jones developed a trait that later had a significant influence upon his career: an ability to speak in public. Reciting lessons and Bible verses in Sunday school, Jones remembered adults peering through the windows to hear him. He also "preached" to other groups of children and would often go into the woods to practice speaking. Alex Jones encouraged this in his son, having the boy memorize and recite Bible passages, newspaper articles, and poems. Often Alex had his son recite to visitors in the Jones home, an exercise that helped Bob overcome a certain initial timidity and self-consciousness. A traveling minister was so impressed with the young Jones that he arranged for Jones to attend school on a nine-month basis. Jones credited these experiences with preparing him for an evangelistic career.[26] At fourteen he was preaching revival services and was licensed to preach at fifteen.[27]

While conducting small revival services in Alabama, Jones also found time to further his education. Beginning in 1900, he attended Southern University, a Methodist school in Greensboro, Alabama. (The school is now in Birmingham and has been renamed Birmingham-Southern College.)[28] Jones paid for his education with the offerings he received from preaching in different churches.[29] Jones spent three years at Southern, and while he did not graduate, he received important exposure to a liberal arts environment. He remembered, however, that these liberal studies took place in a strict, theologically orthodox setting. At Southern, Jones remarked, "there were no modernists. Everybody believed the Bible in those days."[30] Undoubtedly this memory of a "sound" educational environment influenced Jones later, when he built a college.[31]

Evangelistic preaching, meanwhile, increasingly occupied Jones as he entered his twenties, in the first decade of the new century. By his own admission, Jones did not plan to become an evangelist. It was a matter, he said, of "entering open doors."[32] Swamped with speaking invitations, Jones found his ministry almost by default, and his career as an evangelist made lasting contributions to his life. At a revival service in Uniontown, Alabama, in 1908, the evangelist met Mary Gaston Stollenwerck, daughter of a prominent

Uniontown family. They were married shortly thereafter. Their only child, Bob Jones Jr., was born on October 19, 1911.[33]

Jones had begun his evangelistic career in an era characterized by large revivals and flamboyant preachers.[34] Among the most notable of the period were Billy Sunday, J. Wilbur Chapman, "Gypsy" Smith, William E. Biederwolf, and Sam P. Jones. It was Dwight L. Moody, however, evangelist of the mid-nineteenth century, who had most decisively set the stage for turn-of-the-century revivalism.[35] Moody introduced the practice of conducting revival services virtually as a business enterprise. Speaking in numerous American cities in the 1870s, Moody "advanced" his revival campaigns with finance, publicity, and prayer committees several weeks prior to his appearance. He enlisted the assistance of a song leader, Ira Sankey, to recruit choirs for the revival and to conduct congregational singing before Moody launched into his message. Moody forcefully preached what he called the "three r's": "ruin by sin, redemption by Christ, and regeneration by the Holy Spirit." After the sermon, an "invitation" was given so that people could respond to the offer of salvation. Moody was tremendously successful, attracting huge crowds and securing thousands of decisions for Christ.[36]

Two of Moody's most successful imitators—and two of the biggest influences upon Bob Jones—were Billy Sunday and Sam Jones.[37] Sunday, a professional baseball player turned revivalist, was most prominent from 1895 to 1920. He attracted huge crowds, thanks both to professional advance work and to his own theatrical style. During his sermons Sunday would "do push-ups on the platform while preaching at his full rapid force. Darting to the side of the pulpit, he might suddenly grab a chair, and while shaking it in the air, call the devil every name he dared."[38] Sunday not only preached salvation, he also advocated certain social and political ideas, especially Prohibition. He attacked what he perceived as a decline in traditional morality, corruption in the cities, and the increasing inroads modernism was making in the orthodox churches. Although never as flamboyant as Sunday, Bob Jones reiterated many of the same themes in his own preaching. The two men appeared together several times on the same platform, and on at least one occasion, Jones helped "advance" a Sunday crusade through the South. Jones illustrated his high regard for Sunday when, after the latter's death, Jones placed Sunday's widow on the Bob Jones University Board of Trustees and named a campus building after her.[39]

Sam Porter Jones, a Methodist evangelist from Georgia, was also a significant influence upon Bob Jones. For Bob Jones, "God raised up Sam Jones down South to shake the formality out of the church people."[40] Sam Jones preached the old-time gospel message along with a vision of a world in which there would be "no liquor, no laziness, no unseemly entertainments, no high society frivolity."[41] In his preaching Bob Jones repeated many of the same themes. Sam Jones also offered character-building witticisms in his preaching and published a small book of them, *Sam Jones' Sayings*.[42] Bob Jones followed suit later when he published *Chapel Sayings of Dr. Bob Jones*.[43]

Bob Jones's evangelistic career spanned his entire life, even though after 1927 he was primarily occupied with his college. The years of full-time evangelism spanned 1900 to 1927. Jones began with meetings throughout Alabama, where his reputation as a forceful evangelist emerged. In 1908, in Dothan, the response following a Jones revival resulted in city officials closing the local liquor dispensary.[44] Jones recalled that after some of his meetings "some of the towns actually opened headquarters downtown for people to restore money or property they had stolen." Such occurrences after revivals were not uncommon. Jones soon began receiving speaking invitations outside Alabama.[45]

Jones followed the organizational format established by Moody. Meetings took place in large municipal buildings or in hastily constructed "tabernacles."[46] An advance man, Willis Haymaker, accompanied Jones on his travels. There was always a rousing song service before the preaching. Jones's sermons predominantly concerned salvation, and an invitation to the "lost" was always given at the end of a sermon. One group of ministers praised Jones for "his ability to draw and hold by his messages large audiences. . . . Hundreds have been converted and thousands of church people renewed in their spiritual life."[47]

Jones's years as an evangelist coincided with one of the most pronounced transition periods in American history. Change could be found almost everywhere, as the nation's cities grew at a phenomenal rate, as a flood tide of immigrants changed the complexion and religion of the cities, and as the advent of the automobile and radio revolutionized American life. Many Americans were not comfortable with these changes. They feared that nineteenth-century Protestant values were being undermined by the "loose" morality endemic in the cities and by the wave of Roman Catholic immigrants coming to the United States from southern and eastern Europe. The sense of instability was exacerbated in the post–World War I years, as the popularity of Freudian psychology and the divorce rate rose and as the optimism and idealism of the pre-war years seemed to collapse into narcissism.[48]

Jones's activities and sermons during these years demonstrated that he was part of that conservative Protestant coalition beginning to fear the demise of Protestant cultural and moral values. Their reaffirmation of traditional values expressed itself in such movements as Prohibition, resurgent nativism, and a virulent anti-Catholicism. Jones had long been active in the Prohibition movement. As early as 1911, he traveled as far away as Montana to speak for Prohibition.[49] Jones once turned a funeral service for an executed murderer who had killed his wife on a drunken rampage into a speech for Prohibition.[50] With Prohibition, Jones asserted, "the hour has come when God-fearing men shall rule."[51]

The rise of nativism in the post–World War I years also influenced Jones. A fresh wave of eight hundred thousand immigrants between June 1920 and June 1921 intensified nativist feeling and helped fuel the second Ku Klux Klan.[52] While Bob Jones was never a member of the Klan, he clearly shared their antipathy to foreigners. Since most of the immigrants congregated in the large cities, Jones and other nativists concluded that they were at least partially responsible for urban immorality. "Only twenty percent of Chicago's population is native-born," Jones observed in 1927. "If I owned Chicago and Hell I would sell Chicago and live in Hell."[53] He denounced "degenerate, unassimilated foreigners" and advised his listeners that "the boats run both ways, and these folks who are here for our loaves and fishes can go back to Russia or someplace else."[54]

Xenophobia was closely linked with renewed anti-Catholicism. As Jones traveled the evangelistic circuit in the 1920s, Alabama considered a law requiring the state to inspect convents (where arms might be hidden), and Michigan and Nebraska legislators considered proposals banning parochial schools.[55] The high point of anti-Catholicism in the 1920s was the 1928 campaign against New York Governor Alfred Smith's presidential candidacy. A more inviting target for conservative Protestants could scarcely be imagined. Smith was an opponent of Prohibition, a stereotype of the urban politician, and a Roman Catholic.[56]

Jones actively participated in the campaign against Smith. He toured Alabama in the fall of 1928, blasting Smith and Catholicism. Opposing the Democratic presidential nominee in the solidly Democratic South was a bold political act. The *Montgomery Advertiser* attacked Jones for his Republican stance and intimated that the Klan had hired Jones to misrepresent Smith.[57] Endorsing Herbert Hoover in an October 1928 editorial in his *Bob Jones Magazine,* Jones revealed the way in which Smith's candidacy had become a symbol of the changes sweeping the nation. Smith represented Roman Catholicism, and for ministers like Jones that church stood "for ignorance, superstition and slavery of the human soul. The things that made America great are the very things Al Smith's religion opposes." Smith was a symbol of the flood of immigrants entering the United States who, Jones told his readers, congregate "in the big cities . . . and hold to their foreign traditions. They are for Al Smith." Smith was associated with the "city idea of American government," a concept opposed to the "country idea," which supported "God and decency." Smith's candidacy, Jones concluded, "is a challenge to pure, old-time, honest-to-God Americanism."[58]

Jones also delivered a sermon/lecture during the 1920s entitled "The Perils of America." Given in numerous revivals and church services, "The Perils of America" was an excellent reflection of the cultural upheaval many Americans felt during this decade. The sermon revealed Jones as a man uncomfortable with the direction of the new century and anxious to return to what he regarded as a more idyllic time. Jones linked the transition of the 1920s with spiritual crisis.

In his sermon Jones envisioned a world in which there was no ambiguity. It was a world uncorrupted by large cities and their baneful moral influence, a world where the Bible functioned as the supreme authority, providing not only firm moral guidance but accurate historical accounts of humanity's past as well, and a world where young people were educated with moral and theological absolutes. For Jones, this world had in fact once existed in America. Its architects were the early settlers and "old-time Americans" who "watched through the key-holes of their homes with one eye on the Indians and with the other eye they read the Bible. . . . They wrote the name of God on everything they touched . . . when they laid the foundations of this civilization."[59] For conservative Protestants of the 1920s, recovery of this lost world became their paramount social purpose. Formidable obstacles stood in the way, however: rapid urbanization, immigrant Catholics' great numbers, and the new moral ambiguity. Jones also feared the forces of theological modernism that were divesting the Bible of its authority. There was a new concern which became acute for Jones: state universities and even denominational colleges appeared to be destroying the faith of thousands of young people from Christian homes.

Large cities were a favorite Jones target. They were contagious dens of iniquity abetted by technology. "Picture shows, automobiles, and modern travel," Jones thundered, "have taken the influences of the cities to the country." As a result, even "country girls" now wore "paint," the "latest bob," and silk dresses and hose. The Sabbath was no longer respected; people preferred to go to the picture shows in the city on Sundays. The issue was simple: "if the cities go to hell, they take the country to hell with them."[60]

"The Perils of America" also assailed modernism's inroads within many denominations. The 1920s were the years when the fundamentalist-modernist controversy reached its peak. Bob Jones's involvement in this phase of the struggle was tangential. As a well-traveled evangelist, however, Jones was aware of the growing controversy and was actively involved in at least one organization that was decidedly fundamentalist, the Winona Lake Bible Conference, based at Winona Lake, Indiana. Founded in 1896 by evangelist J. Wilbur Chapman, the Winona Conference functioned as a sort of trade organization for evangelists, a place where they gathered every summer to discuss "trade secrets . . . new techniques . . . and the problems facing the profession."[61] The conference brought together such well-known men as Billy Sunday, William Jennings Bryan, and William E. Biederwolf. In the summer of 1920, the Winona Conference sponsored a resolution by Bob Jones and William Biederwolf stating that evangelists associated with the conference would not preach under the auspices of theological liberals.[62]

In "The Perils of America," Jones asserted that modernist preachers did not preach "repent or perish" but instead "are giving a little message on ethics or talking about social service."[63] This statement revealed the increasingly popular line among fundamentalists equating social activism with theological liberalism. The statement was ironic, considering that Jones's advocacy of Prohibition had made him an ally of many theological liberals who considered Prohibition part of the Social Gospel agenda.[64] It was also ironic in that many nineteenth-century revivalists had been among the most prominent social activists. In any event, Jones's rhetoric signaled the increasing affinity between post–World War I theological conservatism and social and political conservatism.[65]

Modernists also came under fire because they did not appeal "to the authority of the Bible to back their utterances." Modernism, Jones charged, was given to explaining away the Scripture in terms of myth, reducing it in effect to just another collection of Hebrew documents. For Jones, not preaching an authoritative, inerrant Scripture was the most crucial error of the modernists. His rhetoric on this point illustrates well the way in which the theological crisis also had cultural overtones. Without an authoritative Bible, almost any heresy could be entertained. More ominously, without the unquestioned authority of the Bible, modernists created a vacuum into which Roman Catholicism, the religion of the immigrants, would move. Rome offered an infallible Pope, a magnet to "crowd [people] into your Roman Catholic churches." Conversely, liberal Protestant ministers were emptying churches as they planted doubts about the Bible's reliability. The modernists were therefore "enemies to Protestantism. They are destroying the foundations under all our Protestant civilization."[66]

A third concern expressed in "The Perils of America" was Jones's growing conviction that both state and some church-related colleges were becoming secularized, undermining Christian beliefs and the morals of young people. Jones correctly perceived a trend that had been underway since the Civil War. Prior to that time, most colleges were religiously affiliated, administered by clergy and dedicated to the inculcation of ethics and "mental discipline."[67] After the war, as industrial growth accelerated, funds from the federal government and private industry flowed to higher education. Churches became less important to schooling. In private and public institutions businessmen and other laymen began replacing ministers on boards of trustees and as college presidents. Further, adoption of the German graduate training model with its emphasis on scholarship and freedom, as one writer put it, meant that many institutions became concerned less with "transmission of the old than with experimentation with the new."[68] President Charles Eliot of Harvard University articulated the new attitude when he observed that "a university cannot be founded upon a sect."[69]

Darwinism was an important catalyst in this move toward secularization. Championing investigation and hypothesis, Darwinism revolutionized academic life by making science the preeminent discipline and by creating an atmosphere in which new social sciences such as psychology and sociology proliferated. Most important, Darwinism encouraged the assumption that academic research, in Mark Noll's phrase, "carried with it no antecedent commitments to a world view."[70] By the early twentieth century it became increasingly apparent that American higher education, rather than buttressing the religious order as it had since colonial times, was now instead a competitor with religion.

Even denominational colleges soon felt the effects of this revolution. In the later nineteenth century at least three faculty members—one each from Vanderbilt (Southern Methodist), Southern Baptist Seminary (Southern Baptist), and Columbia Theological Seminary (Presbyterian)—were dismissed for holding heretical views on evolution and the origins of the Bible. By 1914 the liberal president of Vanderbilt University, James Kirkland, had successfully wrested control of his board of trustees away from the Southern Methodist bishops, and during the 1920s a self-proclaimed evolutionist, William Louis Poteat, was the president of North Carolina's largest Baptist school, Wake Forest College.[71]

Kirkland and Poteat seemed so dangerous to conservatives because they articulated a vision of Christian education that incorporated the new educational model and the new discoveries in science. Kirkland, the driving force behind the formation of the Southern Association of Colleges and Schools in 1895, vigorously rejected the notion that a Christian institution had to be chained to dogma, asserting instead that the duty of all schools was "to teach the truth, so far as it is known, and then to discover more truth."[72] When the evolution controversy rocked Tennessee in 1925, President Kirkland called for the "establishment on this campus of a school of religion, illustrating in its methods and organization the strength of a common faith." This was, he said, the best "remedy for a narrow sectarianism and belligerent fundamentalism."[73] Poteat of Wake Forest, speaking at Chapel Hill in 1925, assailed the fundamentalists for equating "the new learning with heresy. . . . Did not the King of the truth-seekers say, 'Ye shall know the truth and the truth shall set you free?'"[74] The fundamentalists, Poteat argued, "were making it difficult for intelligent, educated men to be Christians."[75] For conservatives, such rhetoric was merely a smokescreen to hide attacks upon the Bible. They registered their alarm by launching faculty purges and passing doctrinal creeds at denominational gatherings.[76]

Bob Jones shared this alarm, arguing in "The Perils of America" that "the educational institutions in America are sleeping over atheistic volcanoes." For Jones, the chief culprit in the destruction of the schools was Darwinism. There could be no reconciliation between evolution and the Bible. "Is this old book," Jones asked, "written with the finger of inspiration . . . to flee the stage because Mr. Darwin guessed about how everything was made?" Evolution was far more than an attack upon the Bible; it was wreaking havoc among the current generation of college students. Jones maintained that since evolution entered the curriculum, young people in universities were "talking about birth control, race suicide, trial marriages, etc." Jones painted a picture of the nation's universities overrun with atheism. He vowed to battle this trend "if Jesus Christ tarries his Coming and spares me in good health."[77]

If evolution posed a threat to Christian education, so did the new academic model with its emphasis upon more freedom for both faculty and students. The elective system, for example, was not merely a new educational innovation, it was a threat to the character of college students. "When I went to school," Jones related, "we had no elective system . . . we were taught to do the hard things. . . . Times have changed. Now young folks go to school and take what they want to take. They have come to believe that whatever they want, they have a right to have." Instead, Bob Jones recommended "good, old-time iron-handed discipline" for young people who were at the "most impetuous period of their lives." Indeed, it was a crime to do otherwise.[78]

As Jones traveled the evangelistic circuit in the 1920s delivering his sermon, his indictment of modern education began to take on a special urgency. Jones met parents who related stories of their children's defection from the faith in state universities and church colleges. One instance particularly influenced Jones: visiting with a missionary after one of his messages, Jones learned that the man had helped found a denominational college. When his son was ready for college, the missionary sent the boy to the school, thinking "he will come back to us as good as when he left us." Instead, the missionary related, "while I had been preaching in my country churches, the devil had been sowing tares in the college. A skeptic had gotten in the science department. . . . My boy came home an atheist." The man urged Jones to "go up and down this country and tell this story."[79]

Such complaints were echoed elsewhere. Theodore T. Martin, a prominent conservative Baptist, lamented in 1920 that "bitter tears over the wrecked faith" of young people were being shed, thanks to modernism in Baptist schools.[80] H. C. Morrison, president of the Methodist Asbury College, warned that in colleges where modernists and Darwinists were employed, "the Word of God is discarded, the Son of God is rejected, and the Holy Spirit is grieved away."[81] Even the liberal Protestant observer Edwin Poteat Jr. observed that "a generation of young people is arising that knows not the shibboleths of early orthodoxy."[82]

Clearly, of all the concerns Jones expressed in his famous lecture, his analysis of education elicited the greatest response from his listeners. In a world perceived as increasingly out of control, the education of their young was for many fundamentalists the last opportunity to turn back the tide of secularism. The vigor of the antievolution crusade was a testament to this near panic. For Bob Jones, the greatest frustration was, as he related to one group, "leading boys and girls to Jesus Christ and then seeing them attend institutions which shake their faith."[83] Thus the declining state of American education became, from Jones's perspective, an encapsulation of the many ills he saw besetting Protestant values. Interestingly, in the middle 1920s, as his attacks upon colleges drew ever more enthusiastic responses, Jones did not advocate the "purging" of established schools, as his counterpart J. Frank Norris did in Texas in the early part of the decade. Rather, by 1926, Jones was entertaining the idea of establishing his own school, one that he envisioned becoming the "greatest interdenominational, orthodox educational center in the world."[84]

Jones's ambition corresponded to a larger development within the fundamentalist movement. Repeatedly defeated in efforts to reform what they regarded as apostate denominations, the victims of national laughter during the Scopes Trial, many fundamentalists concluded that persistence in these efforts was futile. Separation was their recourse. A fundamentalist subculture began to grow as conservative schismatics broke from the Baptists and Presbyterians and as the Bible institute movement received new momentum.[85] Not only did the Bible institutes train preachers and evangelists, they also spawned an ever-growing number of evangelical periodicals and, in the 1920s, radio stations, such as WMBI, the voice of Moody Bible Institute.[86] This growth surge in the late 1920s indicated the existence of a constituency to which the idea of an orthodox, "safe" college would appeal. Jones clearly sensed this as he traveled the nation. Jones knew people would readily send their children to such a school. His more immediate problem was acquiring the capital to build a college.

As a nationally known evangelist, Jones had become one of southeastern Alabama's more prominent citizens. This status brought Jones into contact with powerful figures who, even if they were not religious fundamentalists, might be persuaded to support a venture such as a local college. In addition, Jones's advocacy of conservative social ideas in his sermons undoubtedly endeared him to others who might support a college dedicated to those ideals. Among those Jones could count as friends were the soon-to-be governor of Alabama, Bibb Graves; S. H. Blan, Alabama state auditor; Georgia congressman William Upshaw; and *Atlanta Constitution* columnist Sam Small. With the exception of Small, all of these men would serve on the Bob Jones College Board of Trustees. Their names lent Jones's efforts a status they might not otherwise have enjoyed. This was especially true with Alabama governor Bibb Graves.

Graves, elected in 1926 with the endorsement of the Ku Klux Klan, became in his two terms a supporter of child welfare, public health services, and higher taxes on corporations.[87] He also gained a reputation as an opportunistic politician, accepting Klan support in 1926 and leading a crackdown upon the order the next year. He could also support Prohibitionist evangelist Bob Jones without being a "dry" by conviction.[88] Helping the noted evangelist begin a college would reap dividends with more conservative voters. In addition to serving on the board of trustees, Graves gave the keynote address at the ground-breaking for the school in December 1926. Most importantly, Graves enabled Jones to solicit funds for his school with members of Birmingham's financial community. Graves himself once approached the prominent Birmingham businessman Donald Comer for funds on behalf of Bob Jones College.[89] Jones's trust in Graves was such that in 1930, as economic conditions began adversely to affect the school, Jones asked Graves to serve on a committee to investigate financial options. When the school was forced to leave Florida in 1933, Jones turned once again to Graves, telling the governor that "I am depending upon your brains and advice." Graves may also have been instrumental in introducing Jones to a Wall Street lawyer, Raymond Crane, who served on the board and contributed substantial amounts.[90]

Jones's acquaintance with Atlanta congressman William Upshaw and columnist Sam Small also insured other valuable connections. Upshaw had been active both in Prohibition and the antievolution campaigns and was well known to those constituencies. He had also once published a journal in Atlanta, *The Golden Age,* which advocated "patriotic education."[91] Small reached a sizable audience with his column in the *Atlanta Constitution.* Praising Jones as "a clear-headed businessman, an inspirer of confidence and courage," Small also informed his readers that "cultured and financially competent men and women in many states are giving encouragement to the Bob Jones College enterprise."[92] These connections gave Jones valuable publicity and undoubtedly eased his fundraising chores. With this kind of support Jones could turn his attention to the problems of locating and funding his college.

The middle 1920s witnessed a major land boom in the state of Florida. In 1925 a businessman visiting Miami found "real estate madness. . . . Everyone seemed to be shaking hands, offering cigars, studying mysterious diagrams of 'desirable subdivisions'."[93] Though this mania was largely burned out by 1926 in southern Florida, land speculation continued to surge forward in northwestern Florida where, a local historian noted, it was "not uncommon for $5,000,000 worth of real estate to change hands weekly."[94]

Panama City, located in Bay County, was one of the hottest spots in northwestern Florida. The Tallahassee *Florida State News* in 1927 labeled Panama City a scene of "prosperity and optimism. . . .

Homes are being built everywhere . . . businesses are being erected and the city has every outward and inward appearance of being one of the livest places in all Florida." By 1926 two major new hotels had been constructed to accommodate the town's growing tourist industry, and a major rail line was completed the same year, linking Panama City with Dothan, Alabama.[95] With the local economy booming and, most importantly, with land plentiful and still cheap, Bob Jones decided upon Panama City as the location for his school. Jones was already well known in the area for his evangelistic crusades, and Panama City, only eighty-five miles from Jones's home of Dothan, was close enough for Jones to continue to cultivate the Alabama business community for funds.

The site chosen for Bob Jones College was known as Long Point, a promontory projecting into North Bay. Long Point was part of a 2500-acre property owned by New York real estate developer Minor C. Keith. Early in 1926, when Jones and Keith discussed the possibility of building a school on this land, Keith Properties was already dividing the land into residential lots. Although complete details of their discussions are not available, it is reasonable to infer that the deal they struck enabled Keith to expedite the sale of residential lots and enabled Jones to acquire land for his college without an enormous outlay of money. The arrangement called for Bob Jones to advertise the land—another indication of his reputation in the region—and to connect this promotion with fundraising for his college, widening the market of potential buyers to include those sympathetic to Jones's fundamentalism. For services rendered in heading the publicity campaign, Jones was entitled to 25 percent of the proceeds from sales on three hundred acres. He handed the commission over to his trustees to invest in the construction of the college's physical plant.[96] The college was to have 470 acres surrounded by private residences, including Jones's own two-story home.

In the spring of 1926 Jones launched an advertising campaign with the slogan, "Give Till It Hurts." Posters advised the residents of Bay County that "by buying lots you . . . make a safe investment, line your pockets with profits, boost your community and endow a college."[97] Minor Keith advised a buyer that lots ranged from "$1,000 for a 50×50–foot lot to $2,000 for [a] 50×300–foot lot on the water front." These sales were successful enough to allow construction of the college to begin in April 1926. In the spring and early summer of that year, Jones scheduled numerous evangelistic meetings in southeastern Alabama and northwestern Florida to further publicize his plans for Long Point, now renamed College Point. The finale of the land publicity campaign came on July 5, 1926, designated "College Point Day." Festivities included a 175-car motorcade through Panama City, addresses by local officials and Bob Jones, and a tour of the new homes and the college campus.[98]

Though the subdivision sale was an enormous success and helped offset an expensive land purchase for Jones, he still needed funds to complete construction, hire a faculty, and cover other expenses. Jones launched a bond sale. Speaking to local business leaders in Dothan in February 1927, Jones outlined the program. The bonds were to mature in ten years with an annual interest rate for the investor of 6 percent. To guarantee the bonds, Jones announced that the college possessed 470 acres of prime land. In addition, Jones informed the businessmen that he had taken out a $500, 000 life insurance policy on himself as an additional guarantee.[99] Another source of income for the college was a small farm that occupied twenty acres at College Point. In 1927 Jones announced plans for both a dairy and a truck farm.[100] Later the college sold vegetables and dairy products to, among others, the U.S. naval base at Pensacola, Florida.[101] It is also possible that the 2500-acre tract of College Point contained wooded areas from which Jones may have sold lumber, a lucrative industry in Bay County during the late 1920s.[102]

Ground-breaking ceremonies for Bob Jones College were held on December 1, 1926. The newly elected governor of Alabama, Bibb Graves, delivered the keynote address. Asserting that "godless education is a curse," Graves praised the new school as a "monument . . . dedicated to Jesus Christ." Bob Jones also spoke, informing his audience that Minor Keith had given him the deed for all the land connected with the college and that there were "no strings, but that it stands absolutely free from any encumbrance whatever."[103] Construction of the campus continued throughout the spring and summer of 1927. W. E. Patterson, professor of education from the University of Alabama, assisted Jones in recruiting faculty.[104]

Those present at the opening for the 1927–28 school year, held on September 14, 1927, included Governor Graves, congressmen Henry Steagall and William Upshaw, and representatives from the Alabama and Florida departments of education, University of Alabama, University of Florida, and the Alabama Polytechnic Institute.[105] Finally, after years of preaching against the ills of modern religious liberalism, evangelist Jones had "flung down the gauntlet to modernism."[106] Jones had already informed his audiences that his was "a college where no evolutionist need apply."[107] The opening day ceremonies clearly reinforced this direction. To the strains of "Faith of Our Fathers," all the board and faculty members filed past the podium to sign the college creed.[108] This document, still unamended in 1993, was a firm declaration of the "fundamentals of the faith." Proclaiming the mission of Bob Jones College to do combat with "all atheistic, agnostic, pagan . . . adulterations of the Gospel," the charter also reaffirmed the "inspiration of the Bible, the creation of man by the direct act of God, [and] the incarnation and virgin birth of Jesus Christ." The college's creed also contained a provision stipulating that the doctrinal statement "shall never be amended, modified, altered or changed."[109]

This uncompromising attitude indicated that from its inception Bob Jones College stood in stark contrast to other colleges and universities, both state and denominational. Bob Jones's raison d'être was to provide an alternative to the direction of American education since the Civil War. Research and academic freedom were not priorities; instead, as the 1927 Bob Jones College catalog stated, the purpose of the school was to provide a place "where the student's religious faith would not be shaken by questionable teachings." The school considered its mission accomplished when a student had "attained the intellectual requirements and attained a firm grip . . . of the great fundamental truths of the Christian religion."[110]

In this sense Bob Jones College represented an attempt to recover the early nineteenth-century ideal of a college as the transmitter of values and "mental discipline." This attempt to recover a lost world was also illustrated in the rules governing the student body. Student life was strictly regulated, especially in relations between the sexes. Women were not allowed off campus except in the presence of a family member or an "authorized chaperon." One student from the first class remembered that in chapel services (which were compulsory), the men sat on the right side of the auditorium and the girls on the left. The student also remembered that "during the day the boys could only say 'hi' to the girls. . . . The only free dating time each weekday was during the 15 minutes before supper." Dancing, card playing, or dice throwing brought a hundred demerits. The rule book also imposed twenty-five demerits on any student caught listening to "music considered 'jazz'." Bob Jones College was to be a safe haven for both religious orthodoxy and the morals of young people.[111]

The new school's existence was soon known within the fundamentalist community. In addition to advertising in periodicals such as *The Sunday School Times* and *The King's Business,* Bob Jones also publicized his college in his evangelistic travels. Jones continued a heavy speaking schedule that carried him as far away as Kansas and Maine.[112] Such activities linked Bob Jones College with a national network of religious conservatives who shared Jones's appraisal of American education, and this helped attract to Bob Jones College a constituency that transcended both regional and denominational boundaries. Within a year of the school's opening, Massachusetts, Ohio, and Indiana along with eight southern states were represented among the student body. Typical of the response Jones evoked when he announced his college was the reaction of a New Jersey high-school senior. Having heard Jones speak in an evangelistic campaign in Newark, Jessica Crane echoed the feelings of many in the fundamentalist subculture when she remarked, "it just didn't seem possible that such a place could be found in this day and age."[113]

Interestingly, while many fundamentalists applauded the new college, one significant element within fundamentalism voiced dismay. J. Oliver Buswell, president of Wheaton College in Illinois, then the only other fundamentalist liberal arts institution, wrote sternly to Bob Jones shortly after the September 1927 opening. The letter is not available, but according to Bob Jones Jr., Buswell informed the elder Jones that he "objected to his founding Bob Jones College, since Wheaton was a biblical institution and doing everything that needed to be done. . . . There was no need for another institution."[114] Buswell's early expression of hostility was a harbinger of conflict to come between the two institutions. In the next two decades, as we shall see in the next chapter, they would represent opposing strains within conservative Protestantism.

From its beginning, Bob Jones College was a liberal arts institution offering instruction in English, mathematics, biology and chemistry, history, and Bible.[115] Each of ten faculty members held at least a master's degree in his respective discipline. The college in its early years granted a bachelor's degree in only three areas: music, speech, and religion. The college limited its four-year program to those areas because they were most easily adapted to full-time Christian work. Students not majoring in those subjects were advised to transfer after their sophomore year. The academic program grew rapidly. By 1931 the school offered courses in philosophy, political science, and education. Also, beginning with the 1931–32 academic year, the Religion department offered a master's degree in religious education. The college also expanded its curriculum to include premedical and prelaw courses.[116] The student body expanded rapidly as well. Beginning with eighty-eight students in the fall of 1927, there were more than two hundred for the 1928–29 school year.[117] In the spring of 1929 a five-member inspection team from the University of Florida sent a report to the state superintendent, W. S. Cawthon, approving the academic program of Bob Jones College.[118]

In the 1927–28 catalog Jones stated that the new school also sought membership in the Southern Association.[119] The college already followed the curriculum outline suggested by the association as a model for its own academic program.[120] However, Bob Jones Sr. later declared that after further deliberation the college decided not to seek admission because it feared potential outside control of its internal policies.[121] There may have been other reasons as well. Jones asserted that from the school's beginning no other institution would "excel Bob Jones College in the efficiency of scholastic training."[122] He was later rebuked for this statement by no less than his friend and financial backer, J. S. Mack. Mack, after discussions with unnamed educational authorities, found "your school didn't rate so high."[123] The former Bob Jones registrar and assistant to the president, Theodore C. Mercer, later said the reason Jones did not seek accreditation was because the founder regarded accrediting associations as "educational trusts." Mercer also argued that Jones Sr. opposed accreditation because then he would be unable to "run the school in the same ironhanded manner."[124] Though Bob Jones College did not become a member of the Southern Association, that did not prevent members of the first graduating class from entering the graduate schools of the University of Pittsburgh, University of Chicago, and Colorado State University.

The first priority for Bob Jones College remained the spiritual. At the school's beginning Jones declared "there are some things that education alone cannot do. Nothing but God in the soul through the miracle of regeneration can save the individual."[125] Jones held revival services at the beginning of every term. Heeding the admonition of Asbury College president H. C. Morrison to "keep the chapel platform hot," Jones required mandatory chapel attendance and brought in noted evangelists to encourage the students' spiritual development.[126] The students responded to Jones's evangelistic zeal. The "preacher boys" of Bob Jones, those students intending to become ministers, formed a ministerial association in 1927. Adopting the slogan "Bay County for Christ," these young men traveled through northern Florida and southwestern Alabama holding revival services and volunteering in local churches.[127]

Students not in the ministerial association formed a volunteer prayer group. The group met daily to pray and to discuss ways in which laypersons could witness for Christ to their coworkers and neighbors.[128] Jones, encouraging his students in their outreach efforts, organized the Young People's Fellowship Clubs in 1931, both for his students and the converts they might reach. The clubs, according to one evangelical periodical, "visited the sick and shut-in, distributed tracts, and taught in Daily Vacation Bible schools." The clubs also served as a support network for Bob Jones students when they were away from school.[129] Jones himself remained the supreme example, remaining on the evangelistic circuit six months out of the year.[130]

In addition to academics and evangelism, Jones set one other major goal for the school. He wanted to combat the stereotype, popularized in the 1920s, of fundamentalists as people who, in Jones's words, "had greasy noses, dirty fingernails, baggy pants and who never shined their shoes."[131] None fueled this stereotype more than H. L. Mencken, when he observed that the typical fundamentalist "knows nothing of the arts; of the sciences he has never so much as heard. . . . When he hears by chance of the battle of ideas beyond the sky-rim, he quite naturally puts it down to Beelzebub."[132] Such talk infuriated Jones. According to his longtime associate and business manager, R. K. Johnson, Jones fervently believed that Christians should be "better doctors, better lawyers, better singers, better businessmen and better athletes."[133] Christians were to do everything "as unto the Lord." Summing up his attitude, Jones declared that "here at Bob Jones we believe in educating the whole person. It is just as important for a man to know how to get in and out of a lady's parlor as it is for him to have book learning."[134]

Mary Jones, Jones Sr.'s wife and the daughter of a prominent Alabama family, was raised in an environment that valued social refinement.[135] Helping further the cultural emphasis at the school, she gave lectures in etiquette to the students and organized formal banquets and parties for the development of social skills.[136] Her mother, Estelle Stollenwerck, lived with the Joneses and, besides making substantial financial contributions to the school, also exerted a significant cultural influence.[137] Perhaps Stollenwerck's most important contribution was her early tutoring of Bob Jones Jr. He later credited his grandmother with introducing him to the world of the classics and opera.[138] Reflecting this influence, Jones Jr. later became active in the "Classic Players," a drama club on campus that regularly performed Shakespeare's plays. Within fifteen years of the school's founding, the Bob Jones University Opera Association, another reflection of the Stollenwerck influence, produced annually a major opera in conjunction with singers from the New York City Metropolitan Opera. Bob Jones Jr. oversaw much of this and toured on his own as an interpreter of Shakespeare. The exposure brought him an invitation, which he declined, to take a Warner Brothers screen test in the early 1930s.[139]

As the college developed its academic, evangelistic, and cultural emphases, the nation entered the Great Depression. The elder Jones financed the school through three principal means: student fees, bonds, and real estate mortgages—plus whatever incidental contributions he could solicit as he traveled. Most of the money came from bonds. They covered the initial expenses of the school, and more were sold periodically as the need arose.[140] In the summer of 1928 Jones launched another major fundraising drive with bonds to construct a new residence hall, laundry, and auditorium on campus. Jones kept his bondholders supplied with good news; by 1930 he boasted that other universities accepted Bob Jones College premed and prelaw credits.[141]

But in the spring of 1929 a worsening local economy exacerbated by poor crops and heavy floods forced Jones to ask the bondholders for an additional ten thousand dollars. In this same appeal Jones informed them that increasing numbers of students were unable to pay for tuition and board.[142] Then, as the northwestern Florida land boom finally collapsed, Minor Keith told Bob Jones that he was withdrawing his real estate development company from Florida. In a settlement worked out between the two, Keith purchased bonds to help Jones finish construction of the campus, and the college assumed $500,000 in mortgages belonging to individuals who purchased land in the same area as Bob Jones College. As the depression worsened in 1929–30, many of these individuals could not keep up their mortgage payments. By the fall of 1929 the amount from these mortgages due Bob Jones exceeded $200,000. Jones now found it increasingly difficult to pay interest to his bondholders. In November 1929 he asked those who felt they could to return their bonds to the college.[143] Despite such budget-cutting measures as a faculty pay-cut, Jones informed his bondholders late in 1930 that the college could no longer pay interest on its bonds. Payments from the mortgages would more than cover the school's bonded indebtedness, but Jones was unable to collect, forcing him to default on his interest payments.[144]

As student payments dwindled and mortgage collections failed to materialize, Jones's troubles multiplied. In 1928 Jones fired Bible professor W. J. Hall. According to Bob Jones Jr., Hall had denied "portions of the Word of God" in his classes.[145] The disgruntled Hall became pastor of a local church and evidently began to speak out against the college. By 1932 he had convinced a group of local Bob Jones College bondholders to file suit for interest from the college. Since Jones could not at this point pay interest on the bonds, there was no way he could meet the demands of Hall and his followers. In January 1933 the college filed for bankruptcy.[146]

The crisis in Florida brought about changes in the school's approach to its finances. Jones determined to run the school on a cash basis and also revamped the way in which faculty were paid. Originally, teachers were paid according to the degrees they held and their standing within the faculty. When by 1930 Jones could no longer afford this arrangement, he informed his teachers he could only offer "a place to live and something to eat, plus a little cash."[147] Sixty years later, Bob Jones University executive vice-president Bob Wood confirmed that faculty at Bob Jones are still not paid according to their academic achievements. Most faculty live on campus and take their meals in the university dining hall. Pay increases are made on the recommendation of the administration based upon its own criteria.[148] Bob Jones later acknowledged that serious mistakes were made in the early years of the school. He advised a Bob Jones University graduate years later that "if you have to raise money to pay operating overhead, you are going to get into trouble."[149] The most immediate consequence of bankruptcy resulted in Bob Jones College leaving Florida.

Bob Jones Jr., returning from graduate school at the University of Pittsburgh in 1932, noticed during one of his drives home the deserted property of Centenary College, a Methodist school for women, in Cleveland, Tennessee.[150] Jones Sr. traveled to the location early in 1933. He learned that the Methodists still owed money on the property to a Cleveland businessman, who agreed to sell it to Jones for $33,000.[151] Learning of Jones's interest, the Cleveland chamber of commerce invited him to relocate the school there, and Jones told them that if they would contribute $7500 he would do so. The sum was raised in a single afternoon.[152] Cleveland ultimately contributed more than ten thousand dollars to renovate the Centenary campus in preparation for Bob Jones.[153] Under the terms of the sale, Jones had until 1936 to pay the remaining $25,500. The Methodists, who still owed money on the property, agreed to pay off what they owed as well.[154]

Bob Jones College graduated its last class in Florida in May 1933. One month later a local turpentine operator purchased the college property, once valued at $350,000, for only $7500.[155] A faculty member, Grace Haight, and businessman and trustee Raymond Crane each gave the school three thousand dollars to finance the move to Cleveland.[156] Though the move was a forced one, Jones Jr. later reflected that had those events not taken place, "we would still be there in northwest Florida; but our God had brought us now into a broader field of service and opened wider doors for us."[157]

Bob Jones College grew significantly during the Cleveland years (1933–1946). While in Tennessee the college expanded into five schools: Bob Jones Academy for Kindergarten–12, the College of Liberal Arts, the School of Business, the Graduate School of Religion, and the Graduate School of Fine Arts. By 1945 a student at Bob Jones College could earn a B.A. or B.S. in the liberal arts, a business certificate, a Ph.D. in religion, or a Master of Fine Arts degree.[158] An enlarged student population accompanied this growth. Beginning with three hundred students in the fall of 1933, the student body expanded to four hundred by 1936, representing students from 38 states and three foreign countries.[159] When the school left Cleveland in 1946 the student body numbered more than one thousand, with four hundred enrolled in the ministerial program alone.[160] The physical plant never quite accommodated such growth. During the fourteen Cleveland years the college built four men's residence halls, two women's residence halls, a new classroom building, a new library, a new auditorium/gymnasium, and off-campus apartments for older students.[161]

The school also achieved fiscal stability in Cleveland. Business manager R. K. Johnson asserted that at the end of the 1933–34 school year the college had paid for new equipment and given the faculty a bonus.[162] This new-found financial health was rooted in several sources. The growing student body obviously brought in funds, but the city of Cleveland also aided the college financially. Looking upon the school's presence as a boon to the local economy, the chamber of commerce mounted an annual fund-raising drive to help Jones pay off what he owed on the property.[163] A large local crowd invariably appeared at opening exercises every year and may well have contributed money to the college.[164] Jones's own frenetic speaking schedule, which in the first half of 1939 alone took him from New York and Philadelphia to Los Angeles and Seattle, netted the college money from collections taken in his meetings.[165] Jones also acquired large new financial benefactors while in Cleveland, most notably C. W. Harle, president of Merchants Bank in Cleveland, and J. S. Mack of G. C. Murphy stores. Mack regularly dispensed financial advice to Jones along with substantial contributions. In addition to giving the college more than eight hundred shares of G. C. Murphy stock, Mack also regularly matched whatever funds Jones was able to raise, and when Mack died, Bob Jones College received funds from his estate. The Mack Library and the Margaret Mack residence hall for women on the campus of Bob Jones University today attest to his influence upon the school. Sometimes funds arrived from unexpected sources. In a two year period, R. K. Johnson reported, Bob Jones College received $500,000 from the wills of various individuals Jones had met over the course of his evangelistic travels.[166]

One of the most important developments for Bob Jones College during the Tennessee years was the emergence of Bob Jones Jr.[167] The only son of Bob and Mary Jones, the young boy had accompanied his parents on revival crusades, where he heard not only his father but other well-known evangelists. After graduating from Bob

Jones College in 1931, Jones Jr. entered the history program at the University of Pittsburgh. Writing his M.A. thesis on "The History of Evangelism in America," Jones Jr. did additional summer work at the University of Chicago.[168] In 1933 the board of trustees elected him as college vice-president and assistant to his father. After the school moved to Cleveland, Jones Jr. chaired the history department, coached the drama team, and acted as president during his father's absences.[169] Under the leadership of Jones Jr. the college continued to build a strong drama and opera program. The younger Jones traveled to England with members of the speech faculty in the summers of 1935 and 1936 to study at Stratford-upon-Avon. Other faculty members under Jones Jr.'s direction took summer study at institutions such as Northwestern and Columbia.[170]

So in the worst of economic times Bob Jones College enjoyed great growth. The larger fundamentalist community grew significantly in the 1930s and 1940s, as well. The increased circulation of such periodicals as *Moody Monthly,* the rise in the number of such radio programs as Charles Fuller's "Old Fashioned Revival Hour," and the surging enrollments at such colleges as Wheaton and Bob Jones all attest to this expansion.[171] Despite these heartening developments, fundamentalism began to experience an internal tension growing from the issue of separatism from denominations that tolerated liberalism. Many fundamentalists felt that the established denominations were too riddled with modernism to be worth saving, and during the 1930s groups of fundamentalists created the Independent Fundamental Churches of America, the General Association of Regular Baptist Churches, and the Orthodox Presbyterian Church. Conversely, other fundamentalists remained active in their denominations, hoping to act as a brake upon liberalism.[172]

Bob Jones Sr. doubtlessly regarded himself as a separatist. His sermon "The Perils of America" left no question regarding his feelings about theological modernism. Within two years of founding Bob Jones College he fired a faculty member for propagating modernism in Bible classes. In 1934 Jones told the *Baptist Bulletin* that "if we entertain a modernistic minister in our house or support him with our money we are a party to the program of that minister."[173] Yet Jones's primary concerns in these years were evangelism and building his school. While erecting Bob Jones College was an act of separating from the public and denominational colleges, Jones did not involve himself in any efforts to purge or break away from his own denomination, the Methodist Episcopal Church, South. Rather, while Baptist and Presbyterian fundamentalists left to form new, separatist bodies, Bob Jones Sr., as he told a fellow pastor in 1939, decided "to remain in the denomination . . . supporting that which is orthodox and . . . refusing to support that which is not." Jones further acknowledged that his stance had caused him embarrassment in orthodox circles.[174]

Indeed, Jones found his course increasingly untenable. When the school moved to Tennessee, Jones moved his church membership to the Broad Street Methodist Church in Cleveland. Assuming the pastor there to be a conservative, Jones contributed toward his salary but refused to contribute to larger denominational efforts, considering them modernistic.[175] Jones managed this balancing act for six years, from 1933 to 1939. In September 1939 Bob Jones Jr., also a member of the Broad Street Church, reported to his father that the pastor had allowed a modernist to preach in a Sunday morning service. The visiting speaker, Dr. W. A. Smart, was a professor in a Methodist seminary. According to Jones Jr., Dr. Smart preached from the Book of Revelation, and in the course of his sermon "denied the inspiration of Scripture, the necessity of the New Birth, the reality of Satan, the deity of our Lord, and almost every other doctrine of the faith." Confronting the pastor after the service, Jones Jr. demanded his church membership certificate, asserting that he would not be a member of a church that allowed "this kind of infidel." Jones Sr. concurred with his son.[176] Both resigned from the Cleveland body.

Shortly after withdrawing from the Broad Street Church, Jones Sr. found himself embroiled in another conflict with Methodist officials. One of the denomination's papers, the *Alabama Christian Advocate,* refused to carry advertisements for Bob Jones College. The editor insisted that the advertisement, which highlighted the commitment of Bob Jones College to orthodoxy, was really a concealed slap at Methodist schools. Jones informed the editor that "the college can do without the *Alabama Christian Advocate*." Since the paper's refusal to carry the Bob Jones advertisement, said Jones Sr., "I am more convinced than ever that there must be a place in God's program for the Bob Jones College."[177]

Interestingly, following his withdrawal from the Broad Street Church and his encounter with the *Alabama Christian Advocate*, Jones Sr. still led no militant, separatist group out of the Methodist Church. Even after acknowledging that he had met Methodist ministers who denied the virgin birth of Christ, Jones insisted upon maintaining his membership in the Methodist denomination. Rather, he resolved to find "some good, uncompromising, orthodox Methodist pastor" and place his membership in that man's church.[178] Jones's stand is remarkable in light of Bob Jones University's later militance over the necessity of complete separation from all forms of apostasy.[179] Staying within the Methodist Church, even while acknowledging that modernism had gained significant influence in it, ironically put Bob Jones Sr. in company with those who felt conservatives might still be a positive force in the denominations. Nonetheless, Jones's act of withdrawal from the Broad Street Church was a first, small step in a journey that would take him, his son, and Bob Jones College to the leadership of militant, separatist fundamentalism.

CHAPTER TWO

Separatism Unleashed

The Joneses' decision to leave the Broad Street Church in 1939 coincided with a growing debate among fundamentalists over the question of separatism. Since the days of the fundamentalist-modernist controversy, many fundamentalists, such as William B. Riley, had elected to stay within their denominations and fight modernism there. Others, such as J. Gresham Machen, regarded continued fellowship in a modernist denomination as intolerable and promptly withdrew.[1] Though adopting divergent approaches, both groups of fundamentalists were united by the common enemy of modernism. But as theological modernism began to decline in the 1930s, many fundamentalists wished to adopt a less strident and more inclusive attitude. Others still held to the warlike attitude of the 1920s and insisted on maintaining complete separation. By the early 1940s this division could be neatly charted with the formation of the extreme separatist American Council of Christian Churches (ACCC) in 1941 and the more moderate National Association of Evangelicals (NAE) in 1943.

Although their withdrawal from the Broad Street Church gave them the appearance of separatism, the Joneses' separatist tendencies were held in check by two personal and philosophical circumstances. The first was Bob Jones Sr.'s strong advocacy of evangelism and his continued leadership of the school. The second was the growing belief among fundamentalists in the 1930s and 1940s that revival was indeed possible, a perception shared by both Bob Jones Sr. and Bob Jones Jr. Both these factors led them into alliance with the moderate NAE in the 1940s. By the end of the 1950s, however, these goals had been replaced by a virulent separatism that led the Joneses to sever their ties with the NAE, Billy Graham, Moody Bible Institute, and several smaller evangelical organizations. This remarkable and paradoxical journey, spanning the years 1941 to 1958, was fueled by the increased prominence of the more aggressive Bob Jones Jr., an internal crisis in 1953 that shook Bob Jones University to its foundations, a growing incompatibility with the NAE, and a personal and philosophical clash with the evangelist Billy Graham.

Despite the dimming prominence of modernism, the division in fundamentalism became increasingly pronounced at the end of the 1930s. Until that time, many fundamentalists accepted *Baptist Bulletin* writer Oliver Van Osdel's advice to "keep our eyes on the rejected Son of God in these days of declension and compromise."[2] Even Wheaton College, soon to be a center of the new attitude, billed itself in the 1930s as "a lighthouse for education in the midst of the increasing darkness of infidelity."[3] A series of schisms accompanied this defeatist rhetoric as separatist groups, such as the General Association of Regular Baptist Churches (GARBC) formed in 1932.[4] More dramatically, a group of fundamentalists in the Presbyterian Church, led by J. Gresham Machen (who had already left Princeton Seminary to form the separatist Westminster Seminary), were brought to "trial" before the national synod in 1936. Believing the denomination's foreign missions board to be modernist, these fundamentalists had created a rival board, and for this they were charged with "not being zealous and faithful in maintaining the peace of the Church." Stripped by the synod of their ordinations, the defrocked fundamentalists formed their own denomination, the Orthodox Presbyterian Church. Eventually even this group experienced division when dissidents broke away to form the Bible Presbyterian Church.[5]

Convinced of their possession of absolute truth, these fundamentalists regarded their mission as not only protecting their beliefs but also actively attacking unbelief. For them, the war of the 1920s was still very much in progress. (Robert Ketcham, for example, the leader of the separatist GARBC, was still publishing "exposés" of modernism within the Northern Baptist Convention as late as 1949.)[6] In the late 1930s Rev. Carl McIntire, one of the defrocked Presbyterian fundamentalists, rose to the leadership of the militants. Pastor of a church in Collingswood, New Jersey, McIntire was described by one writer as a man who regarded any "departure from his doctrines as the rankest form of soul destroying apostasy." He articulated the attitude of many fundamentalists when he observed that "dialogue, rapprochement, reconciliation have become the weapons of a corrupt church to aggravate and intensify its apostasy."[7]

Having separated from the Presbyterian Church, USA, to help Machen form the Orthodox Presbyterian Church, and having then separated from Machen to form his own Bible Presbyterian Church, McIntire was a man constantly in search of a foe. In the 1930s he and other like-minded fundamentalists found another enemy in the Federal Council of Churches (FCC). The FCC, created in 1908 by churchmen dedicated to the Social Gospel, was the organization that, as Martin Marty describes it, "became the chief agency for uniting efforts in support of social, as opposed to private, Christianity."[8] The FCC, composed of 33 denominations, deemphasized doctrine with a brief statement calling Jesus Christ "Lord and Savior." Establishing a Commission on the Church and Social Service, the FCC embarked upon an unabashedly liberal agenda.[9]

McIntire and his followers attacked the FCC on several counts. First, they accused the FCC of advocating "pacifism" and "a new social order and radicalism." Second, the FCC was laying false claim to the historic Christian faith. Its one-line doctrinal statement calling Jesus "Lord and Savior" was too weak for the fundamentalists, for whom virtually any heresy could be entertained under such a broad statement.[10] Further, when fundamentalists separated from denominations affiliated with the FCC, they found themselves embroiled in property battles, as denominations sought to deny them their church buildings on the grounds that the buildings belonged to the denomination, not to local congregations. Also irritating many fundamentalists was the fact that the radio networks gave the FCC free air time, while nonmembers had to pay.[11]

In the fall of 1940 leaders from the Bible Presbyterian Church and the Bible Protestant Church, under McIntire's guidance, met to consider ways to counter the influence of the FCC. After a year of study these leaders formed the ACCC in September 1941. The ACCC adopted a strict constitution requiring all members to subscribe to the fundamentals of the faith and forbidding membership to churches that had any affiliation with the FCC. As McIntire commented, "the line of separation would have to be clear. This requirement was demanded in God's Word." In September 1941, with the creation of the ACCC, McIntire said, "little David went out to meet the great Goliath."[12]

Although the ACCC began initially with support only from the Bible Presbyterian and Bible Protestant churches, other separatist groups soon flocked to it. The most notable of these were the Independent Fundamental Churches of America and the GARBC. Significantly, the support garnered by the ACCC came from those groups that had been among the first to separate from their denominations in the late 1920s and early 1930s. In this sense the ACCC was a continuation, albeit more organized, of a movement that had been extant for some time. Even more significantly, the ACCC did not confine itself to denunciations of the FCC. Fundamentalists who had remained in liberal denominations to try to counter liberalism were also criticized. McIntire flatly stated the ACCC position: "God's people cannot support or be a part of a fellowship with unbelievers, such as is represented in the modernist Federal Council." Those fundamentalists who stayed in liberal denominations were "not being obedient to the plain commands of our Lord." Because of this, members of the ACCC could not work even with other fundamentalists who persisted in staying in the FCC.[13]

Not all fundamentalists shared the goals or mentality of the ACCC. The Bob Joneses were not among the supporters of the ACCC. Almost simultaneous with the creation of the ACCC, another group of fundamentalists were considering what might be done to increase their influence. These fundamentalists, like their counterparts in the ACCC, were resolutely committed to the fundamentals of the faith. They, too, had passed through the fundamentalist-modernist war. But as the heat of that controversy dissipated, these fundamentalists saw an opportunity for conservative theology to stage a comeback—not in continuing to fight defensively, but rather in proposing a more positive alternative.

Developments during the 1930s spurred optimism in this camp. One was the significant growth experienced by fundamentalist churches and institutions. Colleges such as Bob Jones and Wheaton recorded growing enrollments, evangelical periodicals such as *Moody Monthly* gained larger circulations, and fundamentalist radio preachers such as Charles Fuller gained larger audiences.[14] This was in stark contrast to the experience of mainline FCC churches, for whom the 1930s were a decade characterized by lower attendance, reduced budgets and program cutbacks, and displaced ministers.[15] In 1935 the liberal *Christian Century* observed that "the Christian church has come into the depression wholly unprepared to take account of it, and to minister to the deepest human need which it discloses."[16]

Another source of optimism for fundamentalists was a renewed interest in orthodox theology on the part of many modernists. In 1935, from the pulpit of the Riverside Church in New York City, the great modernist Harry Emerson Fosdick delivered the sermon, "The Church Must Go beyond Modernism." While in no way reverting to fundamentalism, Fosdick nonetheless conceded in his sermon that modernist theology had become too preoccupied with intellectualism and had become too sentimental. Fosdick advised his congregation that "we must stop acting as if the highest compliment that could be paid to Almighty God is to have a few scientists believe in Him." Moreover, modernism had accommodated itself so well to the idea of progress that the moral judgment of God had been forgotten. "Sin," Fosdick said, "personal and social, is real, just as our forefathers told us, and we can see, as they told us, sin leads men and nations to damnation."[17] Fosdick's critique of modernism contained elements of an increasingly popular school of thought, imported from Europe, called neo-orthodoxy.

In the 1920s, as modernism infiltrated American denominations and American theologians optimistically preached the Social Gospel, Europe was recovering from the devastation of World War I. Europe, the home of liberal theology, now in the aftermath of the war began to produce critics of liberalism. In 1919 Swiss theologian Karl Barth shook the theological world with his commentary on the book of Romans.[18] The war and its immense toll shattered, for Barth, the liberal view that man by his own efforts could bring the Kingdom of God to this earth. Barth now understood that liberal theology, in remaking Jesus into a simple teacher of ethics and a good example for people to follow, had in fact destroyed what humans needed most: a savior to rescue them from their fallen, sinful natures. "Man is as he is and cannot make himself any different. He is the cause of his own trouble," Barth asserted, and he advised his readers to return to the God of the Bible "who has sought and found the way to us . . . [through] Jesus Christ, no other, and nothing else."[19] Barth, like Fosdick, was no fundamentalist, for he accepted many of the findings of the higher critics relegating a good deal of the Bible to mythology, but liberalism had gone too far and had missed the essential point that the Bible in fact contained God's revelation to humanity. The key difference between Barth and liberal theologians was that Barth emphasized the Bible and Christ as God's efforts to reach humans, while the liberals tended to see the Bible and Christ as useful reference points for their task in constructing an ideal society.

Barth's critique of liberalism began to reach the United States in the 1930s just as the full force of the Depression struck the nation. Many American theologians, notably Reinhold Niebuhr of Union Theological Seminary in New York, began to pay attention to the critics of liberalism. It was becoming painfully obvious to such teachers as Niebuhr, as the Depression gripped the land and as totalitarian states began to rise in Europe, that the boundless progress proclaimed by the liberals was not going to materialize. Rather, events seemed to confirm the orthodox view that humans were indeed depraved and in need of help from outside themselves. Shocked by these developments and by the suffering he saw in the factories of Detroit while a pastor there, Niebuhr returned to classical Christianity. In his *Beyond Tragedy,* Niebuhr asserted that "the cross, which stands at the center of the Christian world view, reveals both the seriousness of human sin and the purpose and power of God to overcome it."[20] Like Barth, Niebuhr did not accept a literal interpretation of the Bible, but rather held that God's truth was expressed through the many mythical stories in the Bible. Niebuhr, through his prolific writing and speaking, became the key leader of a movement calling itself "neo-orthodoxy," which rejected both fundamentalism and liberalism.

In addition to the decline of mainline churches and the internal reevaluation undertaken by liberals, fundamentalists had a third cause for optimism. This came about as twentieth-century biblical scholarship began to confirm certain ideas in the Bible. Archaeology, for example, now discredited the German critic Julius Welhausen's thesis that Israel was not monotheistic at the time of Moses. Scholars also began to reconcile the teachings of Jesus and Paul, long regarded as evidence that the Bible lacked unity. As William Horndern has pointed out, "nineteenth-century scholarship was analytical; it took the Bible to pieces and analyzed the parts. Twentieth century scholarship, using the results of analysis, went on to synthesis, and discovered that the Bible . . . represented a unity. Paul's gospel about Jesus is not radically different from Jesus' gospel about himself."[21]

As scholarship moved toward friendship with orthodoxy, the liberalism of the early twentieth century received a further battering from World War II. Humans, it appeared, were nowhere near to ushering in God's kingdom. By 1950, the *Christian Century* asserted that liberalism had entered "a blind alley. In clinging stubbornly to the earliest conclusions from modern science, biblical criticism, the psychology of religion and comparative religion, those who still wear the label of liberalism as a partisan badge are essentially dogmatists. Their liberalism is the victim of an arrested development."[22]

The disorder within liberal ranks, coupled with their own sub-stantial growth during the 1930s, convinced many fundamentalists that perhaps all was not lost. They were still in a position to influ-ence the theological world and society. The question confronting them now was how to organize in order to make their influence felt. One of these fundamentalists, James Murch, aptly summa-rized the situation when he observed that in the 1930s and 1940s there existed "a tremendous constituency accomplishing great things for the Lord but without cohesion, or means of united action."[23] Significantly, these fundamentalists were becoming more critical of their own tradition. In 1937, Donald Grey Barn-house, editor of the fundamentalist periodical *Revelation*, com-plained that too often "born again men are bitterly quarreling with each other over secondary matters." J. Elwin Wright, a Boston pastor and head of the New England Fellowship, a group of co-operating fundamentalist churches, echoed this observation when he stated that many fundamentalists were "hypercritical and in-tolerant."[24]

For fundamentalists such as Wright, Barnhouse, and Murch, the idea of a broader evangelical organization of their own had been growing for some time. Wright's own New England Fellowship had at its 1937, 1940, and 1941 conferences passed resolutions call-ing for some kind of united action. In the winter of 1940–41 an in-terested group of ministers sent out a letter to fundamentalist pastors and leaders in an attempt to gauge support for a national organization. J. Elwin Wright, on a national speaking tour in the spring of 1941, reported "an evident eagerness to give active sup-port to such a movement."[25]

Meeting in Chicago in October 1941, fundamentalist leaders gathered to discuss the creation of a national association. Also pre-sent in Chicago were representatives of the newly formed ACCC, led by Carl McIntire. They had come to present the ACCC pro-gram and to persuade the Chicago group to join forces with them. McIntire feared the FCC would be strengthened if there were two fundamentalist organizations. In Chicago the divergent paths of the two groups quickly became apparent. After McIntire presented the plans and purpose of the ACCC, J. Elwin Wright, representing the others, informed McIntire that they did not wish to join the ACCC. The Chicago group was concerned that the ACCC's purpose was completely negative, to harass the FCC. They envisioned something larger and more positive.[26]

The Chicago meeting issued a call for a national conference of evangelicals to be held in St. Louis in the spring of 1942. Asserting that "there are millions of evangelical Christians who feel at present they have no corporate means of making their wishes known," the Chicago evangelicals proposed the creation of a national organization that among other goals would strive for "evangelism, united efforts of evangelical churches, and Christian education." Churches could join as long as they accepted the "traditional evangelical position." Among the signers of the letter was Bob Jones Sr.[27]

Meeting in St. Louis in April 1942, representatives from forty denominations launched the National Association of Evangelicals. Once again, Carl McIntire was on hand to urge the delegates to join the ACCC. Once again, he was rebuffed.[28] The organization that emerged from St. Louis was, like the ACCC, firmly against liberalism. The NAE shared the ACCC's assessment of the Federal Council, calling the latter a group of "vociferous liberals" at their first annual convention in 1943. Like the ACCC, the newly formed NAE found it unacceptable that FCC ministers received free radio time.[29] In St. Louis the evangelicals voted to express their "unqualified opposition" to organizations that purporting to represent Protestant Christianity, had nonetheless "departed from the faith of Jesus Christ."[30] Although both the ACCC and the NAE were opponents of the Federal Council, and although both had identical doctrinal statements, two key differences quickly became apparent, differences that would define the split of fundamentalism into "fundamentalists" and "evangelicals."

The first major difference, and the one destined to become the chief point of contention, involved the issue of separation from apostasy. The ACCC resolutely forbade membership to any denomination or individual church that retained any ties whatsoever with the FCC. Conversely, the NAE, while denying membership to denominations affiliated with the FCC, nonetheless admitted individual congregations that might be part of those same denominations.[31] The second major difference was the willingness of the NAE to concede that fundamentalism, as it had been defined so far, was not taken seriously by outsiders and that oftentimes fundamentalists had only themselves to thank for this state of affairs. Harold Ockenga, president of the NAE, observed that "a terrible indictment may be laid against fundamentalism because of its failures, divisions, and controversies. . . . Now is the time to forget all of these differences and join together as one with the Crucified One."[32] The NAE was thus the first organization that, while thoroughly fundamentalist in its doctrine, was not dedicated solely to fighting liberalism but rather to a positive presentation of evangelical Christianity.

The enthusiasm and new direction of the NAE quickly became apparent. Meeting in Chicago in May 1943, the NAE created a Committee on Policy and Fields of Endeavor. From the recommendations of this committee, others were established dealing with evangelism, missions, education, moral and social welfare, quotas for chaplains in the armed services, and radio broadcasting.[33] Plans for ministry in war industrial communities and for a weekly paper were also announced.[34] In 1944 the NAE formed a commission to coordinate evangelical efforts in overseas postwar relief. In 1949 members of the NAE created the Evangelical Theological Society, composed of college professors and ministers and dedicated to challenging, in James Murch's phrase, "the assumption and claims of liberalism that believing in the historic Christian faith . . . can only be done at the sacrifice of the intellect." In 1950 an Evangelical Welfare Agency was established in Chicago and a year later the first NAE Forum on Social Action convened.[35]

In stark contrast to these efforts, the ACCC established its program of confronting the FCC. McIntire and ACCC representatives began shadowing the FCC by scheduling simultaneous meetings in the same cities where the FCC met in conference. In 1948, for example, when the World Council of Churches, the international counterpart of the FCC, met in Amsterdam, McIntire was on hand to hold a conference in a deliberate effort to create confusion. The next year, when an ecumenical program for raising funds for the homeless and sick was announced, the ACCC denounced it as "socialistic propaganda" and the "greatest drive ever to advance the socialistic world."[36] Thus, with the formation of the ACCC and the NAE, the fundamentalist coalition of the 1920s was effectively sundered.

As these two divergent paths opened in the 1940s, the Bob Joneses cast their lot with the NAE. The influence of Bob Jones Sr. was crucial in this decision. No one could question Jones Sr.'s opposition to modernism—he had promptly fired a faculty member in the 1920s who spoke favorably of Harry Emerson Fosdick—but Jones Sr. was first and foremost an evangelist. Indeed, a corollary to his founding Bob Jones College was that modernists in colleges were undercutting his evangelistic ministry by destroying the faith of his young converts.[37] Jones held evangelistic services at the beginning of every school year in order to give his students the opportunity to respond to the gospel, if they had not done so already. It is reasonable to infer that a new organization dedicated to evangelism would be attractive to Jones, even if it did not take a hard-line separatist stance. Further, it is even possible that Jones Sr. in the late 1930s and 1940s was wary of organizations whose only trademark was a harsh separatism. He had, after all, remained in the Southern Methodist Episcopal Church and expressed sympathy for conservative pastors within that denomination struggling against liberalism.[38] Given these factors, Jones Sr. appeared an ideal candidate for such an organization as the NAE.

Jones Sr. shared many of the same concerns of the founders of the NAE. He signed the October 1941 Chicago letter calling for a national conference of evangelicals, and in a letter to a fellow evangelist shortly thereafter, Jones voiced some of those concerns: "I feel greatly disturbed about the whole situation in America for two reasons: first, our fundamental crowd is so divided and fighting each other so hard, many of us are losing out spiritually; second, the division in our groups hurts our testimony in all sections of America." Jones pointed out further that "if England, America and Russia can get together on how to win the war and each nation retained its own form of government, it would seem to me that our fundamental groups, since we believe the same doctrines, could get together."[39] These were certainly not the sentiments of a schismatic bent on ideological purity. It is significant that Jones shared these concerns nearly two years after the founding of the ACCC. Obviously, that organization, with its strident separatism, was not solving what Jones regarded as a major problem, namely, division in fundamentalist ranks. The NAE, with its emphasis on unity, was an attractive alternative.

The belief that fundamental Christianity was on the rebound from the disastrous 1920s also motivated the men who founded the NAE. The growth of fundamentalist institutions in the 1930s fueled their optimism. Bob Jones Sr., having seen his school recover from bankruptcy and go on to expand its programs and enrollments, could personally attest to this growth. The founders of the NAE were also confident that the United States was ripe for a religious revival. Will Houghton, president of Moody Bible Institute and a NAE member, voiced this sentiment when he observed that "God has a stake in this nation and He is concerned that His word of warning and invitation shall be given forth."[40] Jones Sr., having spent his entire adult life preaching on the need for revival, would undoubtedly have found this rhetoric appealing.

Jones Sr. revealed his enthusiasm for the NAE in an article written shortly after he attended the 1944 NAE conference. Praising the NAE for representing "the cross-currents of evangelical orthodoxy in America," Jones noted that it was "remarkable how far all orthodox Christians can walk together." He noted the wide diversity of denominations represented within the NAE. There were Calvinist and Arminian elements, those who practiced full immersion in baptism and those who practiced sprinkling, and those who believed in different forms of church government, all working together in one organization. While they shared these differences, they also shared a common belief in what Jones termed the "great essential fundamental truths of God's Word": the incarnation and deity of Christ, his vicarious death and his resurrection. For Jones, this demonstrated that "if orthodox Christians would magnify the things about which they agree as much as they emphasize the things about which they disagree, there would be more harmony among God's people."[41]

Jones's comments regarding the NAE are illuminating in several respects. First, nowhere did he argue that the NAE must be militantly separatist. He took it for granted that any person or church in the NAE was fundamentalist in doctrine. For Jones, that meant agreement on the person and work of Christ. This is even more remarkable considering that at the time Jones wrote his article, the NAE accepted into its membership churches still affiliated with the FCC, a fact of which Jones was undoubtedly aware. Second, Jones's comments reveal that he was distressed over the division in fundamentalist ranks. While he did not mention the ACCC by name, it is possible to infer that Jones Sr. was alarmed over its increasing harshness, no longer directed solely at the FCC, but now also at the NAE.

Relations between the NAE and the ACCC had never been very comfortable. It was obvious from the beginning, when the founders of the NAE rejected McIntire's invitation to join the ACCC, that the two groups were starting from different premises. As early as 1944, McIntire had accused the NAE of "expediency and compromise."[42] McIntire based his accusation on the fact that the NAE would not repudiate any and all connections with the FCC. J. Elwin Wright summed up the position of the NAE when he commented that fundamentalists "must speak with courage against apostasy. . . . We must, at the same time, be gracious and wise." Conversely, for McIntire and the ACCC, "controversy is nothing to be ashamed of when it is in the holy cause of righteousness and of the faith."[43]

This division deepened, as McIntire kept up a steady drumbeat of criticism for the NAE. Because the NAE accepted churches still in the FCC, McIntire concluded that "Dr. Ockenga, Dr. Wright . . . and other leaders of the NAE are all in the apostate FCC." McIntire went on to label the Northern Baptist Convention, the Methodist Church, and the Presbyterian Church, USA, as "apostate." Members of the NAE, as far as McIntire was concerned, might be fundamental, Bible-believing Christians and still be in league with

Satan since they would not oppose the FCC with the same vigor as the ACCC. The next year, at its 1949 convention in Denver, the ACCC passed a resolution condemning the NAE for not taking a "clear-cut stand" on separation.[44]

These criticisms apparently did not bother the Joneses or limit their involvement in the NAE. While McIntire was criticizing the NAE for its soft separatist stance, Jones Sr. served on the first NAE commission on evangelism and was later asked to chair the commission.[45] Jones Jr. was equally active. In the spring of 1947 he was elected for a three-year term to the NAE's board of administration. In accepting this position Jones was obligated to sign both a doctrinal statement and a statement endorsing the NAE's constitution and by-laws.[46] Evidently Jones Jr. felt comfortable, at this point, in accepting the NAE position on separation.

The next year the NAE leadership felt obliged to counter the growing criticism of the ACCC. The NAE executive board adopted a resolution stating that while the NAE certainly believed in separation from apostasy, it nonetheless felt that the decision to leave or stay in a church or denomination should be up to the individual. In other words, a Christian brother might remain in the NAE and in an FCC church if he felt God could use him as a moderating influence against liberalism. A letter explaining the NAE statement was sent to the board members, including Jones Jr., who accepted it.[47] In this same year, 1948, Jones Jr. accepted an invitation to give the opening address at the NAE conference in Chicago, and two years later he was elected one of two vice-presidents for the NAE.[48]

Although both Joneses appeared comfortable in the NAE, changes were occurring within the organization and within Bob Jones University that would ultimately make their alliance untenable and would move the Joneses into the ultraseparatist camp. Among these changes were a personal misunderstanding between the Joneses and NAE officials, a growing uneasiness over the NAE's identification with the "new evangelicalism" and all that it entailed, the increasing influence of Bob Jones Jr. in the school's administration, an internal crisis in 1953 that fundamentally altered the school, and the rising prominence of former Bob Jones student

Billy Graham. Together these factors, between 1949 and 1958, enabled a latent separatism to assert itself at Bob Jones University.

The first fissure between the Joneses and the NAE occurred in the spring of 1949. That year Bob Jones Jr. invited the NAE to hold its annual conference in Greenville, South Carolina, where the school had relocated in 1947. The invitation was refused, and a flurry of correspondence ensued between the Joneses and NAE leaders. The letters are significant because they reveal that much more was troubling the Joneses. Writing to R. L. Decker, president of the NAE, Jones Sr. complained that "some of the brethren felt that if the NAE held its convention in connection with Bob Jones University, it would create jealousy on the part of other educational institutions." The NAE was invited to Greenville, Jones stated, because he felt that large evangelistic meetings might have been held in connection with the NAE. Jones then criticized the NAE for its evangelistic techniques. While the details are not completely available, Jones Sr. had, at the first meeting of the NAE evangelism commission, proposed some sort of plan that was rejected. "I was," Jones said, "the only well-known evangelist in the convention. I had in mind a plan for evangelism that would have appealed to all evangelicals . . . but the brethren had their own plans." Jones Sr. also recalled the fact that when the NAE was forming its committee on education, no one from Bob Jones University was asked to serve on it, and "Bob Jones University . . . is the fastest growing Christian educational institution in the history of America." It also irritated Jones Sr. that "certain brethren connected with the NAE look on us as if we were a liability rather than an asset."[49]

President Decker also heard from Bob Jones Jr. Despite the fact, Jones Jr. wrote, that "both my father and I have tried aggressively to boost the NAE and to extend its membership and influence, . . . because of the personal jealousies of certain individuals . . . we have not sometimes been able to render the service we could have rendered." Jones Jr. wanted the NAE to meet in Greenville because he wanted southern fundamentalists to "become acquainted firsthand with the NAE" and because he felt the NAE would be popular with his students. Jones Jr. felt that his opportunities for further service to the NAE were limited by "the friction and strain which membership [in the NAE] has come to entail."[50] Obviously, then, by 1949 there were elements within the NAE not entirely comfortable with the identification with Bob Jones University that a Greenville convention would bring. While the Joneses ascribed this to "personal jealousies"—and there may indeed have been some—there was another, more philosophical reason why an identification with the Joneses might have been less than appealing to a growing, influential group within the NAE.

When the NAE was founded in 1942, its primary emphasis was upon evangelism, upon making it easier for evangelicals to organize and propagate their message. The early NAE committees dealing with evangelism, securing free radio time for evangelical ministers, and obtaining their share of the chaplain quota in the armed forces, all attested to this emphasis. Throughout the 1940s the NAE steadily expanded to include not only evangelistic goals, but also more diverse concerns such as social welfare and education. One reason this expansion was possible was because the NAE was not founded primarily as a defensive, separatist organization. Closely related to this new attitude were two further developments: first, many fundamentalists were now dissatisfied with that name and wished for something less offensive; and second, in the 1940s a younger generation was coming to maturity within fundamentalist ranks whose roots were not in the revival circuit of the early twentieth century or in the fundamentalist-modernist wars of the 1920s.[51] Together, these factors created an atmosphere in which the Joneses felt distinctly uncomfortable.

By 1947 the new trend was unmistakable, as more fundamentalists began referring to themselves as "new evangelicals." The term, coined in 1947 by Fuller Theological Seminary President Harold Ockenga, was meant to demonstrate the new attitude among conservatives.[52] Ockenga, a Boston pastor and a founder of the NAE, in a sermon to his Boston congregation, spelled out the dimensions of the "new evangelicalism."[53] He first made it clear that in doctrine he was a fundamentalist. Indeed, for Ockenga, new evangelicalism was "a movement of self-criticism that has come out of the fundamentalist movement." He asserted that fundamentalism, because it had suffered repeated defeats, had now "grown suspicious of people who do not hold every doctrine and every practice that they hold." Fundamentalists had now begun to turn on each other. "Too often," Ockenga said, "there has been less charity and courtesy shown . . . than there has been in the liberal camp." Ockenga also attacked the fundamentalist penchant for separation. This search for absolute purity was endless. "Where in the world," Ockenga asked, "will you find the person or the church that is totally pure?" Asserting that fundamentalism had lost every battle with modernism for the last fifty years, Ockenga asked, "Is this the power of God? . . . Where is the power of God in that?"

New Evangelicalism offered an alternative. While fundamentalists argued and separated from one another, new evangelicals believed in "positive preaching of the Word," confident that "this Gospel is intellectually defensible and respectable." The new evangelical was "willing to face the intellectual problems whether they deal with creation, or with the age of man, or whatever it is, examining the claims of the Bible . . . in the light of the best knowledge of the day." New evangelicals were also eager, Ockenga stated, to apply the gospel to social problems. To do otherwise, to present a message concerned only with personal salvation, was to present a "truncated Christianity." New Evangelicalism, then, was a movement affirming the fundamentals of the faith but was not content merely to affirm them, hoping rather to reintegrate them into the social, academic, and religious worlds.

Foremost among the new evangelicals was a group of young men coming to maturity in the 1940s, trained in secular graduate schools, and eager to defend conservative Christianity as an intellectually viable system. Their numbers included Harold Ockenga (Ph.D., University of Pittsburgh), Carl F. H. Henry (Ph.D., Boston University), Edward J. Carnell (Ph.D., Harvard University), George Ladd (Ph.D., Harvard University), and Bernard Ramm (Ph.D., University of Southern California). Their attitude was best expressed by Bernard Ramm, who observed that within fundamentalism a "movement has developed . . . that has given the word an odious connotation. Men . . . frequently lacking in education or cultural breadth . . . took to the stump to defend the faith."[54] The new evangelical effort to correct this took place on a number of fronts. In 1947, for example, Carl Henry published his *The Uneasy Conscience of Modern Fundamentalism*, in which he decried the lack of a social ethic among fundamentalists.[55] Also that year Fuller Theological Seminary was established in Pasadena, California. The new seminary was dedicated, in George Marsden's words, to "raising the level of biblical, theological, and apologetical awareness in fundamentalist churches."[56] In 1956 evangelicals also launched *Christianity Today*, a periodical intended to serve as a counterpart to the liberal *Christian Century*.

In March 1956 a seminal article, "Is Evangelical Theology Changing?" appeared in *Christian Life*. The article charted the progress of the new evangelicals, identifying several ways in which new evangelicalism differed from fundamentalism. First, the authors noted a more charitable attitude toward science among evangelicals. For example, Bernard Ramm's *The Christian View of Science and Scripture* had appeared in 1955. Ramm ventured that perhaps the "days" in Genesis 1 were really ages (thus allowing for the evolutionary process). Ramm also speculated that Noah's flood was a local one, not universal. That an avowed conservative could make these assertions did indeed presage a new attitude. The article also noted that the new evangelicals were less dogmatic on such issues as dispensationalism and biblical infallibility.[57] Perhaps the surest sign that the new evangelicals were accomplishing their aims came when Arnold Hearn, a liberal theologian, noted in the *Christian Century* that there was indeed a "remarkable renascence of intellectual activity" in conservative ranks. Praising the evangelicals for presenting conservative Christianity in "terms more sensitive to the integrity of the modern mind," Hearn urged his fellow liberals "not to dismiss them."[58]

The Joneses lamented this trend within Protestantism for two reasons. First, they feared that the new emphasis upon research, critical thinking, and dialogue with liberals was diverting evangelical Christianity from its primary mission of evangelizing. Liberals

were to be converted, not debated. Second, despite the protestations of the new evangelicals that their methods were simply
another means of evangelism, the Bob Joneses feared that this intellectual approach was creating an attitude of superiority in which
some fundamentalists were looked down upon. It is not surprising
that the Joneses reached these conclusions. Research and analytical
thinking had never ranked as high priorities at Bob Jones University. Conceiving their mission to be one of protection and indoctri-
nation, the Joneses did not place much value upon scholarship if it
did not buttress what was already regarded as the truth.[59]

A sharp exchange in the pages of *United Evangelical Action*, the
official periodical of the NAE, between Bob Jones Sr. and a writer
named J. Carl vividly illustrated the Joneses' growing breach with
the NAE. J. Carl, in a letter to the editor, expressed dismay that
within conservative evangelical ranks there were several Christian
colleges that, Carl felt, "favor the anti-intellectual forces at work
within evangelicalism." Referring to Bob Jones Sr. without naming
him, Carl cited the founder of one of these colleges who "recently
made the statement that everytime they hired a Ph.D., they had to
have a revival to offset it." Carl also criticized Jones for remarking
that too much time spent reading history or science texts made a
student "lose his passion for souls." Asking "can you imagine any
serious academic work being done in an atmosphere of that kind?"
Carl further wondered why evangelical colleges such as Calvin and
Wheaton "turn out dozens of men who have gone into the pagan
university world to make names for themselves . . . whereas this
other type of school has turned out almost no one of such ability?"[60]

In his rebuttal Jones Sr. both defended his school and criticized
the new evangelical efforts to appear intellectually respectable. His
letter reveals Jones to be, philosophically, miles apart from the faction gaining increasing power in the NAE. Jones flatly stated, "I am
sick and tired of certain supposedly orthodox Christians casting
slurs upon institutions that give first emphasis to evangelism." He
stated further that Bob Jones University, in addition to its evangelistic emphasis, also had high academic standards. Still, for Jones, the
purpose of a Christian college was to "teach practical Christian phi-

losophy." Then he launched into his attack upon the new evangelicals. "We are not," Jones said, "going to save men by matching wits with them. There is no saving power in education." Jones cited the Apostle Paul, who "was not won to Jesus Christ by scholarship. . . . After Paul was saved he did not go out to match wits with the pagan world. He went everywhere telling men that . . . Jesus died for them." As far as Jones was concerned, "we have come to bad days in orthodox circles when some men exalt the training of the intellect and scholastic research as the hope of our day." Jones advised the new evangelicals to "get on their knees and ask God to deliver them" from their intellectual pride.[61]

The NAE refusal to meet in Greenville, coupled with the growing philosophical differences between the Joneses and the new evangelicals, occurred at a time when Bob Jones University was also experiencing a transition in leadership. The elevation of Bob Jones Jr. to the school's presidency in 1947 had significant consequences for BJU and its move toward separatism. While his father had the reputation of a fiery evangelist, Jones Jr. was in many respects more aggressive and confrontational.[62] This personality characteristic made Jones Jr. less patient than his father and more willing to sever ties with those with whom he disagreed. He also inherited the leadership at a time when he and his father, long active in the largest evangelical organization in the nation, suddenly found themselves scorned by some as a detriment to the movement. This development exacerbated Jones Jr.'s pugnacious traits. Adopting a separatist position fit more naturally with his temperament.

By the time Bob Jones Jr. assumed the presidency in 1947, there was already ample evidence of his confrontational style. In 1939, when the Joneses broke their association with the Broad Street Methodist Church, it was the younger Jones who confronted the minister and who recommended leaving the church to his father. In his memoirs, Jones Jr. recounted the service in which he decided to break his ties with the Broad Street Church. Describing the minister as attacking "every other doctrine of the faith," Jones Jr. "sat there shaking my head and saying 'no, no, no.' The 'no's' got louder the longer he preached." The speaker, according to Jones, "grew redder and redder until finally he said 'I cannot continue this message because of the rudeness of one man in this congregation.' For the first time in my life, I cried full voice, 'hallelujah! Praise God!'" After the service Jones Jr. asked the pastor to "send me my [membership] letter first thing in the morning."[63]

Jones Jr. could be equally assertive when someone attacked his school. A former student, then at Wheaton, informed him that elements at Wheaton were criticizing BJU for supposedly having lower academic standards. Jones Jr. responded with a blistering letter. Attributing the criticism to "egotistical feeling," he observed that "anyway, we have not had a lot of internal trouble like Wheaton has had. We have a loyal crowd of students and God is blessing the school. If Wheaton doesn't come down off its high horse it will have more trouble than it has had already." The letter carried the obvious implication that God was blessing BJU, and if Wheaton persisted in its arrogant attitude, they could expect trouble from the Lord.[64] Jones's conduct in the Broad Street Church and his reaction to criticism from Wheaton reveal him as a man quick not only to make judgments but also to express them in a very straightforward manner.

With his father, Jones Jr. became active in the NAE. He spoke at the national meetings throughout the 1940s, and in 1950 was elected vice-president of the organization. Jones recalled that when the NAE was formed, its purpose was to "unite Bible-believing Christians for a strong witness and testimony. The idea was that it would be able to get radio and television time for the biblical viewpoint."[65] Attempting to obtain television time for fundamentalists was particularly attractive to Jones Jr. because he was working to develop BJU into a center for Christian filmmaking. In 1950 BJU purchased $300,000 worth of production equipment and launched a new program called "Unusual Films." Jones Jr. asserted that "our young people can't escape the movies, radio and television. But they can learn to use these things, control them, make them talk for the Master."[66] Jones hoped eventually to see Unusual Films productions on national television.[67] The NAE was a valuable ally in working toward that goal. Thus Jones Jr. remained active within the NAE even as the organization was taking heavy criticism from separatist fundamentalists.

Jones Jr.'s attitude changed quickly in the aftermath of the NAE refusal to meet in Greenville and the growing criticisms of the educational philosophy of Bob Jones University. In his 1985 memoirs, Jones was unsparing in his condemnation of the NAE. Reflecting upon his election as NAE vice-president in 1950, Jones claimed he was being "used" by some in the NAE to "deceive the fundamentalists" into thinking the NAE was a fundamentalist organization. Jones also claimed that there "was no hope from the beginning" for the NAE because its leaders were "traitors to the separatist cause. . . . That means traitors to the cause of Christ and the Word of God." He was particularly scornful of the new evangelical effort to cultivate the secular academic world. The new evangelicals, he said, "simply had to have liberal recognition. They said to the enemies of the Christian faith, 'we will call you Christian brothers if you will call us "doctor," "professor," and "scholar." '"[68] Jones severed his ties with the NAE in June 1951.[69]

Two years later, in a letter to *United Evangelical Action,* Jones Jr. criticized the NAE for failing "to take a firm and uncompromising position on matters important to the defense of the faith." With this statement, Jones echoed the criticisms hurled at the NAE by separatists during the time Jones himself had been active in the organization. Robert Schuler, a Methodist evangelist active in the NAE and a friend of Bob Jones, noted the growing change in Jones Jr. In a letter to *UEA,* Schuler urged evangelicals to pray for "the ugly-spirited hyper-fundamentalists." He lamented the fact that Jones Jr. was "apparently leaning in their direction."[70]

In the summer of 1953, as Jones leveled his harsh criticism at the NAE, an incident occurred at BJU that resulted in the firing of a key administration official and the subsequent resignation of several faculty. In May 1953 the registrar and assistant to the president, Theodore C. Mercer, was dismissed for allegedly forming a faculty clique hostile to the Joneses. There were also intimations that Mercer was involved in homosexual activities.[71] The Mercer episode is important because it occurred at a time when the Joneses were increasingly on the defensive within the evangelical community. An internal crisis of this magnitude could serve only to heighten the Joneses' sense that they were indeed alone in a hostile world. As the Mercer affair engulfed the campus in the summer of 1953, Jones Sr. remarked that "every orthodox, fighting Christian institution is today under the most terrible satanic attack that has ever been carried on since I have been preaching."[72]

For sixteen years, Theodore Mercer had been connected with BJU in various capacities: first as an undergraduate and graduate student, then dean of men and registrar, and finally as assistant to the president.[73] He very favorably impressed Jones Sr. "Mercer was a man," Jones Jr. recalled in 1989, "whom my father thought had great possibilities. I did not." Jones Sr. urged his son to appoint Mercer as assistant to the president. Reluctantly, Jones Jr. assented to his father's request, asserting that "I hated to block my dad on something like that."[74] Despite Jones Jr.'s misgivings, the relationship evidently worked for a time. In 1950 Mercer was given full executive authority whenever both Joneses were away from campus.[75]

The chain of events leading to Mercer's ouster began in the spring of 1951. At the end of the 1950–51 academic year Jones Jr. held a meeting with the deans. The problem discussed, according to Mercer, was "our inability to get the proper number of qualified faculty and our apparent difficulty in holding those whom we did get." The deans informed Jones Jr. that the faculty pay system, based solely upon need and requiring faculty to live on campus, was largely responsible for discouraging prospective faculty. Jones Jr. accepted their assessment and appeared ready to discuss changes until, Mercer remembered, "Jones, Sr. came into the office as he customarily did when Dr. Jones, Jr. was having a conference with any group." The patriarch saw no need for changes and shortly thereafter incorporated the school's salary system into the university charter.[76]

Mercer was also concerned with the administrative morass caused by the father making policy contrary to his son's. Writing a letter to the younger Jones, Mercer informed him that often the university executives did not know whom to follow. At their next meeting, according to Mercer, Jones Jr. told the executives that he was the president and "we were to take orders from him, not his father." Several of the men apparently mistook the president's statement and began to laugh. Jones became angry, and Mercer recalled that he "pounded on his desk to emphasize he was running the school. He knew, as we did, that he would give us orders until his father pleased to give us other orders." Jones Jr., in the fourth year of his presidency, had not only to contend with deteriorating relations with the evangelical community, but also with a leadership transition that was not yet complete. Now, in addition, his faculty was growing restive under their salary and living arrangements.

At the end of the 1951–52 academic year, seventy staff and faculty members left, including the deans of religion and arts and science. While this number included many who were retiring, there was enough discontent in this group to lead the Joneses to investigate. Mercer remembered a series of faculty meetings in which Jones Sr. demanded "to know who had been heard to complain about housing, salary, etc." According to Mercer, the resignations of the two deans were prompted by the treatment they had received at the hands of the administration. Morale further plummeted when it was revealed that a history professor, Morton Brown, was fired for writing a letter to the administration criticizing a recent decision. The wave of departures, resignations, and firings produced, in Mercer's words, "a terrible mental and emotional climate on the campus."[77]

Further evidence that the Joneses felt increasingly insecure came in the spring of 1952, shortly after the mass exodus of seventy employees. The Joneses proposed, and the board of trustees adopted, a revised version of the charter and by-laws. The new version formally empowered the president to "appoint, employ, and discharge all members of the faculty . . . and fix their respective compensation." Moreover, all faculty and staff were instructed not to complain "to anyone with whom he or she associates in this institution. . . . As long as one is employed by the institution, such employee must not criticize the administrative policy of the institution except to the president or the proper executive." The new by-laws further stated that if a staff member could not be loyal to the school, then the "relationship with the institution ends immediately." Husbands and wives of employees were expected to manifest the same degree of loyalty to the university. As far as salaries were concerned, the system of pay according to need was formally codified. Staff members who demonstrated "a cooperative spirit" would be entitled to bonuses.[78]

Mercer, already alarmed over the departure of so many staff, became further disillusioned when Jones Sr. informed him of the reason for the new by-laws. According to Mercer, "Dr. Jones told me expressly that any time we did not want any person to remain with us, all we had to do was call him in, point to the by-laws and tell him he was no longer satisfactory and that no reason had to be given." Mercer later speculated that the arbitrary treatment of faculty was one reason BJU did not receive accreditation. Committees from the South Carolina board of education visited the campus several times and questioned the peculiar pay system and the workloads placed upon the faculty. Mercer maintained that the visiting educators proposed changes in the pay system and several other unspecified academic policies. Evidently the Joneses promised changes but, Mercer recalled, "most of the things were never fixed." As for faculty pay and workloads, Mercer remembered Jones Sr. recommending that the faculty be worked "so hard . . . they'll be too tired to complain about anything."

Significantly, it was during this time of internal turmoil that the first criticisms of evangelist Billy Graham were made. Five years before Graham held his 1957 New York crusade with the help of "modernists," when he was still very much a part of the fundamentalist community, the Joneses were already criticizing their former student. Mercer remembered Graham labeled in a faculty meeting as "shallow, superficial, and not having real revival." These early criticisms by the Joneses suggest that their later harsh separatist rhetoric against Graham may have been a defensive action motivated in part by the turmoil the school experienced in the early 1950s. Mercer suggested in 1953 that anyone connected with BJU who got "in the limelight [met] with disfavor."[79]

By May 1953 Mercer's days were numbered. During the 1952–53 academic year, according to Jones Sr., the dean of women, the dean of students, and the new dean of the School of Religion all informed him that "there was something wrong with Mr. Mercer's conduct in his position as assistant to the president." Upon further investigation, the executive committee met and agreed to fire Mercer. Mercer was charged with forming a faculty clique who, Jones Sr. maintained, "worked with him to dig into the foundations upon which BJU [was] built." Mercer was also accused of allowing a student couple to date in his office in his absence, and of arranging to have a "special friend" dismissed from classes so the student could "spend time in [Mercer's] office with him."[80] The gender of Mercer's "special friend" was not disclosed, but in 1989 Jones Jr. recalled that Mercer had a number of student friends and "they were all boys."[81]

Upon his termination at BJU, Mercer promptly printed two pamphlets in which he recounted what he regarded as abuses at BJU. Sending copies to all the students at BJU, Mercer also, according to Jones Jr., wrote to the textbook companies that supplied BJU and urged them to stop doing business with the school.[82] In the wake of Mercer's firing, the dean of fine arts, Karl Keefer, resigned, arguing that at BJU one must "actively or tacitly agree with all decisions and actions, or leave." Mercer also charged that after his release at least two BJU students were dismissed when it was discovered that they had written to him.[83] In December 1953 a group calling itself the Joint Alumni–Former Student Committee issued a call for Mercer's reinstatement.[84] After Mercer was released, Jones Sr. preached a series of chapel messages on Judas. Jones identified Mercer with Judas but, Mercer remembered, "made clear that Judas was a much finer fellow, for he did have the grace to hang himself and he did not write letters back to his school."[85]

The analogy to the traitor Judas fit well in the minds of the Joneses. The Mercer affair reinforced their growing defensive mentality. The school was now beset from within and without. As Jones Sr. informed the alumni shortly after the firing, "Jesus had a Judas

Iscariot. Paul lost practically all of his following." He asked them to pray "as you have never prayed in your life. We are fighting a hard battle. . . . We are not going to let the devil have BJU."[86] Mercer's opposition, coupled with the criticisms of other faculty concerning administrative policies, served in the end to convince the Joneses that their path was indeed the correct one. From their perspective, the opposition really emanated from Satan. In dismissing Mercer they were fighting the devil, and if that left them in the minority, they could point to Jesus and Paul as having suffered similar fates.

The personal and philosophical differences with the NAE, Jones Jr.'s ascension to power, and now the Mercer upheaval all clearly altered the direction of BJU. The Joneses' denunciation of the NAE for being insufficiently separatist after they themselves had been a part of the organization and the comparison of their opponents to Judas suggested a new course for the school: separation was the next logical step. Ironically, it was the work of a former Bob Jones student, Billy Graham, that finally moved BJU into the camp of ultraseparatism.

The evangelical periodical *Christianity Today* once observed of Billy Graham that "the great irony of his career is that his most vehement opponents are fellow Bible believers."[87] Indeed, it was the controversy over Graham's evangelistic campaigns and methods that brought to a climax the struggle that had been waged since the formation of the NAE and the ACCC in the 1940s. Born in 1918 into a strongly Presbyterian North Carolina family, William Franklin Graham Jr. showed no inclination to be an evangelist during his youth. At age sixteen, after hearing the noted southern evangelist Mordecai F. Ham, Graham was converted. Following his conversion, his parents pressed him to enter the ministry. After a summer of playing semiprofessional baseball, Graham consented and enrolled in Bob Jones College, then in Cleveland, Tennessee.[88] This first encounter with the Joneses did not go well. Graham told his biographer in 1979 that "I didn't have the slightest idea what kind of school [Bob Jones] was." His mother, having heard Jones Sr. speak in a revival, had been the great proponent of BJC. Graham stayed for only one semester. During that brief time,

Graham remembered, "I never did fit in. . . . I couldn't believe the rules there . . . there were demerits for just about everything."[89]

Although Graham stayed for just one semester, he did come to the attention of the Joneses. Jones Jr. remembered the young North Carolinian as "determined to make himself a campus leader." He contended that Graham failed in this effort because the "student body was . . . too intelligent and too spiritual to be taken in by his charm." When Graham informed the school of his decision to transfer to Trinity Bible Institute in Florida, Jones Sr. warned him that if he left BJC for a little-known Bible College, "the chances are you'll never be heard from again."[90] According to R. K. Johnson, Jones Sr. was already suspicious of Graham after an incident in which Graham violated school rules by leaving campus without signing out.[91] Even before Graham gained any celebrity, it was clear that there was a personality conflict between him and the Joneses.

Leaving Bob Jones for Trinity, Graham was ordained as a Southern Baptist minister and shortly thereafter transferred to Wheaton College in Illinois. During his Wheaton years Graham not only earned a degree in anthropology, he also gained exposure by preaching over the radio and by working as a representative for Youth for Christ.[92] His speaking ability brought him to the attention of William B. Riley, president of Northwestern Bible College in Minneapolis. Riley was a warhorse from the 1920s, his major contribution then being the organization of the World's Christian Fundamentals Association. Riley asked Graham to serve as vice president of Northwestern, and upon Riley's death in 1947 Graham assumed the college presidency.

Graham's years at Northwestern also coincided with a growing interest on his part in mass evangelism. Not suited by his education to serve as a college president, Graham resigned the office in order to pursue this interest. Mass evangelism had fallen into disrepute, the term loaded with connotations of tent revivals laden with sensationalism, emotionalism, and very often financial irregularities. Early in his crusade ministry, Graham established two firm rules to help reverse this public perception. First, in order to hold a crusade, Graham requested an invitation from a majority of local churches. Also, all crusade finances were to be handled by a committee of local businessmen. After the meetings an audit was prepared revealing how much money was received and how it was spent.[93] The first Billy Graham crusade, held in Los Angeles in 1949, was a great success. The meetings attracted crowds of three hundred thousand and much of the city's religious leadership. Graham was also the beneficiary of overwhelmingly favorable publicity. Generous coverage was given to him in *Time* and *Life*. From this time on Billy Graham became a permanent fixture on the American religious scene.[94]

Graham's rise to prominence paralleled the widening division within the ranks of conservative Protestantism over the issue of separation. While the new evangelicals would eventually make Graham's ministry one of the shining examples of their phenomenon at work, in the early years of his ministry Graham still displayed the harsh edge of fundamentalism. Writing his first column as president of Northwestern in the January 1948 issue of the college magazine, *The Pilot,* Graham asserted his intention to make the school "militant in its stand against modernism in every form." When *The Pilot* inadvertently carried an advertisement for a book by the great modernist Harry Emerson Fosdick, Graham published an apology and assured his readers that the paper still represented "the orthodox, conservative, fundamental theological position. We do not condone nor have fellowship with any form of modernism."[95] Graham also displayed his fundamentalist leanings at the 1948 Conservative Baptist Association convention. Asked what he thought would be the result of the upcoming meeting of the ecumenical World Council of Churches, Graham answered flatly, "I believe they are going to nominate the anti-christ."[96]

Despite their earlier uneasy relationship, Graham also attempted to cultivate the Joneses. Shortly after becoming president of Northwestern, Graham wrote Jones Sr. assuring him that "we are trying to do here in the great Northwest what Bob Jones University has done 1200 miles away." Bob Jones signaled his approval by awarding his former student an honorary doctorate. After his successful Los Angeles campaign had launched his evangelistic career, Graham wrote to the elder Jones and called him the "model toward which we are patterning our lives. Your counsel means more to me than that of any individual in the nation." Graham also tried to make amends with Jones Jr. Again writing to the father, Graham asked him to "give my love to Dr. Bob Jr., as there is no man in the world that I love more than I do him. You may rest assured that if the Lord should take you Home first, I shall stand by Bob with everything I have."[97]

Graham's efforts to win the Joneses' favor worked. Jones Jr. asserted that by 1949 he and Graham had become "rather close friends." The younger Jones substituted for Graham at an evangelistic meeting in California in 1949 when Graham had another commitment.[98] Further endearing Graham to the Joneses was the fact that most of Graham's evangelistic team were Bob Jones graduates. Graham's song leader, Cliff Barrows, was a BJU graduate and a man described by Jones Jr. as "so separated when he came to this institution that he would not even attend a Southern Baptist Convention church."[99] Other Bob Jones graduates on Graham's team included T. W. Wilson and Willis Haymaker, who had worked in many of Jones Sr.'s evangelistic rallies. In the spring of 1950, Graham held a crusade in Columbia, South Carolina. The Joneses invited him to Greenville, and Graham held a rally of six thousand people in Rodeheaver Auditorium on the BJU campus. Jones Jr. later entertained Graham and his associates in his home and allowed Graham to use the auditorium for another rally that evening.[100] During his 1950 visit to South Carolina, Graham approached Jones Jr. and asked him, according to Jones, to "warn me if you see me doing anything that will hurt the cause of Christ." Jones promised to do just that, and the two prayed together.[101]

At what point the Jones/Graham relationship began to deteriorate is difficult to identify. By the time of their 1950 meeting in Greenville, the barbs Jones Jr. was enduring from certain members of the NAE had put him on the verge of leaving that organization. Two years later, the school was embroiled in the Mercer controversy. Theodore Mercer asserted that he had heard Jones Jr. label Graham as "shallow and superficial, and not having real revival."[102]

If Mercer's charge is true, then in the space of two years, from 1950 to 1952, Jones Jr.'s opinion of Graham had drastically changed. One plausible explanation for this alleged change is the fact that Graham remained active in the NAE and had encouraged the new evangelical element in it; Jones Jr. may have harbored ill-will toward Graham for that continued involvement. Another possibility, one the Joneses vehemently denied, is that they were jealous of Graham's meteoric rise.[103] Whatever the case, by 1956 Bob Jones University and its leadership had turned against Graham.

In November 1956, the Billy Graham Evangelistic Association contacted Jones Jr. regarding the possibility of holding a rally in Greenville. This was to be part of a nationwide effort to garner publicity for Graham's proposed Spring 1957 crusade in New York City, but by 1956 Graham had already begun to seek the support of avowed modernists in planning his crusade. Earlier, he had rejected an invitation from a committee of fundamentalists to preach in New York but had accepted one from the Protestant Council of New York, a group associated with the National Council and World Council of Churches.[104] Jones Jr. informed the Graham organization that the university could not support a rally because Graham was "seeking the sponsorship of modernists and liberals. . . . Billy is going to wreck evangelism and leave even orthodox churches, if they cooperate, spineless and emasculated."[105]

Fundamentalists were alarmed over the changes in Graham. Even before accepting the invitation of the Protestant Council, Graham had begun to offend them. He had spoken in the chapel of the liberal Union Theological Seminary in New York and then announced what a spiritually profitable time he had while there. Graham had also asked that his name be dropped from the cooperating board of the *Sword of the Lord,* a militantly fundamentalist periodical that regularly criticized new evangelicals. A sure sign of the change in Graham came when he told an interviewer in 1956 that he did not care for the term "fundamentalist"; rather, Graham said, "I much prefer being called a 'Christian'." Shortly before his New York crusade, Graham flung down the gauntlet to the fundamentalists. "I intend," he told the 1957 NAE convention, "to go anywhere, sponsored by anybody, to preach the gospel of Christ. . . . We often think that a person is not a Christian unless he pronounces our shibboleths . . . exactly the way we do. I have found born-again Christians . . . who do not know our particular evangelical language."[106]

Bob Jones Sr. wrote a reply to the numerous inquiries the university received regarding its stance on Graham and his ecumenical sponsors in New York. Jones Sr. charged that by including such ministers as Henry Van Dusen, president of Union Theological Seminary, and Dr. Norman Vincent Peale in his crusade, Graham had "violated the Scripture." Jones could not understand how "Billy Graham says he believes the Bible is the Word of God and can be sponsored by preachers who do not believe the fundamentals." Thanks to Graham and his sponsorship, "evangelism is in the greatest peril it has ever been."[107] The Joneses' stand cost them support. J. Elwin Wright, for example, one of the founders of the NAE and a BJU board member, resigned in protest from the board because of the Joneses' position. In a vitriolic letter to Jones Jr., Wright accused him of joining with "communists, modernists and ultrafundamentalists in condemning the work of Billy Graham." Wright warned Jones that since Graham was obviously one of "God's anointed," Jones with his attacks had "placed your school and your own soul in mortal peril." Wright urged Jones to "repent and confess your sin."[108]

Graham proceeded with his New York crusade despite the protests of the fundamentalists. Without question, Graham's 1957 crusade was a watershed event in the deepening division between fundamentalists and new evangelicals. Graham's inclusion of liberal Protestants in his evangelistic efforts was a microcosm of the new evangelical strategy of reestablishing dialogue with those once dismissed as "modernists." Graham's personal evolution from a Bible-wielding fundamentalist who vowed to "oppose modernism in every form" to one who vowed to "go anywhere, sponsored by anybody" is also representative of the journey taken by many in the fundamentalist camp.[109]

One observer noted that shortly after New York, "at the grass roots level the question soon became simply, 'are you for or against

Graham?'"[110] Individuals like the Bob Joneses, evangelist John R. Rice, and denominations such as the GARBC quickly aligned against Graham, while J. Elwin Wright, Carl F. Henry, and the NAE supported him. Twenty years earlier, they had all been allies united against modernism. Graham's ministry also hastened the redefinition of the once synonymous "fundamentalist" and "evangelical." Graham himself disavowed the fundamentalist label. A *Christianity Today* editorial put the matter starkly. Evangelicalism, the editorial stated, derived from the New Testament Greek word *euangelion,* gospel or glad tidings. To call oneself an evangelical was to identify with the "whole gospel as set forth in God's holy word." Fundamentalism, conversely, did not "possess the biblical background nor has it gained the . . . well-defined content that history has bestowed on evangelicalism." The term fundamentalism had become identified with "bitterness and pettiness of spirit."[111]

The Graham controversy was the last in a series of events that moved the Bob Joneses into the separatist camp. After the 1957 battle with Graham, there was a marked increase in the militant rhetoric and action emanating from Greenville. This militancy had, of course, been on the rise throughout the 1950s, propelled successively by the Joneses' break with the NAE, Jones Jr.'s rise to the presidency, the Mercer affair, and now the Graham controversy. The Joneses, enthusiastic supporters of and participants in the NAE in the 1940s, could now scarcely abide their old allies. Instead, the Joneses loudly proclaimed their separation from compromisers such as Graham and the NAE. This change heralded a new period in the history of BJU, as soon became apparent in the aftermath of the Graham controversy.

One area in which the new militancy was most readily noticeable was in the university's advertising. In 1958 the university began running a notice entitled "ultrafundamentalist." Informing prospective students that "if it were possible to be more fundamental than the fundamentals, that is what BJU would be," the announcement warned students against "modernists, infidels, and the disciples of the new evangelicalism." The message stood in contrast to previous university advertising, which stressed the academic and personal opportunities available to students at BJU. When the university submitted the copy to *Moody Monthly* for publication, the *Moody* editorial staff refused to run it. They were bothered by the Joneses' apparent equation of "modernists" and "infidels" with "disciples of the new evangelicalism" and wanted further explanation. Eventually Jones Jr. and William Culbertson, president of Moody Bible Institute (MBI), debated the issue in correspondence.

Culbertson canceled *Moody Monthly*'s contract with BJU after Jones Jr. apparently accused the *Moody* staff of unethical business practices. He concluded sorrowfully, informing Jones that "I wish matters were different, particularly when we have so much in common in heritage and devotion to the fundamentals of the faith." Jones Jr. wrote a strong letter back to Culbertson that demonstrated the militant, separatist, besieged mentality now in place in Greenville. Moody's refusal to carry the BJU advertisement, Jones Jr. stated, was abundant evidence that MBI "is no longer willing to 'contend for the Faith' or align itself with those who condemn compromise." Jones also attacked Culbertson's administration, observing that "ours was only a faint hope that MBI would draw back from the path of compromise upon which you . . . had set. . . . I have been aware for some years that the administration of Moody lacked either courage or conviction." BJU, by contrast, "is associated in the minds of people . . . with a firm stand for the faith and with an unrelenting battle in its defense. . . . MBI is plainly not willing to be lined up with an institution that is aggressive in its attack upon modernism and compromise." Clearly for Jones, being a fundamentalist entailed not only doctrinal orthodoxy but also a willingness to fight.[112]

In December 1958 Jones Jr. and other separatist leaders held a conference in Chicago explicitly to reaffirm the fundamentals and to condemn new evangelicalism. In a statement revealing just how far Jones Jr. had traveled in ten years, he asserted that the "greatest religious danger in our modern world is not modernism. It is compromise with modernism on the part of Bible-believing

Christians."[113] The enemy, for Jones, was now in the camp in the guise of compromising believers such as Billy Graham and Moody Bible Institute.

As they became more aggressive and militant, the Joneses began to use the "separateness" of different Christians and Christian organizations as a litmus test for associating with them. In 1960 Jones Jr. severed the university's ties with Youth for Christ, an organization that had been part of the postwar evangelical growth spurt. Jones parted company with the group because its leader, Ralph Engstrom, had begun, in Jones's estimation, to "surround himself with the compromise crowd." Jones was also upset because *Youth for Christ Magazine,* like *Moody Monthly,* had refused to carry a BJU advertisement. Despite Engstrom's desire to meet with him, Jones informed two Youth for Christ board members that "there is no point in the world in his coming [to Greenville]." Jones concluded that "there is no hope for Youth for Christ under the present leadership. . . . Youth for Christ is sold out to compromise." A year later, Jones Jr. separated from Child Evangelism Fellowship (CEF), an organization that presented the gospel to preteenagers by, among other methods, holding week-long "clubs" in neighborhoods. In a letter to the organization, Jones Jr. concluded that CEF "no longer takes a stand against compromise with apostasy. . . . I cannot consistently permit my name to be associated, even in an advisory capacity, with [CEF]."[114]

The Graham episode had opened the floodgates for the Joneses' militant separatism. After 1957 there was a clear pattern of the Joneses separating from other conservative Christians they deemed insufficiently separatist. The tension that had been building for more than a decade at BJU had finally found an outlet. Separation also recovered some crucial psychological territory for the Joneses. Ridiculed by some other conservatives for being a hindrance to evangelical Christianity, the Bob Joneses could now point to those same conservatives and accuse them of not being as "pure" or "separate" as they, the Joneses, were. Moreover, by calling the university "ultrafundamentalist" in its defense of the faith, they negated the charges of anti-intellectualism leveled at them by the new evangelicals. Which was more important, scholarship or standing true to God?

The Joneses had, of course, always been separatist in a sense. Because American higher education was increasingly secular, the founding of the university was an act of separation. The firing of a faculty member in 1928 for propagating modernism was an act of separatism. Yet despite these episodes, the Bob Joneses had always endeavored to cooperate with other conservatives. Jones Sr., for example, continued his affiliation with the Southern Methodist denomination long after it was apparent that modernism had made significant inroads there. Their long involvement in the NAE further illustrates this point. From 1941 to 1957, however, the course of events outlined in this chapter altered the Joneses' separatism, intensifying it and transforming it into their most distinctive characteristic. Separation became, after the events of that sixteen-year span, the Joneses' way of dealing with the rapidly changing American religious environment. The Joneses' increasing insularity also resurrected many of the tenets of seventeenth-century separatism, as we shall see. Separatism became, for the Bob Joneses, much more than ecclesiastical separation. It afforded them the opportunity to construct their own subculture and to deal with the increasing change characteristic of American society in the 1960s and 1970s.

CHAPTER THREE

The Separatist Path

The clash with Billy Graham and the new evangelicals inaugurated a new and important phase for the Bob Joneses and their university. Militant theological conservatism remained their chief distinguishing characteristic as they entered the decade of the 1960s. Over the period of the next twenty-five years, the Joneses continued to sever alliances with such avowed fundamentalists as John R. Rice and Jerry Falwell, the main objection being, as always, that they were insufficiently separatist. With this rigid adherence to separatism, the Joneses began to resemble such groups as the Donatists and Anabaptists. Most strikingly, they began to resemble the seventeenth-century Calvinist separatists, who regarded not only the Church of England but fellow separatists as suspect.

The extreme separatism practiced by the Joneses throughout the 1960s and 1970s resulted in two major consequences. First, as the Joneses publicly disassociated themselves from such well-known fundamentalist separatist leaders as John R. Rice over the separation issue, the fundamentalist camp became thoroughly polarized. By the 1970s, as we shall see, the Joneses were considered the theological policemen of the fundamentalist movement. As such, they alienated a major segment of the movement. Second, the political activities of fundamentalist Jerry Falwell, who sought to build a political coalition of fundamentalists, Catholics, and Mormons, compelled the Joneses to consider how their separatism applied outside the ecclesiastical realm. Concluding that Falwell had violated separatist tenets, the Joneses broke with him as well. The charge against Falwell in 1980, coupled with the numerous attacks launched by the Bob Joneses against other fundamentalists in the 1970s, convinced many in the fundamentalist camp that if the movement were ever to be effective, the ceaseless infighting had to stop. Falwell and others, including many with previous ties to Bob Jones, began consciously cultivating a new, less strident image for fundamentalism as the 1980s began. Labeling the new movement "pseudo-fundamentalism," the Joneses found themselves at the head of the opposing faction. As they had done first with the modernists, then with Billy Graham and the new evangelicals, and now with Jerry Falwell and other fundamentalists, the Bob Joneses claimed once again to be contending for the true faith.

The separatism practiced by the Joneses had ample precedent both in Scripture and in church history. Separation from evil was an idea inherent in Christianity. As a philosophical system, Christianity posited a division between the forces of light led by God and the forces of darkness led by Satan. There could be no ambiguity when the choice was between absolute good and absolute evil. Ultimately, for the orthodox Christian, everything was defined against the backdrop of this climatic battle. This philosophical premise fueled the separatist mentality.

Throughout Scripture, true believers were repeatedly warned to refrain from evil associations and reminded that they were different, that they were a people "set apart." In the Old Testament, for example, God told the nation of Israel that "I the Lord am holy, and have separated you from the peoples, that you should be mine" (Lev. 20:26). Because of this special relationship, God explicitly warned Israel not to intermarry with or emulate the heathen peoples they might encounter (Deut. 7:3–4). When the Israelites failed to keep their associations pure, God dealt with them severely, delivering them as captives to their neighbors because they had "feared other gods and walked in the customs of the nations whom the Lord drove out" of the Promised Land, Canaan (2 Kings 17:1–8). Also in the Old Testament, the Psalmist advised God's people not to walk "in the counsel of the wicked," nor to "stand in the way of sinners" (Ps. 1:1).

The New Testament continued these admonitions. The Apostle Paul, writing to the Corinthian church, commanded the believers there not to be "mismated with unbelievers. For what partnership has righteousness and iniquity? Or what fellowship has light with darkness?" (2 Cor. 6:14). Christians were warned also to "avoid" those who preached "contrary to the doctrine which ye have learned" and they were reminded that "whosoever will be a friend of the world is the enemy of God" (Rom. 16:17–18, James 4:4). The Scriptures prophesied that at the end of time God would indeed prevail over Satan and his forces, who would be "thrown into the lake of fire" and "tormented night and day forever and ever" (Rev. 20:10). It was abundantly clear that there could be no accommodation with the kingdom of darkness.[1]

Church history was replete with examples of Christians attempting to heed these separatist commands. The result was an almost continual succession of schisms and divisions. In the fourth century, for example, the Donatists, led by Donatus, bishop of Carthage, practiced separation from other professing Christians who, in times of persecution, had denied the faith. The Donatists argued that before these individuals could be received back into fellowship, they needed to be rebaptized. Conversely, leaders such as Augustine argued that after a proper penance these believers could be restored. For the Donatists, a church with impure members was intrinsically impure. For them the church was, as one scholar noted, "a visible society of the elect separate from the world."[2] Impure elements had to be purged.

The separatist impulse was also seen in groups such as the Anabaptists ("rebaptizers") of the sixteenth century. Sydney Ahlstrom has defined Anabaptism as "widely separated yet interrelated efforts to restore or revive the primitive church."[3] One of the many distinctive doctrines of this diverse group was a rejection of infant baptism. Baptism was a symbol reserved only for those who had consciously accepted Christ and renounced the world. For the Anabaptists, the true Church was really composed of, as Roland Bainton suggested, "a handful of saints. . . . The unworthy must be cast out, the tepid and doubting must never be forced to come in."[4] The Schleitheim Confession, composed by Swiss Anabaptists in 1527, admonished believers that "all creatures are in but two classes, good and bad, believing and unbelieving, darkness and light. . . . From this we should learn that everything which is not united with our God and Christ cannot be other than an abomination which we should shun and flee from."[5] While the Bob Joneses were in many respects light-years removed from the fourth-century Donatists and sixteenth-century Anabaptists, they most certainly did come to share these groups' devotion to purity and separation from apostasy.

The ideas and practices of the seventeenth-century English separatists, however, provide the strongest comparison with the separation practiced by the Joneses. These separatists were originally part of the Puritan faction within the Church of England. The Puritans, as their name implied, sought to "purify" the Church of England from the last vestiges of Roman Catholicism. Some in their number, however, eventually concluded that the only hope for true believers was to abandon the Church of England and form a new, separate church. A group of separatists formed their own church in Norwich, England, in 1581.[6]

One of the most articulate separatists was Henry Barrowe, who spelled out the separatist case in a series of tracts. Barrowe objected to the Church of England on four counts. Attacking the Church of England's use of the *Book of Common Prayer*, Barrowe argued that the church perpetuated Romanist practices by encouraging people to rely on prayers offered in a mechanistic, superstitious manner. Second, Barrowe felt that the episcopal organization of the Church of England resembled too closely the Roman Catholic Church. Ecclesiastical hierarchy fed yet another concern, that the ministers in the Church of England were not themselves pure. They were "forced" on churches by the bishops. Finally, Barrowe criticized the Church of England's practice of allowing the unconverted to belong to parish churches.[7]

Several key themes ran through the separatists' argument. First, the church was being ruined by impure elements, whether they

were remnants of Roman Catholicism or an unregenerate membership. Second, the only option open to true believers was to "come
out" of the Church of England. Persistent worship beside the unconverted was a sin. Third, the true separatist must denounce the
Church of England for its apostasy in the strongest possible terms.
Barrowe urged Christians "without any delay to forsake those dis-
ordered and ungodly and unholy synagogues, and the false teachers of these times." "Our communion," he continued, "must be in
the faith, and not in error or transgression. . . . [Members should]
leave their fellowship, [rather] than to partake with them in wickedness." In true separatist fashion, Barrowe tolerated no ambiguity.
"There is no comparison," he observed, "between these holy
churches of God . . . and these confused idolatrous assemblies."[8]

Having concluded that the Church of England was hopelessly
overrun with apostasy, the separatists then turned their fire upon
the Puritans, who had chosen to remain within the church as a
force for reform. Although ostensibly objecting to many of the
same things as did the separatists, the Puritans obviously lacked
the courage of their convictions. True Puritanism, the separatists
maintained, inevitably led to complete separation. Those staying
within the church to reform it were compromising themselves
mortally. In 1644 Roger Williams argued that "the grounds and
principles of the Puritans . . . must necessarily, if truly followed,
lead on to and enforce a separation."[9]

Williams provided an excellent example of extreme separatism,
his rhetoric and lifestyle presaging the Joneses in several respects.
Williams fully shared the belief that leaving the Church of England was insufficient. It was also necessary to continue denouncing
it. For Williams, the true separatist must, as one writer put it,
maintain "a constant alertness."[10] Williams actively asserted his
separatist principles. He refused a call to pastor a Boston church
because it had not, though separated from the Church of England,
renounced and repented of its former association. As Williams explained, "I durst not officiate to an unseparated people, as, upon
examination and conference, I found them to be."[11]

Eventually Williams denounced the Puritan churches in Massachusetts because they were all, to borrow Edmund Morgan's phrase, "tainted with Roman corruption." As Morgan has noted, Williams also drew a distinction between "godly persons" and "godly persons who had renounced their participation in the Church of England." To worship beside even a "godly person" who had not "renounced" the Church of England was tantamount to worshipping with the unconverted. As for the unconverted, it was a sin to "join with unregenerate men in any act of worship, whether oath, prayer, or simply being taught by a preacher." In Williams's view, apostasy had resulted in "a total routing of the Church and Ministry of Christ Jesus, put to flight, and retired into the Wilderness of Desolation." Although he believed that in the end Christ would triumph over his enemies, Williams held that in the meantime Christ's followers should expect to suffer, just as Christ did.[12]

The Bob Joneses, with their militant separatism and stringent criteria for association, resembled Williams and other seventeenth-century separatists in several ways. Just as Williams and others had concluded that the Church of England was hopelessly corrupt, so the Joneses and their followers had concluded that the mainline Protestant denominations were past saving. G. Archer Weniger, a fundamentalist pastor and a close associate of the Joneses, summed up this attitude in 1976. Commenting on a recent meeting of the World Council of Churches, an organization composed of the mainline denominations, Weniger asked, "What must God think of the abominable services of worship arranged in the corrupt imaginations of religious leaders and used to decorate the meetings of the World Council of Churches[?] . . . What will be the answer given at the Judgement Seat of Christ for . . . such men as Methodist liberal E. Stanley Jones, the late Union Seminary President Henry Van Dusen . . . Presbyterian liberal John Bonnell?"[13] As far as the Joneses were concerned, there could be absolutely no association with denominations tainted with liberalism, or "false teaching." A pamphlet written by the Bob Jones University Bible department stated flatly that anyone "who advocates fellowship with apostasy and who cooperates with . . . false teachers, unbelievers, and Romanists is guilty of a public defiance of God's command."[14] This echoed rather closely Henry Barrowe's admonition of three centuries earlier to "leave their fellowship, [rather] than to partake with them in wickedness."

Also, like the seventeenth century separatists, the Joneses strongly criticized their fellow fundamentalists who neglected to denounce apostasy with the same vigor as they did. This had been a particularly important issue for Roger Williams. He had, as we have seen, distinguished between "godly" people, that is, people who believed doctrinally as he did, and "godly persons who had renounced their participation in the Church of England." The Joneses agreed with Williams. As Bob Jones Jr. explained, "There is a difference between orthodoxy and fundamentalism. A man who believes the Bible and accepts it in its entirety as the Word of God is orthodox. A fundamentalist . . . is a man to whom . . . the Scriptures are important enough to warrant his *contending* for them. . . . If a man is a fundamentalist he is a contender for the faith."[15]

The seventeenth-century separatists also argued rather strenuously that the Puritans' efforts to reform the "apostate" Church of England were inconsistent with the true meaning of "puritan." Williams argued in 1644 that true puritanism led to separation. Bob Jones III, writing in 1985, observed that ultimately one could not "stay in and reform that which is corrupt and spiritually apostate. It will never happen. . . . Any believer who wants to be God's mouthpiece in this world must be a separatist."[16] The separatist attitude toward the Puritans was also analogous to the Joneses attitude toward the National Association of Evangelicals. The NAE, as we have seen, wanted to reestablish contact with the mainline denominations and work within them as a reforming force. Bob Jones Jr., after his break with the NAE, labeled the organization and its leaders as "traitors to the separatist cause."[17] Roger Williams could easily have said the same thing about the Puritans. Finally, although the Joneses never experienced Williams's physical banishment, they found themselves effectively "banished" from conservative evangelicalism in the 1940s, as we saw in chapter 2. This induced in the Joneses, as it did in Williams, a heightened sense of aloneness.

The Joneses, similar in so many ways to the seventeenth-century separatists, were heirs also to other separatist movements and ideas in eighteenth- and nineteenth-century American church history. Like their European counterparts, American churches experienced a seemingly endless succession of divisions. The first Great Awakening, for example, while in many respects a unifying force, fostered significant divisions in colonial churches. One of the chief issues in the Awakening was, once again, the presence of impure or "unregenerate" elements within the church. Advocates of the Awakening were offended by the presence of unconverted church members or ministers whom they also regarded as unconverted. George Whitefield articulated the conviction of many when he stated that congregations were spiritually destitute because "dead men preach to them."[18] Such rhetoric, positing the existence of evil alongside the good, invariably incited separatist sentiments.[19]

In addition to the Great Awakening, there have been numerous other schisms within American churches. Some have suggested, in fact, that separatism is the common denominator in American church history, citing the flood of schisms in the nineteenth and twentieth centuries.[20] Almost no denomination has escaped unscathed. The Methodists experienced major doctrinal divisions in 1843 and 1860. Later still, in the nineteenth century holiness groups emerged from Methodist schisms. The issue of slavery effectively sundered the northern and southern wings of the Baptist and Methodist denominations. American Presbyterians divided into two major factions with their tumultuous 1837 general assembly, over the issues of abolition and theological doctrine. The Churches of Christ divided in the early twentieth century over church polity.

Separatism received further impetus late in the nineteenth century as dispensationalism, or premillennialism, became increasingly popular. Premillennialism posited a steady increase in apostasy culminating in the return of Christ and the beginning of the millennium. Looking for Christ's reappearance easily translated into cataloging the alleged compromises of other beliefs. The inroads of biblical criticism and modernism into American churches in the late nineteenth century also heightened this alertness. The Jones family stood clearly in the premillennial tradition. Bob Jones Jr. remembered that "my dad was a strong premillennialist and always identified himself as such."[21] Certainly in his sermon, "The Perils of America," Jones Sr. was acutely aware of what he regarded as a decline in the theological fidelity of American denominations, especially in their colleges. Both Bob Jones Jr. and Bob Jones III expressed concern over the years with men and movements that they believed hastened the coming of the Antichrist and a one-world church, two key conditions, in premillennial doctrine, for the Second Coming.[22] Jones III observed once that "this ecumenical movement in religion . . . is all part of the plan to get the people of the world together for the take-over of the Antichrist." Jones Jr. also expressed confidence that "the devil has been doing everything he can . . . to try to break down the lines of ecclesiastical separation. . . . As one of [his] devices to build the world church of Antichrist."[23]

The Joneses' militant separatism, having led them to sever any association with Billy Graham and the new evangelicals, now led them into conflict with fellow fundamentalists. From the beginning of the 1960s until the middle 1980s, the Joneses practiced a separatism that led them to ostracize two of their long-time associates, evangelists John R. Rice and Jack Van Impe, whose separatism they viewed as inadequately contentious. It was also within this period that Jerry Falwell replaced, for the Joneses, Billy Graham as the "most dangerous man in America."[24] The continued strong leadership of Bob Jones Jr. throughout this period also encouraged the increasingly harder line taken by the university.

The break between the Joneses and Rice and Van Impe provides a look at both the way the Joneses now defined separation doctrinally and the manner in which they implemented this conviction. The disagreement between the Joneses and John R. Rice was perhaps most surprising of all. Rice, evangelist and editor of the fundamentalist periodical *Sword of the Lord,* had long been a noted separatist. As early as 1932, Wheaton College invited Rice to speak in chapel on the subject of separation.[25] Like the Joneses, Rice broke with Billy Graham over the separation issue. In 1958, Rice joined with the Joneses in the separatist meeting in Chicago, called specifically to denounce ecumenical evangelism, and Rice served as chairperson of the resolutions committee that issued a separatist manifesto.[26] Rice also strongly denounced the new evangelical movement. In a 1956 article in the *Sword,* Rice decried the new evangelical penchant for "playing down fundamentalism and the defense of the faith, to poke fun at old-time fundamentalists, and to quote with glowing terms of appreciation the weighty pronouncements of infidel scholars."[27]

Rice's close identification with Bob Jones University further bolstered his credentials as a separatist. He served on the BJU board and regularly promoted the school in his magazine by printing advertisements and sermons by the Joneses. He praised BJU as an "out-and-out Christian college of the kind to gladden the hearts of all true Christians." BJU, according to Rice, was doing "magnificent work of training young people for Christ, rearing up Christian leaders in these terrible and apostate days."[28] In a truly bizarre episode in which one fundamentalist leader charged BJU with encouraging "worldliness" in students because of the school's emphasis on Shakespeare and drama, Rice rushed to the school's defense. He assured his readers that "you can trust the high moral and spiritual standards held there [at BJU]."[29]

Rice also enjoyed a close personal relationship with the Jones family. He and Jones Sr. joined each other often in evangelistic meetings. The patriarch required all the ministerial students at BJU to read the *Sword* and write reviews of the sermons printed in the magazine. The onset of the new evangelicalism brought them even closer. In 1959, Jones Sr. invited Rice to speak at BJU on separatism, a sermon later printed as a tract entitled *Christian Cooperation and Separation.*[30] Also that year, when Billy Graham held a rally in Chicago, Rice staged a counterrally featuring Jones Jr. as the speaker.[31]

Given this history of close cooperation against Graham and New Evangelicalism, it is all the more ironic that the Joneses and Rice broke over the issue of separation. That they did is a clear indication of how far to the right the Joneses had moved on the issue. It seems significant that the break occurred after Jones Sr.'s death in 1968, when the younger and more combative Jones Jr., who had already separated from conservative organizations with any new evangelical ties, became firmly in control.

One of the first intimations that Rice's relationship with BJU had changed came in 1969, when he returned to BJU to preach, once again, the sermon on separation that he had delivered in Greenville in 1959. Rice recalled that he "preached the same message from the same outline. To my shocked surprise, Dr. Bob Jones Jr. did not like it."[32] In his sermon, Rice stated that on fundamental doctrines of the faith, such as the deity and sacrificial work of Christ, "there is no room for difference, no room for cooperation." Rice could not support Billy Graham because Graham welcomed modernists, "Christ-deniers" to Rice, to his platform. But Rice could associate with a fellow Christian who stayed in the increasingly liberal Southern Baptist Convention but who refused to support the Convention's liberal programs.

This last position was no longer tenable for Jones Jr. In a 1971 pamphlet, he stated that Christians must separate themselves from other believers who, though fundamentalist, had not dissociated themselves from liberal organizations. As Jones put it, "the fact that such a man stands in the pulpit and 'preaches the Gospel' or seems to be winning souls does not justify or excuse his alliances and his unscriptural position in relation to apostasy." Jones also declared that BJU Press would not publish a book written by anyone who remained in apostate circles, even if the book was "completely scriptural." Simply put, for Jones any fundamentalist who remained in a liberal denomination was, by his continued presence, placing a tacit seal of approval upon that denomination's liberalism, even if the fundamentalist refused to support liberal programs. Jones further reasoned that to continue in fellowship with such a fundamentalist would mean that he, Jones, was also tacitly supporting liberalism. This was not an option for Jones because, as he stated, the Bible "does command separation from those who aid and encourage compromise with apostasy."[33]

The immediate point of contention between Rice and Jones was that Rice continued to print sermons by such well-known Southern Baptist leaders as W. A. Criswell and R. G. Lee in the *Sword*. Many fundamentalists concluded that liberalism had overrun the Southern Baptist Convention (SBC). Rice himself criticized liberalism within the SBC. He noted that the SBC published works by modernist theologians in *The Broadman Commentary* and observed that SBC seminaries invited known liberals, or "infidels" as Rice called them, to speak in their chapels. Many of the SBC colleges, Rice concluded, were guilty of "false teaching." This notwithstanding, Rice could not oppose, in his words, "sound, Bible-believing, soul-winning Southern Baptists." He saw no problem in printing sermons by Criswell and Lee because they were "two men of the whole SBC most ardently and vocally opposed to modernism in the whole Convention." Their sermons on the "inspiration of the Bible, the deity, virgin birth, bodily resurrection of Christ we have published with great joy and with blessing to many."[34]

After the 1971 publication of Jones Jr.'s pamphlet, *Scriptural Separation,* in which Jones criticized Rice without directly mentioning him, Rice left the BJU board of trustees. The next year, when Rice organized the International Conference on Biblical Evangelism, Jones Jr. publicly opposed it. According to then-BJU-faculty-member George Dollar, "Jones charged that the conference, largely under Rice's influence, would not encourage men now taking a fully separatist stand but would cater to the uncommitted pastors who should by now have made their commitment." Jones's opposition resulted in the cancellation of the conference, since numerous pastors followed Jones's lead.[35]

The division between Jones Jr. and Rice introduced two new terms into the separatist debate, "primary" and "secondary" separation. Primary, also called "first degree" separation, was separation from a modernist. Secondary, or "second degree" separation, was disassociating oneself from a fellow fundamentalist who was not sufficiently separatist. Jones Jr. dismissed these distinctions as "folly" and asserted that "there is no such thing as first degree separation, second degree separation. . . . There is only scriptural separation."[36]

Rice argued that Jones Jr. and his allies, in insisting that all fellowship be broken with believers who stayed in modernist denominations, were teaching doctrine that was "not in the Bible and it was not held by the great Christians of the past." Rice observed further that for all his protestations of ecclesiastical purity, Jones Jr. was not entirely consistent in his own associations. Noting that Jones Jr. had Southern Baptists on the BJU board of trustees, and that a BJU graduate who was an ardent proponent of the SBC had recently been named "Alumnus of the Year," Rice concluded that "to fellowship with those [whom Jones Jr.] likes is okay; to fellowship with those devoted men of the same affiliation he does not like is 'compromise and deceitful.'" Finally, Rice argued that Jones Jr. had departed from historic fundamentalism. Rice pointed out that noted fundamentalists such as J. Frank Norris and William B. Riley had remained in liberal denominations and that Jones Sr. had left a local Methodist church with a liberal pastor but had stayed within the Methodist denomination.[37]

Jones Jr. responded to Rice's charges by asserting that Rice had always been "weak" in his separatist stand. Reproducing letters from his father to Rice urging him to be more aggressive against Billy Graham, Jones Jr. argued that "my father tenaciously held to the Bible position and, through sheer force of influence, forced Dr. Rice to a reluctant and belated stand." His father also "shared with me," Bob Jr. insisted, "his concern about Dr. Rice's weaknesses and his fears that without my father's influence, Dr. Rice would become so weak on . . . separation that it might be impossible for . . . the university to continue to work with him." Jones Jr. labeled as slander Rice's contention that Rice and Jones Sr. had shared the same attitude toward separation. Such a belief demonstrated that Rice "is a hindrance to those who fight for biblical principles."

Jones maintained that nothing had changed at BJU, that he was merely continuing his father's strong separatist stand. The correspondence between Rice and the elder Jones, which Jones Jr. reproduced, did in fact show that the two men had disagreed initially over

Graham's evangelistic methods. Eventually Rice supported the Joneses on the Graham issue. Jones Jr. also countered Rice's assertion that the elder Jones had not completely separated himself from the liberal Methodist Episcopal Church, South. Jones Jr. admitted that this denomination, with its publishing house and seminaries, had "sold out to infidelity," but he hastened to add that "we must bear in mind that 30 or 40 years ago the terrible apostasy, declension, and unbelief so apparent now . . . had not reached their present extreme." In any event, Jones stated that his father had indeed entirely withdrawn from the Methodist church before his death.

As for Rice's statement that the Joneses were inconsistent because they had Southern Baptists on the board, Jones Jr. responded that "we kept these men on our board while they were still in the Convention . . . [because] they were headed out of the Convention, and their contacts with BJU helped to bring them out." As for the presence of Senator Strom Thurmond, a Southern Baptist, on the BJU board, Jones wrote "there is no compromise in receiving advice from and fellowshipping on an individual basis with a Southern Baptist layman. There is compromise in promoting . . . and printing sermons of men who are promoting a compromise program."[38] This estrangement over separation, which began in 1971 when Rice left the BJU board, continued until Rice's death in 1980.[39]

The controversy is illuminating in several respects. First, it reinforces the idea that Jones Jr.'s aggressive, confrontational style was a key factor in moving BJU in the direction of ultraseparatism. In his rebuttal of Rice's arguments, Jones persistently used provocative language. He dismissed Rice's disagreements as "bitterness toward his strong separatist brethren" and attributed Rice's opposition to the fact that Rice "was peeved and frustrated. I, frankly, have no idea to what ends this frustration will lead him." Another problem with Rice, according to Jones, was that he was "usually 15 to 25 years behind the times," an elderly man struggling unsuccessfully, perhaps with the onset of senility. Asserting that "all across America true fundamentalists are grieved by the conduct of his later years," Jones insisted that "we tried to shield Dr. Rice in his old age from humiliation and embarrassment." That became impossible, however, when Rice's weak separatism threatened to "stir up the Lord's friends and His enemies into a common cauldron—into a compromise soup that only the Devil enjoys the taste of." Rice defended himself by observing that "many of Dr. Bob's friends are concerned about his tendency to careless speech. It has recently gotten him in trouble." Bob Jones Jr., however, was not troubled by his growing reputation for pugnacity.[40]

Second, the battle with Rice marked the emergence of Bob Jones III as a separatist in the mold of his father. Assuming the BJU presidency in 1971, Jones III's tenure began with the Rice controversy. He accused Rice of "repeatedly and viciously" insisting that the present BJU leadership did "not practice the brand of separatism subscribed to by the founder." As we shall see, Jones III's strong stance against Rice was a clear indication that he would continue the journey into ultraseparatism. Third, the clash with Rice once again underscored the primacy of separatism for the Joneses. They had in effect staked separatism as the center of their theology. Jones III stated the matter bluntly in 1977: "The school's position on separatism is a vital, basic issue concerning not only whether BJU can be trusted but, what will happen to Bible Christianity. Where the Church stands ten years from now will be decided by what it believes concerning separation today."[41] Finally, Jones Jr. confirmed that, just like the seventeenth-century separatists, he believed that apostasy, once begun, always grew worse. This belief reinforced his conviction that he and his school were among the last defenders of the faith. "The decline in the New Testament standards of Christian separation," he wrote, "has intensified. . . . The speed of that decline in these last 15 years has been three or four times what it was. . . . Conditions have not changed except to grow rapidly worse. BJU has not changed."[42]

The Joneses' break with Rice in the early 1970s presaged a decade of ever more intense preoccupation with the issue of separatism within fundamentalist ranks. The appearance in 1973 of BJU church historian George Dollar's *A History of Fundamentalism in America* is indicative. Dollar's book included a list of fundamentalist colleges and organizations that could no longer be regarded as militant in defending the faith. Schools that, in Dollar's estimation, refused to "expose error" and did not have a "war psychology" included Cedarville College (affiliated with the separatist General Association of Regular Baptist Churches), Moody Bible Institute, and the independent Baptist school, Tennessee Temple University. Dollar enumerated these and other schools "in order that pastors and young people may be alerted to the soft line of these educational institutions."[43] The publication of this polemic by BJU Press expanded the "policing" role the Joneses envisioned for themselves in the fundamentalist community.

Something of the internal dynamics of policing was revealed in evangelist Jack Van Impe's *Heart Disease in Christ's Body* (1984). Van Impe, whose ministry the Joneses supported from 1970 to 1977, found that his BJU backing was a mixed blessing. While it provided him with a national network of BJU-trained pastors who supported his crusades, it also meant a constant monitoring of his associations. According to Van Impe, the BJU alumni kept the Joneses regularly apprised of his contact with other ministers. Van Impe found that "if I wanted Dr. Bob's blessing, I simply had to say, 'yes, sir, I'll forsake that man or group,' whenever, according to his 'convictions,' he felt I had fellowshipped with the wrong person or church." Van Impe eventually broke with BJU, alleging that a "hate movement" existed within fundamentalism. In 1983 Bob Jr. publicly labeled Van Impe a "false fundamentalist."[44]

In establishing themselves as the preeminent separatists in the fundamentalist community, the Bob Joneses found that they were sometimes compelled to consider issues not always directly related to ecclesiastical separation. Nowhere was this more true than in the Joneses' relationship with Jerry Falwell, pastor of the fundamentalist Thomas Road Baptist Church in Lynchburg, Virginia. Falwell rocketed to national attention in June 1979 when, with the help of conservative fundraisers Richard Viguerie and Paul Weyrich, he launched the Moral Majority. The organization, ostensibly, was a nonpartisan, nonsectarian effort to elect political and social conservatives to office. Falwell stated his intentions succinctly: "We are urging morally concerned Americans to unite their political 'clout' to defend the traditional family and the conservative political principles that have made this nation great."[45]

The Moral Majority was in many respects the expression of long pent-up hostility at the direction American life had taken over the previous twenty years. The seeming inability of the United States to "win" in Vietnam, the increased visibility of feminists and homosexuals, the legalization of abortion, and an overall climate of permissiveness in the 1960s and 1970s all combined to produce tremendous resentment and frustration among conservative Americans. By 1979, with the United States once again held at bay by a Third World nation, Iran, and with many conservatives believing that the Carter Administration was encouraging the downward trends, an army of angry voters was ready for mobilization. With the 1980 election on the horizon, organizations such as the Conservative Caucus and the Committee for the Survival of a Free Congress formed. The Moral Majority was yet another in this growing list.

Predictably, the image of a fundamentalist minister organizing a political movement produced a barrage of criticism. The *Christian Science Monitor* condemned Falwell's supposed "moral zealotry," and the *New York Times* noted that Falwell's efforts had "caused considerable consternation among clergy and laymen alike, who feel it threatens the basic separation of church and state." Later, a Carter Administration official labeled Falwell an "ayatollah," and television producer Norman Lear formed People for the American Way to combat the Moral Majority. Despite opposition, the Moral Majority and other conservative groups helped to oust many "liberal" politicians in 1980. On Election night, 1980, President Carter went down to defeat, taking with him such liberal stalwarts as George McGovern, Frank Church, John Brademas, and John Culver. A subsequent *New York Times* poll showed that the victorious Ronald Reagan garnered 61 percent of the "born-again" vote. The hapless Carter, the Baptist Sunday School teacher from Georgia, received a mere 35 percent. Of thirty-eight candidates targeted by the Moral Majority, twenty-three were actually defeated. An ousted Alabama congressman said of the Moral Majority, "They beat my brains out with Christian love."[46]

For Falwell, the 1980 election was a great personal triumph. Only fifteen years earlier, Falwell condemned preachers in politics, observing that "preachers are not called to be politicians but soul-winners." Now, he had been instrumental in mobilizing a significant force in the American body politic. Though Falwell was a doctrinal fundamentalist and an independent Baptist minister, he had not attempted to organize a fundamentalist political movement. Flatly stating that "this is a time for Catholics, Protestants, Jews, Mormons, and all Americans . . . to return this nation to . . . moral principles," Falwell tailored his appeal to calls for morality. It was enormously successful. Thanks, for example, to the Moral Majority's antiabortion position, Roman Catholics eventually made up 30 percent of the organization.[47]

Like Falwell, the Joneses believed that the nation was in the grip of a moral crisis. Unlike Falwell, however, they had been making political pronouncements for a considerably longer period. Jones Sr. actively campaigned for Prohibition and against Al Smith in the 1928 presidential election. In 1951, Jones Jr. organized the Mid-Century World Outlook Conference. Held at BJU, the conference featured diplomats from France, Germany, Egypt, Iraq, Belgium, and Pakistan. Senator Strom Thurmond of South Carolina and Governor (later Senator) Ernest Gruening of Alaska also appeared. At this conference Jones Jr. asserted that because of "our ineffectual and bungling diplomats," the United States had "tossed the forces of democracy in China to the raving wolves of the Kremlin." In 1952, Jones Jr. presaged many of Falwell's later goals when he observed that one of his objectives was to "resell the fundamental principles of Americanism to this generation." Toward that end, Jones organized an annual "Americanism Conference" on campus.[48]

The Joneses throughout the years unequivocally connected conservative religion with conservative politics. A 1962 BJU press release, announcing another Americanism conference, stated that "a by-product of the religious conservatism which characterizes the University is its conservative position [politically]. Dr. Jones considers this 'entirely natural—a good, Bible-believing Christian is by nature a good, patriotic American.'"[49] Billy James Hargis and right-wing commentator Dan Smoot regularly appeared at BJU Americanism Conferences. In 1964, BJU awarded an honorary doctorate to Alabama Governor George Wallace. Jones Jr. praised Wallace as "a David, warring against the giant, Tyranny." When President Kennedy was assassinated in 1963, Jones Jr. voiced the sentiments of many rightists when he declared that the blame for the assassination lay with the Kennedy Administration itself. Jones indicted "a State Department that has been soft in its dealings with Communists, that permitted [Lee Harvey Oswald] to come back to America after he had defected to Russia," a Justice Department that called out "the militia in Mississippi to enforce . . . unconstitutional decisions of the Supreme Court, but could not compel Communists to register as the law requires," and finally Chief "Justice [Earl] Warren and his colleagues who have by their decisions aided Communism."[50]

During the upheavals of the Vietnam years, BJU students organized letter-writing campaigns to the troops. In 1970 the BJU student leadership issued an open letter to the citizens of Greenville, deploring the "disgraceful conduct" of college students in antiwar protests. When National Guardsmen fired upon Kent State students in May 1970, Jones Jr. stated that "those young people got exactly what they were entitled to and what they ought to get out in Berkeley, too."[51]

The University's battle with the Internal Revenue Service (to be discussed in chapter 5), beginning in 1970, also encouraged the Joneses' political rhetoric. The IRS sought to deny tax exemption to BJU because of a university rule prohibiting interracial dating. Bob Jones III told students in 1976 that the IRS "vilified, misrepresented, and fought" BJU because at BJU "truth prevails." Jones III concluded that the school's troubles with the government proved that "everything about your country is phony."[52]

The Joneses and their constituency shared in the conservative alienation of the late 1970s. The same forces that motivated Falwell were at work in Greenville as well. In April 1979, a BJU *Voice of the Alumni* editorial noted that for years, "most Christians have exhibited what amounts to a hands-off policy with regard to local and national politics." Now, however, the declining state of the nation meant Christians must become politically involved, "out of self defense, if for no other reason." The editorial urged Christians to help select candidates and concluded that "you are a part of a significant political force in your community." The April 1979 *Voice* also included an article by South Carolina state representative Rick Rigdon, a 1965 BJU graduate. Rigdon also urged Christian political involvement, asserting that "we must take advantage of every means available to reverse the present trend toward legalized ungodliness." In the 1980 South Carolina Republican primary, the Joneses endorsed Texan John Connally and, after his failed candidacy, announced their support for Ronald Reagan.[53]

Clearly, the history of the Joneses and their rhetoric demonstrates that they believed political activism to be a legitimate, and sometimes necessary, option for the fundamentalist. Yet in 1980, that belief had been reduced in importance by an overriding and more urgent issue, Jerry Falwell's lack of separatism as he actively courted Roman Catholics, Jews, and Mormons for the Moral Majority. That the Joneses felt compelled to attack Falwell, even as Falwell sounded the alarm on many of the issues important to them, suggested again how all-encompassing separatism had become for them. Their opposition to Falwell's ecumenical political activities also suggested that the Joneses now intended to apply their separatist convictions outside the ecclesiastical realm.

By 1980, Jerry Falwell was already suspect in the Bob Jones camp. Four years earlier, Falwell participated in a seminar sponsored by the California Graduate School of Theology. Other participants included Southern Baptists, Seventh-Day Adventists, and Methodists. Jones Jr. described the seminar as one featuring "apostate churches and denominations." Falwell, by participating, had yoked himself "unequally with unbelievers."[54] It is also possible that Falwell, in founding Liberty Baptist College in 1973, irritated the Joneses by creating competition for college students. Jones Jr. denied any jealousy, and in fairness to BJU, their enrollments remained strong after Liberty was founded. Still, it is possible that Falwell's school was an irritant. In any event, by 1980, Falwell found himself under vehement attack from Greenville.

In June 1980, Jones Jr., in a special mailing to all BJU pastors, blasted Falwell as "the most dangerous man in America today as far as biblical Christianity is concerned." Jones asserted that Falwell, by including Catholics, Jews, and Mormons in the Moral Majority, was building "the world church of Antichrist." In recounting the long, sad history of compromise in his letter, Jones demonstrated how thoroughly alienated he had become, not just from liberal Christians, but from the new evangelicals and now fellow fundamentalists. According to Jones, "first the Devil attacked us with cooperative evangelism as exemplified by Dr. Graham." Then Jones "observed at close range how Youth for Christ became an efficient tool in the hands of Satan. . . . I have seen the National Association of Evangelicals [destroyed by] rotteness and decay." Now, as if all this were not enough, "he [the devil] comes along with a moral crusade that incorporates an appeal to patriotism as well." Jones was particularly horrified that Falwell had allowed conservative activist Phyllis Schlafly to speak at Thomas Road Church. Falwell introduced Schlafly to his congregation as a "great Christian woman." For Jones, this could not be true, because Schlafly was also "a devout Roman Catholic."[55]

Bob Jones III joined his father in opposing Falwell. In a September 1980 article, the younger Jones elaborated the case for separatist opposition to Falwell. In doing so, he revealed that attempting to live as an extreme separatist while still being influential in society led to some inconsistencies. Jones III also demonstrated a significant departure from a principle that fueled nineteenth-century evangelicalism and which his own grandfather had maintained, the idea that the Christian must be an active force in social reform. Finally, Jones III's article revealed that he too, like his father, shared in the alienation from other Christians, liberal, new evangelical, and fundamentalist.

In condemning Falwell's willingness to work alongside Catholics and Mormons, Jones III argued that morality was ultimately a religious matter, that a "man's morality is based upon his religious beliefs." Therefore, when religious leaders of various persuasions united to promote "moral reformation," they were really engaged in a religious activity. From this premise, Jones III deduced that "since our morals spring from our theology, the implication is that members of the Moral Majority are in theological agreement." Conceding that a fundamentalist might agree morally with a Catholic on the issue of abortion, Jones III held that to unite on this one common belief was to "imply a basic soundness and commonality in all areas of belief."

Having seemed to dismiss any possibility of a fundamentalist working with a Jew or Catholic, Jones III then tried to establish just when this cooperation might be acceptable. He opposed any union, for example, between a local fundamentalist church and a local Roman Catholic church in fighting abortion. However, according to Jones III, "if there were a secular organization in their city opposing abortion, a godly pastor would feel no hesitancy offering his congregation's assistance to a cause they agreed with. A Catholic priest might do the same thing with his people. If such happened, they would find themselves 'riding the same train' to get to a common destination. There is no compromise in that." According to this argument, then, separation did not apply when a fundamentalist and a Catholic were in a secular organization, fighting for morality. Although the Moral Majority claimed to be just that, a secular organization, both Joneses continued to insist that the Moral Majority was a religious organization and therefore unscriptural, since Moral Majority meetings often featured prayers, singing, etc. Jones III was a man searching for a way to reconcile his separatist beliefs with the need to combat immorality. Jones further revealed his divided loyalties when he observed that "every Christian ought to be in favor of morality and should crusade for it" but later argued that "cleaning up America's morals is not the church's mission."[56]

Jones III's contention that "cleaning up America's morals" was not the church's mission also demonstrated that he (and his father), in their pursuit of theological purity, had departed from a central tenet of historic American evangelicalism, that the church was to be an active force for social reform.[57]

Finally, Jones III, in his opposition to Falwell, demonstrated that he too shared in the alienation of his father from other Christians. In his article, Jones III bluntly stated that "disobedient preachers such as Billy Graham, Jerry Falwell, and others, are . . . responsible for the moral decay in America." If these men really wished to reform America, Jones advised them to "break their ecumenical ties, quit their compromising, confess their sin of spiritual fornication, and then get right with God." Revealing how separatism now completely pervaded his worldview, Jones III declared that "ecumenical religious alliance is the one sin that brings God's patience to an end quicker than all other sins." Jones III's alienation was perhaps best summed up when he observed that "it is best that God's people turn their backs upon the Moral Majority and seek the soul-satisfying contentment of being a scriptural minority."[58]

Jerry Falwell defended himself by asserting that the Moral Majority was a political organization, not a religious one. For a fundamentalist, according to Falwell, joining the Moral Majority was no different "than joining any other politically conservative movement." The Moral Majority, Falwell wrote, fought "to maintain religious freedom in this nation so that we can maintain our religious practices regardless of how different they might be." Falwell also disputed Jones III's contention that the church was not to advocate moral reformation. He asked, "if cleaning up America's morals is not the mission of the church, then whose mission is it?" Falwell also voiced concern over the ultraseparatist direction of BJU. "It seems strange to me," Falwell observed, "that while BJU has been greatly used of God in the past, they have attacked so many good men and movements . . . that one has to question the value of their judgement." Falwell further contended that if one consistently followed the separatism of the Bob Joneses, then it would be "wrong for a Christian to belong to a political party, labor union, civic club or even to hold citizenship in the United States . . . [since] these alignments bring us into affiliation with others who are in theological disagreement with us."[59] Falwell later observed to an interviewer that "a generation from now that [Bob Jones] segment of fundamentalism will either be more moderate or be nonexistent or held in disdain by believers and unbelievers."[60] Falwell himself represented a new strain within separatist fundamentalism that, while retaining clear convictions on ecclesiastical alliances with theological liberals, represented a distinct break with the hyperseparatism of the Joneses. Intimations of this realignment had been evident since the 1970s. The Jones-Rice controversy over the proper parameters of separatism, Jack Van Impe's denunciation of a "hate movement" within fundamentalism in 1977, and the storm over Falwell's 1980 political activities, all attested to this reconfiguration. Falwell's rise to national prominence clearly delineated these two groups of fundamentalists. Flush with their success in the 1980 election and tired of the seemingly endless internal battles of the 1970s, an emergent group of fundamentalists in the early 1980s realized that they could in fact influence the national political agenda and bring about spiritual renewal within their own ranks.

The distinguishing characteristics of this new group included a strong adherence to the fundamentals of the faith, a firm commitment to separation from liberalism, a desire to retain the name "fundamentalist," and a desire to rehabilitate that term by renouncing hyperseparatism. Jerry Falwell, with his associate Edward Dobson, took the leadership of this faction and articulated its agenda. Other significant leaders were Jack Van Impe and Truman Dollar, both with former strong ties to BJU. (Edward Dobson was also a BJU graduate.) Many of the fundamentalist colleges that came to be recognized as part of the new coalition, such as Cedarville College and Liberty Baptist College, included many BJU graduates as part of their staffs. From the beginning of the rift, in 1980–81, as these more moderate fundamentalists made themselves heard, tension mounted between them and the Joneses.

In 1981 Falwell and two associates published *The Fundamentalist Phenomenon*. The book was significant in several respects. First, the title itself demonstrated that this was a group determined to hold onto their identification with fundamentalism. Second, the book demonstrated a capacity for self-criticism not seen before among separatist fundamentalists. Falwell and Dobson, for example, criticized the fundamentalist tendency during the 1960s and 1970s to preach "constantly on long hair, sideburns, beards, wire-rimmed glasses, etc." Conversely, they noted that "very few fundamentalists have taken a strong stand on such matters as health and fitness, contemporary television programming . . . and excessive materialism." More importantly, Falwell and Dobson asserted that "in the desire to be pure from the world, fundamentalists have tended to develop a . . . paranoid mentality toward the world they are trying to reach." Criticizing the "tendency to overabsolutism" and the "excessive labeling and listing of people, groups, and schools," the authors declared that "fundamentalism must become known for what it is for, not just for what it is against."[61]

Shortly after *The Fundamentalist Phenomenon* appeared, Falwell and Dobson launched the *Fundamentalist Journal,* a monthly periodical designed to be the mouthpiece for moderate fundamentalism. Dobson served as editor, and in his monthly columns he clearly stated the goals and positions of the new fundamentalism. A representative sampling of Dobson's editorials gives insight into the mindset of what he and Falwell termed the "real fundamentalist majority."[62] In March 1984, Dobson addressed the ever-present issue of separatism. "Does the Bible really teach separation?" he asked. "The obvious answer . . . is an emphatic yes!" For Dobson, true biblical separation existed between the extremes of the hyperseparatists and the overly tolerant new evangelicals. The former had, in their "quest for absolute purity . . . often divided themselves from other true believers." Conversely, the new evangelicals, with their "hesitance to draw any lines of demarcation," had left themselves open to "gross doctrinal error." The fundamentals were "essential" and "nonnegotiable," and Christians were, without question, to separate from those who "deny the deity of Christ and the gospel of Christ." Dobson also pointed out, however, that the purpose of separation was to reconcile those who had been separated. Dobson observed that fundamentalists "would do well to ask ourselves if we really want to see people . . . restored to fellowship."[63]

Dobson also stressed that the fundamentalist of the 1980s wished to be a positive influence upon society. The issue of race relations provided a case in point. Admitting that fundamentalists had "ignored, and at times opposed, the great civil rights movement of the nineteen sixties," Dobson concluded, "we were wrong. . . . To close the doors of our churches to anyone on the basis of race . . . or anything else—is a contradiction of our commitment to Christ. . . . We must cast off the prejudicial shackles of our past and embrace those we once ignored."[64] Another indication of this desire to influence society positively was demonstrated at Falwell's Thomas Road Baptist Church. Long identified with the antiabortion movement, Falwell and his associates moved beyond simple nay-saying and established both a home for unwed mothers and a Christian adoption agency.[65]

The high-water mark for moderate fundamentalism came in April 1984, with a gathering in Washington, D.C., called Baptist Fundamentalism '84. The movement Falwell and Dobson had begun was called nondenominational, yet probably a majority were independent Baptists, just like Falwell; hence the name for this meeting. Numerous fundamentalist pastors, representatives from fundamentalist colleges, and interested laymen attended the event. Nelson Keener, a spokesperson for Falwell, summed up the importance of Baptist Fundamentalism '84. Keener stated that "the conference showed that a polarization is taking place, with militant fundamentalism on one side and historic fundamentalism on the other." Ministers such as Falwell, Van Impe, and David Jeremiah (GARBC) were "historic fundamentalists . . . committed to improving their effectiveness in relating the gospel of Christ to today's culture." To accomplish this meant first and foremost an abandonment of hyperseparatism. The purpose of Baptist Fundamentalism '84, therefore, according to Keener, was to show respect for "the diversity among fundamentalist brethren."[66]

The Bob Joneses agreed with Keener that a polarization had occurred within the ranks of separatist fundamentalism, but they contended that Jerry Falwell, with his unscriptural alliances, was responsible for this division. Writing in 1980, Jones Jr. stated that "confusion results from the fact that many who are 'new evangeli-cal' in their alliances . . . operate under the guise of fundamental-ism. . . . Many who identify themselves as fundamentalists are very active in the 'Moral Majority,' but so are Mormons and Roman Catholics." Jones concluded that since "the public at large thinks of the 'Moral Majority' as a fundamentalist movement . . . we are going to be forced to abandon the appelation 'fundamentalist' and choose another term that will identify our position . . . clearly." Jones and his followers did not invent a new designation for themselves, but they did find one for the Falwell camp. Because the latter failed to "expose and oppose ecumenical evangelism" and because they failed to separate from those "involved in false ecu-menism [and] apostate denominationalism," they were "pseudo-fundamentalists." This new subversive movement was "new evan-gelicalism in embryonic form and . . . [it] compromises historic fundamentalism."[67]

From the perspective of the Joneses, the moderate tones of Fal-well and Dobson represented a repetition of the division of the 1940s, when the new evangelical movement broke away from fun-damentalism. Falwell's efforts were more insidious, however, be-cause he continued to identify himself as a fundamentalist. The Joneses quarreled with Falwell on two major points. First, the Joneses contended that no one could be a fundamentalist without being a strict separatist. Falwell had abandoned his separatism in the Moral Majority and showed his further disregard for biblical separatism by insisting that it was not necessary for fundamental-ists to separate from one another when questionable associations were at stake. In a 1984 article in *Faith for the Family*, Jones Jr. ar-gued that "men of this kind are not real fundamentalists at all. . . . They certainly are not . . . in the line of historic fundamentalism, which separated itself from religious compromise and apostasy and contended vigorously for the faith." Jones believed that "pseudo-fundamentalism" represented a greater threat to fundamentalist Christianity than anything else. He informed a Des Moines, Iowa, congregation that "the only danger we fundamentalists face is weakness, cowardice and compromise from the inside."[68]

A second major point of contention concerned the "pseudo-fundamentalist" quest for acceptance both by the mainstream religious community and the secular world. The Joneses contended that if fundamentalists consistently obeyed God, they could never be accepted by the "world." Jones Jr. stated the matter this way: "I have no desire to escape the opprobrium of the world and the hatred on the part of religious apostasy which results from a fundamental stand for biblical separation." Jones III echoed his father when he observed that "the separated fundamentalist is . . . not in the mainstream because the mainstream is going against God." According to Jones III, "when a man is willing to abide by the biblical requirements of separation . . . he may have to stand alone." Thus even in the 1980s, as political, social, and religious conservatism experienced a resurgence, it remained important for the Joneses to be perceived as outsiders, as the last defenders of the true faith. In one sense, the conservative revival served to sharpen the Joneses' sense of aloneness. If everyone else had entered the mainstream, they could claim to be the only ones who had not compromised.[69]

In the period after the 1980 election, the differences between the Joneses and those they called "pseudo-fundamentalists" became much more pronounced. Shortly after the 1981 publication of *The Fundamentalist Phenomenon,* the Fundamental Baptist Fellowship (FBF), a group heavily influenced by the Joneses, issued a scathing critique of the book. According to the review, *The Fundamentalist Phenomenon* was "only a reexpression of new evangelicalism, which again will lead right back to modern liberalism." Taking Falwell to task for quoting liberal theologians, for calling for increased fundamentalist social activism, and for calling for renewed scholarship among fundamentalists, the review concluded that Falwell "wants fundamentalism to become respectable and to be acceptable. . . . This is always a death blow to any true type of Christianity." The FBF, led by a group of men of whom many served on the BJU board, mounted a sustained campaign against Falwell in the pages of the *FBF News Bulletin.*[70]

The Joneses and their constituency also criticized the Falwell/Dobson call for unity within fundamentalism and evangelicalism.

Ridiculing Falwell's plea for fundamentalists to "stop 'shooting our wounded,'" the *FBF News Bulletin* observed that the "analogy of 'shooting our wounded' has been used . . . to discredit any criticism or exposure of a brother's compromise." The *Bulletin* stated that "'shooting' is not aimed at any 'wounded,' but at turncoats and deserters." The Joneses further demonstrated their attitude toward Falwell's "unity" as they sponsored resolutions, which passed, at the 1980 and 1983 meetings of the World Congress of Fundamentalists condemning "pseudo-fundamentalism."[71]

With the break with Falwell, the Joneses' separatism had come full circle. Beginning with the split with Billy Graham, the Bob Joneses practiced an ever-narrowing type of separatism that severed them not only from liberals and new evangelicals, but from fellow fundamentalists as well. As their separatism evolved over this thirty-year period, events compelled the Joneses to consider how their separatist convictions applied to the ecclesiastical realm. Jerry Falwell acted as the catalyst in this reappraisal. While they were forced to consider the question of a separatist's relationship to his society, in fact the Joneses had already constructed their own separatist society in Greenville. In the lifestyle rules for faculty and students and in the educational philosophy governing the university, the Joneses demonstrated that they had already given much thought to what the ideal separatist society should resemble. Having considered the development and application of their theological separatism, we now turn our attention to the Joneses' successful efforts to build their own separatist subculture.

CHAPTER FOUR

The World's Most Unusual University

As the Bob Joneses gained increasing notoriety by breaking with such well-known conservatives as Jerry Falwell and Billy Graham, their equally ardent efforts to build a separatist community on their campus also generated much attention. The unique campus environment the Joneses constructed so laboriously over the years earned their school descriptions ranging from the "world's most unusual university" to the "world's most unusual anachronism." One writer referred to the university as the *enfant terrible* among Christian colleges.[1] Unlike the Joneses' strident theological separatism, which appeared rather late in the university's history, the school's educational and cultural separatism was and remains a constant, from the 1926 ground-breaking until today. As with the theological separatism which made the Joneses major players in various fundamentalist schisms, tension, paradox, and irony characterized their cultural and educational separatism.

At BJU, educational and cultural separatism encompasses two major areas: educational philosophy and rules governing student life. In both of these areas the Joneses found themselves torn between conflicting legacies. Their separatist, premillennial doctrine compelled them to announce the inevitable demise of their culture and society, yet they retained the desire to build a "city upon a hill."

While the Joneses boasted that no school would "academically excel" BJU, in the name of separatism they refused the one credential that might have earned them credibility in the secular educational world, accreditation. Further, students are forbidden to attend Hollywood movies, yet the Joneses sent a faculty member to Hollywood to study filmmaking. In the school's early years, intercollegiate sports were discontinued because the Joneses feared the corrupting influences of visiting teams. Yet unconverted opera singers and other performers regularly appear on campus to perform for the students. An examination of each of these areas will reveal that the Bob Joneses have very often been selectively separatist.

In their quest for pristine religious associations and lifestyles, the Joneses are part of a rather long tradition of trying to recover a purer past.[2] BJU history professor David Beale, writing the university's version of fundamentalist history, revealed this influence when he titled his work *In Pursuit of Purity*.[3] The theme of restoring the church's lost purity is not, of course, a strictly fundamentalist phenomenon.

The restoration of purity easily crosses denominational and cultural lines, encompassing such diverse groups as the seventeenth-century Puritans, some orthodox Jewish groups, and twentieth-century Mormons.[4] So while restoration is an important part of the fundamentalist equation, it is modified by other factors that help explain why fundamentalists such as the Bob Joneses are selectively separatist in their dealings with an impure world.

George Marsden, in his *Fundamentalism and American Culture*, provides a useful model for understanding the often paradoxical nature of fundamentalism. Marsden observed that within fundamentalism there was a tendency to "identify sometimes with the 'establishment' and sometimes with the 'outsiders.'" Among the groups to which twentieth-century fundamentalism can trace its roots, two of the most significant were the nineteenth-century revivalists and the seventeenth-century Calvinists. The revivalists provided a heritage of "individualistic, culture-denying, soul-rescuing Christianity." Revivalism also provided the fundamentalists with, in Marsden's words, the presupposition of a "radical separation between the unconverted and converted." Since the stakes involved spending eternity in either heaven or hell, there was no time for the luxury of theological debate and hypothesis. Dwight L. Moody, the nineteenth-century evangelist who greatly influenced Bob Jones Sr., summed up this attitude when he stated "God has given me a lifeboat and said, 'Moody, save all you can.'" Viewing the world divided into the converted and unconverted heightened the separatist mentality.[5]

Conversely, from the Calvinists, fundamentalists inherited "positive attitudes towards intellect . . . and the ideal of building a Christian civilization." Throughout much of the nineteenth century evangelical Protestant thought enjoyed respectability. Many of the nation's colleges also reflected the evangelical outlook, a worldview buttressed by faith in the Bible and a devotion to Baconian scientific principles. This mentality, as we have seen, eventually came crashing down beneath the weight of Darwinism and the higher criticism. Nonetheless, it left conservative Protestants with a legacy of respect for learning and knowledge, so long as intellectual endeavors were for God's glory. Marsden noted that even during the antievolution crusades of the 1920s, many fundamentalists heaped ridicule upon scientists with Ph.D.s, not because they held doctorates, but because in spite of so much education they advocated hypothesis as fact.[6]

These two legacies combined within twentieth-century fundamentalism to produce considerable tension, if not actually a kind of intellectual split personality. Bob Jones Sr. articulated this dichotomy when he observed that he wanted to build a school with "high cultural and academic standards and at the same time a school that will keep in use an old-time, country mourner's bench where folks can get right with God."[7] This divided mentality explains why Bob Jones wanted a school where, in his phrase, a "student's religious faith would not be shaken by questionable teachings," but also a school that would produce "teachers, lawyers, physicians, and businessmen" who would return to the world. It also explains how Jones could remark, half in jest, that every time his school hired a Ph.D. they needed a week of revival meetings, and then state that "an educational institution with the right kind of spiritual standards will maintain the highest possible academic standards."[8] It is this dual legacy that enabled the Joneses to successfully recreate a nineteenth-century educational and behavioral system on their campus, but which also allowed them to copy advanced state university course offerings, including filmmaking and computer technology.

Bob Jones III once remarked to an interviewer that "we're unusual in our objectives to teach the student what he believes. . . . We wouldn't tolerate any teaching in this school that was opposed to the biblical position."[9] To the secular academic in the late twentieth century, such sentiments are an anachronism, harking to a bygone era in American higher education. Indeed, the educational philosophy of Bob Jones University is an anachronism by the standards that have governed higher education since the end of the nineteenth century, when, with the adoption of the German academic model, American colleges and universities came to hold, in the words of one observer, "naturalistic assumptions about origins, a reverence for free inquiry as opposed to religious inculcation, a notion of knowledge or truth as something to be discovered rather than preserved and transmitted from the past."[10]

This ideological transition moved Bob Jones Sr. to remark to fundamentalist audiences in the 1920s that "education with God left out is a curse. . . . If we don't bring back to the schools of this nation the Word of God and the old-time religion, this nation is gone."[11] While Jones expressed sentiments that were considered out of date by the 1920s, his contention that "education with God left out is a curse" had in fact been a major premise of American higher education for much of the nineteenth century. In establishing his college in 1927, Jones meant to restore that missing element in American education. The school's first catalog stated that Bob Jones College existed to insure that students attained the "intellectual requirements and . . . a firm grip and thorough knowledge of the great fundamental truths of the Christian religion."[12] While it is impossible to establish that Jones consciously determined to recreate a nineteenth-century church college, this catalog statement did in fact summarize the educational objectives of nineteenth-century Protestant education.

The influence of the second Great Awakening, an expanding college-age population, and the desire of many local communities for their own colleges all combined to make the period from 1800 to 1860 one of phenomenal growth for denominational colleges. The long list of institutions founded in these years includes Randolph-Macon, Emory, Depauw, Trinity (later Duke), Denison, and Wake Forest. These schools trained ministers, missionaries, teachers, lawyers, and doctors. In addition, colleges served as cultural and financial boosts to their local communities. They also often provided the only secondary education available in the community.

The denominational college was a place where, as Laurence Vesey writes, "educational and theological orthodoxy almost always went together."[13] True scholarship not only acquainted students with facts, it also pointed them to God and endeavored to make them good citizens. D. H. Hill, president of Davidson College (Presbyterian), expressed this philosophical premise when he observed that "mental cultivation alone cannot subdue the corruption of our hearts or restore us to favor with God. . . . To educate the head and leave the heart untouched is to increase the capacity of the scholar to do evil."[14] In order to educate both the head and the heart, students studied a rigorous curriculum of Latin, Greek, mathematics, philosophy, religion, and science. They also lived under a stern disciplinary code designed to regulate what educators considered the sinful tendencies of youth.

Christian liberal-arts education in these years was a unique blend of orthodox doctrine, Baconian scientific principles, and Scottish Common Sense philosophy. Beginning with the presupposition that the God of the Bible created the universe and had endowed humans with the ability to think and create, Christian educators believed that disciplined study, whether of mathematics or the Latin classics, invariably pointed humans to the knowledge of God. The introduction of an expanded science curriculum in many Presbyterian colleges further strengthened this philosophical base. Study of the natural world in all of its intricacy revealed

God's handiwork and His orderliness; scientific study led humans to uncover the laws by which God governed the universe. Within this framework, there was not much room for hypothesis. Common Sense philosophy, imported from Scotland, also undergirded Protestant higher education in the nineteenth century. Thomas Reid and Dugald Stewart, of the University of Edinburgh, articulated this philosophy largely as a reaction to the skepticism of Enlightenment thinkers such as David Hume. In an effort to preserve Christian principles without appealing to church traditions or special revelation, Common Sense thinkers posited that the world humans perceived really existed and that human intuition led individuals to apprehend both the natural world and morality. In other words, just as humans could observe that certain laws governed the physical universe, they could also through reason and intuition see that moral laws also existed.

The curriculum in church colleges reflected the Common Sense philosophy in a year-long course, usually taken in a student's senior year, called "moral philosophy." In most instances taught by the president of the college, moral philosophy courses served as an apologetic for Christianity and encouraged students to become good citizens. One writer called the moral philosophy course a year-long exposure to "systematic arguments for morality, civic virtue, and the existence of God." Nineteenth-century Protestant educational ideals can be summarized, in one scholar's words, as reliance "upon intuition as a defense of morality, on science as an unequivocal road to truth, and on logical arguments as proof for the existence of God."[15]

The denominational college also acted as a parent to the students. This parental role took two forms, to ensure that students behaved properly and that their spiritual needs were met. If discipline in the classroom and study habits were required, so was correct behavior in all other areas. Discipline codes forbade drinking, gambling, swearing, ownership of dice, billiards, and card playing. Students, as one historian of church colleges recounted, were "not to leave school without special permission . . . or [go] beyond the limits of an ordinary walk for recreation without faculty consent."

The rules stipulated three study sessions every day, usually two hours in length, during which students were confined to their rooms. Students were also obligated to report one another when rules were violated.[16]

Church colleges also took measures for the spiritual welfare of their students. Many students who matriculated in church colleges often did so because they were the only schools in the area, not because they wished to receive a Christian education. Cognizant of this fact, many colleges began the school year with revival meetings, with the goal of converting the new students. The parents of one young man, converted in a revival at Wofford College, wrote to the president thanking him for the school's spiritual efforts. "We felt," they wrote, "that if we could attain the means of sending him to Wofford, God would convert him. . . . [The college was] initiating our sons into the highest science—the consciousness of God reconciled in the soul, and in the training of their spirits for heaven."[17] Sunday church and weekday chapel attendance were required, and missionary societies on campus also helped to stimulate spiritual awareness.

Nineteenth-century denominational educators regarded education as an inculcation process to transmit values and uphold the social order. Proper education offered not an intellectual smorgasbord, but rather, a coherent worldview which assumed that absolutes existed and that the God of the Bible had ordained them. Students discovered these absolutes, or laws, as they studied under the direction of a paternalistic teacher who guided their thinking. Whatever the subject, students learned that its methods and findings were buttressed by divine principles.

Just as God's laws provided for an orderly natural world, when obeyed they also provided for a stable society. As the United States expanded its borders and prospered economically, Protestant educators of the nineteenth century assumed, as did most white Americans, that God's blessing rested upon the nation, undoubtedly because God's laws, as Protestants interpreted them, had been followed, or at least acknowledged, in the United States. Thus American society carried divine sanction. For this sanction to continue, schools needed to train students who would understand divine principle and follow it.

From the 1927 opening until today, BJU has, to a remarkable extent, operated from the same philosophical premises. The similarities between BJU and the nineteenth-century church college are often striking. The April 1929 issue of *Bob Jones Magazine*, for example, stated that an education integrated with a study of the Bible "is necessary to complete our wisdom, [and] give us the right inner standards . . . to do our duty to society." Sixteen years later, a college advertisement noted that while "Bob Jones College follows sane modern educational methods," the school "is founded upon the eternal and unchanging truth of the Word of God."[18] In 1978, Bob Jones III commissioned a faculty team to articulate a systematic treatment of the philosophical premises of a Christian education. Their efforts reflected the same presuppositions and conclusions that characterized the nineteenth-century church college.[19]

The faculty authors of *The Christian Philosophy of Education* began with the assumption that the "God of the Bible . . . existed before man and exists independently of man." This transcendent Being revealed to humankind a "system of certain basic truths through . . . His Word, the inerrant, divinely inspired and preserved sixty-six books of the Old and New Testaments." Emphasizing this point, the faculty wrote that "God's written self-revelation is the starting point of all rational inquiry. . . . No concept can be true that conflicts with the statements of the Scriptures." The conviction that God had revealed himself to humankind established perhaps the most important presupposition of Christian education: the existence of absolute truths, not open to speculation. It also presupposed that these truths could be known and discovered by humans.

Of the truths revealed in the Scriptures, two were critical to Christian education. First, the Bible taught that God created humans in his image. This did not imply that humans carried divinity; rather, it meant that they bore some of the same personality traits as God. As the Bob Jones faculty put it, "man reflects God . . . in his moral, intellectual, and emotional capacities . . . also in his aesthetic sensibility, social inclinations, and other qualities of his personality." Because humans bear the stamp of their creator, they are able to think, inquire, and create. Intellectual endeavors became a godlike activity. Second, the Bible taught that God also revealed himself through his creation and, as the Bob Jones writers stated, "that which reveals God is a proper study for man. . . . Indeed, the Scriptures themselves invite man to consider God's earthly handiwork and hold him responsible for recognizing in it the work of God."

The consideration of "God's earthly handiwork" encompassed the study of humans, the epitome of God's creation, and the natural world. According to the writers of *The Christian Philosophy of Education,* "especially is God revealed in his rational creation, man." Therefore, in studying "man's language, his literature, his artistic achievements, the record of his history, [and] the logic of his mathematical reasoning," students would inevitably encounter certain truths about God and about the laws that he established to govern humans. Also, the study of "the vast universe and the myriad wonders of man's earthly habitation testify that their Creator is a God of order, beauty, and of power." Viewed from this perspective, education became the transmission of immutable truths and values. It followed that teachers were consciously to direct their students' thinking to what was right.[20]

At BJU, the treatment given to the social sciences and history provides a good example of the way in which an academic discipline is integrated with biblical principles. In 1978 another faculty committee, also commissioned by Jones III, wrote *The Christian Teaching of History,* which purported to demonstrate how God revealed himself in the social sciences. Not only God's nature, but also the laws that he ordained for a stable social order can be found, according to the writers, in such diverse subject areas as economics, geography, social institutions, and history. A correct treatment of economics, for example, "reveals principles for the responsible use of God-given natural resources, which man cannot afford to squander." In addition, the student should learn that God has created "a work ethic . . . that is, the responsibility of laboring to earn one's sustenance." Geography will reveal "the infinite wisdom and special forethought of God in planning a suitable habitat for man and regulating it for man's benefit and blessing." As students study human relationships, they should learn "of the dignity and sanctity of the family as an institution of God and find a pattern for the home as well as for the school, church, community, and nation."

The study of history, however, provides the sharpest focus of how God's nature and his rules for humans are integrated into the liberal arts. In studying history, "the spiritual mind can trace the character of the divine Maker of the ages and discern his ways." Above all else, God's providence and sovereignty over humankind is emphasized. According to the faculty writers, "the earthly course of events was begun by an act of God; it is progressively unfolding, revealing God's good purpose in his good time, and it will be brought to an end by God." Specific events and ideas in history are evaluated against the backdrop of God's providence and character.

A proper classroom discussion of the Protestant Reformation, for example, "would likely observe the Lord's propitious ordering of events on the eve of that century, making possible the success of that movement." Movable type, introduced in the fifteenth century, permitted rapid distribution of the Bible. European states and princes, competing with one another, also began to resist interference from the papacy. The papacy is identified as a collection of "flagrantly immoral men," who were "incredibly ignorant of the theological issues raised by the reformers." The reformers wished for a "restoration of the primitive Christian church." Once these "facts" were presented to students, they should be taught that God "prearranged [these circumstances] and then used them for his own purposes in destroying the European ecclesiastical monopoly of Rome, reasserting individual responsibility, and restoring individual liberty, both spiritual and political."

Teaching the history of the United States, the Bob Jones writers asserted, should "emphasize the providential circumstances of its founding and associate its prosperity with obedience to God." God, in his providence, brought a "prepared people to a prepared land" and blessed them "with religious, civil, and economic freedom." God also chastened America, often through such events as the Civil War, for "disobedience and faithlessness in the midst of economic prosperity." A correct interpretation of American history should also emphasize that in "the latter part of the nineteenth century, Christians found their society overwhelmed by materialism, secularism, big statism, humanism, and denominational apostasy." This notwithstanding, Americans still wished "to make available to the rest of the world the material as well as spiritual blessings of their society and to protect the freedoms of the peoples of other lands." For these laudable goals the United States fought in two world wars in the twentieth century.

Students not only learn that God providentially controls history, they also learn what personal characteristics God values and which he wishes to see emulated in their lives. "From his study of the lives of the human makers of history," for example, "[the student] derives an appreciation for the heroic qualities of sacrificial devotion, patient endurance, and constancy in hope." Other qualities a student should learn from a Christian teaching of history include "the principle of submission to government as ordained by God and exemplified by Christ" and the ability to "suffer patiently for righteousness' sake."[21]

Educating students from a Christian perspective was pointless, however, if the students themselves were not Christians. Although all humans carried the image of their creator, if they had not accepted Christ as their savior, they were spiritually comatose. For education, this meant that "the mind of the [unconverted] man is capable of intellectual but not of spiritual perception. . . . His mind has been impaired by sin." Without Christ's regenerating power through conversion, humans instinctively gravitated toward a naturalistic explanation for the world. Once converted, however, humans regained the personal relationship with God that had been lost in the Garden of Eden when humans chose disobedience. Education now took on a completely new dimension. Now, to study history, for example, students not only learned how God worked providentially in the rise and fall of nations, they learned what God expected of them personally. Therefore, "Christian education proper begins with spiritual rebirth." Once spiritually reborn, students could reach the ultimate goal of Christian education, the development of "godliness of character and action."[22]

Clearly, from its inception Bob Jones University began with and propagated the same educational principles that undergirded the nineteenth-century church college. Both viewed education as an inculcation process designed to produce graduates sound both in their theology and in their devotion to a Protestant-based social order. Both Bob Jones and the old church colleges demonstrated a commitment to Scottish Common Sense philosophy, the view that nature and history contained God's principles for an orderly world. Both maintained that academic study not only acquainted students with the facts of a subject, but also taught them personal character and discipline.

This Protestant worldview not only provided the Joneses with their own philosophy of education, it enabled them to critique modern educational philosophy. One of the most articulate critics of the philosophical premises for twentieth-century education is Bob Jones faculty member Guenter Salter. Salter, a Vanderbilt Ph.D. in philosophy and dean of the College of Arts and Sciences at BJU, published a series of articles in *Balance,* a monthly periodical published by BJU dealing with various aspects of education. In two articles, Salter has set forth an argument for the superiority of a Christian liberal arts education and a critique of modern secular education.

Both secular and Christian education, Salter maintains, attempt to establish beliefs. The only difference between the two is their presuppositional starting points. The Christian relies upon "the Word of God rather than man's mind as the final arbiter of truth." Therefore, "the vaunted objectivity of secular education is simply the substitution of multiple, ever-shifting human constructs for absolute, eternal verities."

Because Christians begin with a standard of value that never changes, they can "examine the issues rationally, judge their merits critically, and weigh alternatives in order to reach intelligent decisions." The liberally educated Christian should be one who is at home "in the world of the mind and ideas."[23] For Salter, in the final analysis, Christians make better thinkers because they are not dependent upon values that constantly change. They are the true critical thinkers, intellectually and spiritually equipped to discern between good and evil. Their secular counterparts can only hypothesize, never knowing whether or not they have reached true conclusions.

Salter believes that underlying secular education is an insidious philosophy called humanism. Humanism "embraces the doctrine of evolution; declares heredity and environment to be responsible for a person's value system; dismisses all absolutes, [and] makes man the measure of all things." Most important, however, humanism is "entangled in a net of self-contradiction and resultant absurdity." Among its major fallacies, humanism attempts to ridicule the idea of faith in God while simultaneously affirming faith in man and reason. With the academic revolution of the late nineteenth century, the term "faith" suddenly stood in stark contrast to the scientific process. This, Salter argues, has encouraged a fallacy. The secularist, or humanist, now "subjects all knowledge and ideas to the scientific process in order to establish their truth or falsehood. Yet the scientific process is unable to prove in a scientifically acceptable way that reason should be chosen as final arbiter of eternal verities. . . . Thus the humanist . . . must accept on faith that reason is superior to faith."

Salter also ridicules what he calls the uncritical acceptance of "the notion of a self-existing universe" among secular educators. Disparaging the idea that God created the heavens and the earth as the Bible declares, humanists themselves offer, in Salter's estimation, an equally "scientifically unprovable theory." Moreover, according to Salter, "one might question which takes more fantasy and imagination: creation . . . by an eternal God or a noncreated cosmos that somehow has existed forever?"

The humanist's acceptance of evolution also deprives humans of any real meaning. The view of "man as an entity not uniquely created but rather merely occupying the top rung on the evolutionary ladder precludes his accountability to anyone but himself." However, the social order would be destroyed if no standards existed to which everyone was accountable. Therefore humans create their own standards by consensus. In so doing they ignore "the truism that the majority is not always right. Furthermore, in order to consider anything good or better, one must presuppose the knowledge of an absolute best." Yet acknowledging absolutes is tantamount to acknowledging God. Therefore the humanist is always in a dilemma. Salter sums up by observing that "as a philosophy, humanism thus fails the test because of its inconsistency. The Christian is not surprised; for all things undertaken without God are senseless and utterly devoid of value."[24]

The Joneses' theological principles enabled them confidently to judge the culture in which they found themselves. Those principles also compelled them to attempt the restoration of Christian, or Protestant, values in that culture. So while the Bob Joneses built an anachronistic institution, they still wanted that institution to produce graduates who would be at home in, and influence, modern society. Unlike the Amish, who chose complete withdrawal, the Joneses instead chose to walk the tightrope of condemning modern society while being modern themselves in every way except theologically. This balancing act has enabled them to build a university that uses satellite links to create an interactive, multimedia learning service for Christian schools; that has a nationally acclaimed film curriculum; and whose top majors are accounting and business administration. "We need Christians," Bob Jones Jr. said in 1949, "who go out into the midst of the world to face the problems of the world for Jesus Christ." Nearly forty years later, BJU promotional literature described Bob Jones students as "the hope of America as they go forth to serve Christ." That same literature also portrayed Bob Jones students as those who have "turned their backs on the world and its values. . . . These students are . . . strangers and pilgrims in the earth."[25] This is the dilemma which the Bob Joneses have created for themselves: how to separate from corrupt modernity while using it to restore a purer past. It is a difficult challenge, but one to which the Joneses have responded creatively. So while the Joneses practice an educational philosophy long since discarded by American educators, they do so in a school patterned upon the twentieth-century educational model, a model designed to produce lawyers, doctors, and business people.

In 1983, journalist Christopher Connell, writing for the education periodical *Change,* observed that "perhaps the most surprising thing about BJU is not how it differs from most American colleges, but how much it has in common with them."[26] From the beginning, Bob Jones Sr. looked to others to provide the expertise necessary to make Bob Jones College an academically competitive institution. In 1944 Jones told a chapel audience that "I am the founder of this college, but I am not a scholar. I am not a literary genius. I am not an authority on books. I borrow the technical and educational brains to run this college."[27] The academic program experienced steady growth through the Cleveland, Tennessee, years (1933–1946). Beginning with the move to Cleveland, the college began a one-year business program concentrating, in the language of the 1933–34 catalog, upon "bookkeeping, shorthand, typewriting, and related subjects." From 1941 to 1943, the Bachelor of Science degree in Elementary Education and Home Economics was added to the curriculum, and in 1943–44 the college offered both the Master of Arts and Doctor of Philosophy in religion.[28]

With no hope of further expansion in Cleveland because of residential areas surrounding the college, the trustees in 1946 accepted an offer from the Greenville, South Carolina, Chamber of Commerce to relocate the college there. The college opened in Greenville for the 1947–48 school year.

The 1947 move to Greenville resulted in an academic reorganization and the transition from a college to a university. Now the university consisted of six schools, including the College of Arts and Sciences offering the B.A. and B.S. in twelve subjects, the School of Religion offering the B.A., M.A., and Ph.D., the School of Fine Arts offering the B.A., B.S., M.A., and M.F.A. in twelve subjects, the School of Education and the School of Commerce both offering the B.S., and the School of Aeronautics offering flying instruction and aircraft maintenance.[29] With the academic reorganization also came a change in leadership, as Bob Jones Jr. assumed the presidency in 1947. Jones Jr. took a much more active role than his father in the academic life of the university. As we shall see, he served as the catalyst in creating the school's drama and art programs, and he also sponsored other curricular changes. In 1961, for example, Jones Jr. directed that the university's English and history first year survey courses, traditionally taught in small sections, be transformed into the large lecture/small discussion group format common at large state universities.[30]

In 1957–58 the university was reorganized once more into five schools, the College of Arts and Sciences taking over the School of Aeronautics. During Jones Jr.'s administration, the majors offered in these five schools expanded from thirty-three in 1947 to fifty-four in 1971, when Bob Jones III assumed the presidency.[31] Throughout the university's history, the two areas of greatest academic growth have been business and education. From its modest beginning as a one-year program leading to a certificate, the business school has mushroomed into a major division of the university, offering the B.S. in majors including accounting, marketing, financial management, agribusiness, and commercial aviation. Bob Jones graduates can be found working for such diverse employers as Delta Air Lines, Bendix, Merrill Lynch, IBM, Dow Chemical, and the U.S. General Accounting Office. According to Bob Jones historian Melton Wright, "The university has consistently ranked in the top one or two schools in the state (South Carolina) on the Certified Public Accountants examination and on placing accounting majors into the 'big eight' public accounting firms."[32]

The School of Education has also experienced major growth. From its beginnings as a degree program leading to a B.S. in Elementary Education, the School of Education now offers state certification in Elementary and Secondary Education, M.S. degrees in Personnel and Educational Administration, the Specialist in Education degree, and the Doctor of Education. The university claims that its teacher education majors score 10 to 50 percent higher than the national average on the National Teacher Examinations. In 1947, the South Carolina Department of Education approved the teacher education curriculum, and in 1973 BJU received the approval necessary for its education graduates to receive certification through reciprocity agreements with other states.[33] According to *Peterson's Guide to Four-Year Colleges, 1990–1991*, the majors with the highest enrollments at BJU were Business Administration, Accounting, and Elementary Education.[34]

By the early 1990s, Bob Jones University was subdivided into six schools again, including Arts and Science, Religion, Fine Arts, Education, Business Administration, and Applied Studies (a technical program encompassing trades and technology). Each school is subdivided further into divisions, which in turn are divided into departments. The College of Arts and Sciences, for example, has six divisions including English Language and Literature, Foreign Language and Literature, Natural and Applied Science, Mathematical Science, Nursing, and Social Science. The six divisions are then divided into departments. The division of Social Science, for example, includes the departments of Criminal Justice, History, Social Studies, and Psychology.[35]

One of the truly distinctive features of the Bob Jones curriculum is the film production program, aptly titled Unusual Films. Founded in 1950, Unusual Films offers insight into that portion of the Joneses' heritage that compels them to reclaim the culture for Christ. At a time when most fundamentalists roundly condemned anything having to do with the film industry and culture, Jones Jr. stated, "I reason this way: if all good things come down from the Father, I take it that the dramatic instinct came down from God the same as music and literature. Because the devil perverts music in a night club is no reason to throw the choir out of the church." When BJU speech instructor Katherine Stenholm departed for a summer of graduate work at the University of Southern California (USC) in 1950, Jones Jr. told her, "While you're out there, learn all you can about the picture industry."[36] Stenholm returned with a wealth of information. Shortly thereafter, BJU invested more than $300,000 in launching Unusual Films. The company also enjoyed unusual success. Under Stenholm's direction, from 1951 to 1986, Unusual Films won an award at the Cannes International Film

Festival. Stenholm served both as the United States representative and the keynote speaker at the International Congress of Motion Picture and Television Schools in France in 1958.[37]

The feature-length films produced by Unusual Films include "Wine of Morning" (which won the Cannes award); "Red Runs the River" (which represented the United States at the International Book Fair in Krakow, Poland), the story of the conversion of a Confederate general; "Flame in the Wind," dealing with the Inquisition; "Sheffey," the tale of a nineteenth-century circuit-riding preacher; and "Beyond the Night," the story of a missionary doctor in Africa. The most recent Unusual Films production, released in 1991, is "The Printing," which portrays the efforts of the underground church in the Soviet Union to print Bibles and other religious materials.[38]

Closely related to the film curriculum are the drama productions produced at Bob Jones. The school's emphasis upon drama, particularly Shakespearean plays, stems directly from the interests and efforts of Bob Jones Jr. As a college student, Jones Jr. organized a Shakespeare club, the Classic Players, and wrote and produced a religious play, *Pontius Pilate*. Shakespeare held particular fascination for Jones, because, as he put it, Shakespeare "is the most moral of playwrights. His lines may be sometimes blunt and unrefined, but he is never obscene. His spiritual vision and understanding never permit him to make vice attractive. No sin goes unpunished, and vice is always the object of judgement." Daniel Turner, a professor of music at BJU, wrote a detailed study of Jones Jr.'s philosophy of drama, noting some of the moral object lessons that Jones found in Shakespeare. In *King Henry VIII*, for example, "Cardinal Wolsey is both morally and spiritually corrupt and ends up disgraced. In *Hamlet*, the Prince of Denmark suffers the destructive power of revenge and teaches that sin does not only affect the guilty but the guiltless as well."[39]

The drama program has also won accolades, and excellence in film and drama has reaped public relations dividends for BJU. Most importantly, the film and drama programs have enabled the Joneses to dispel the old Mencken stereotype of fundamentalists as ignorant and lacking in refinement. In 1992–93, BJU hosted the New Sousa Band and the Vienna Chamber Orchestra and performed Saint-Saen's opera "Samson and Delilah," featuring guest artists William Lewis, Yuen Deng, and Adib Fazah.[40] Film and drama have enabled the Joneses to demonstrate that orthodoxy and creativity can go together. As Jones Jr. observed, "Real culture and a Christian experience should go hand in hand. Through the ages nothing else so much as Christianity has exerted a gentle, refining influence. . . . We believe that a . . . critical appreciation of that which is best and most ennobling in literature, music, and the arts enriches life and lends weight to Christian testimony."[41]

Another important aspect of BJU's cultural emphasis is the art museum on the Greenville campus. Begun in 1948 with the help of art collector Carl Hamilton, who had been converted in one of Jones Sr.'s revivals, the art museum grew rapidly. In 1965, a symposium on "Culture and the Visual Arts," led by directors of the six largest art galleries in Canada and the United States, was held at BJU. Today the art museum consists of thirty galleries, including European sacred art from the thirteenth through the nineteenth centuries and boasting works by Rembrandt, Tintoretto, Rubens, Van Dyck, and Honthurst. The museum also includes the Bowen Bible Lands Collection, including among its exhibits four-thousand-year-old Egyptian and Syrian vases, an eighty-foot-long Hebrew Torah scroll, and a model of Solomon's temple. The museum also houses Russian icons presented to the Czar, a Renaissance furniture collection which includes a hand-carved choir stall and an oak ecclesiastical throne, and a collection of silk vestments made for the Imperial Chapel in Vienna.[42] Interestingly, there is no modern art in the BJU gallery. A former gallery tour guide and BJU graduate remembered that, because of limited space, the university had chosen to emphasize the Baroque and Renaissance periods.[43] This decision also undoubtedly reflected Bob Jones Jr.'s personal interests.

Despite these considerable efforts to make BJU resemble secular colleges and universities, the paradox of separatism appeared early in the life of the school. Copying secular liberal arts curricula, Jones Sr. and his followers wished also to create a program of interscholastic sports. The Bob Jones football team, called the Swamp Angels, played other small colleges and high schools in Florida and southern Alabama. The team enabled the fledgling college to offer Christian students the same outlet for participation and spectatorship as other schools, and it also offered Bob Jones students another avenue for spreading the gospel. Monroe Parker, retired evangelist and former assistant to Bob Jones Jr., entered Bob Jones College in 1928 and played the fullback position on the football team. In his memoirs, Parker recalled a member from an opposing team remarking that the Bob Jones players "were the best men I ever saw. They would knock us down and then help us up and say, 'God bless you, buddy.' We would take God's name in vain, and they would say, 'We will pray for you, friend.'"[44] At the end of the 1928–29 season the athletic director, John Allison, planned "a heavier [football] schedule for next year." He apparently hoped that intercollegiate sports would play an important role both in gaining Bob Jones College name recognition and in allowing players to share their faith.[45]

Yet the college discontinued intercollegiate sports before the departure from Florida. There is no documentary explanation, but in 1949 Bob Jones Sr. told J. Oliver Buswell of Wheaton College that intercollegiate sports "was not conducive to the spiritual welfare of the students." His grandson, Bob Jones III, told an interviewer in 1983 that interscholastic sports "is by and large a corruptive influence morally. . . . It's wrong to turn your campus over to a bunch of wild people who will come and drink and curse and litter your campus with whiskey bottles. It just doesn't create the atmosphere that we want for a Christian campus."[46] Perhaps, then, sometime between 1929 and 1932 teams visiting Bob Jones College created a stir with unruly behavior, causing the administration to discontinue its sports program. In any event, the decision significantly limited the college's contact with other schools and effectively ended that particular avenue of spreading Christian witness.

If the Bob Joneses would not compete in sports with other schools, they still intended to compete academically. Yet even in academic competition, the separatism of the Bob Joneses exerted a powerfully limiting influence. The Joneses, it appears, decided early that hiring faculty who might not be personally loyal to them could be dangerous to the stability of the institution. J. S. Mack, a substantial contributor to the college in its formative years, advised Jones Sr. to hire trustworthy graduates and train them in the manner the Joneses wished their school to be run. So early on, the Joneses adopted academic inbreeding as their personnel policy. The administration began approaching certain seniors about returning to their alma mater after graduation. They also suggested graduate schools for certain trustworthy students to attend so that, having secured a graduate degree from another institution, the student would return to BJU. Monroe Parker, for example, became Director of Religious Activities at BJU after earning a Ph.D. in Religion from Princeton. Philip Smith, the current dean of Education, graduated from BJU, earned an M.Ed. from Miami of Ohio, and then returned to his alma mater. As BJU developed graduate programs of its own, many stayed at BJU for their graduate work and then became faculty. Thurman Wisdom, for example, dean of the School of Religion, earned his B.A., M.A., and Ph.D. all at BJU. During the 1991–92 school year, the BJU faculty numbered 310 members, of which 252 were BJU alumni. Only 49 had doctorates, and ten of those were doctorates awarded by Bob Jones.[47]

Perhaps the best example of the Joneses' conflicting loyalties is their refusal to seek accreditation. While they may boast of excelling other schools academically, their lack of accreditation surely undercuts this claim. As we observed earlier, Bob Jones Sr. initially sought accreditation from the Southern Association of Colleges. The opening statement written by Jones in the 1927 catalog clearly attests to this. Whether the college was refused accreditation or simply withdrew its request is not clear, but the college remained unaccreditated. In a 1950 article Bob Jones Sr. wrote that "every educator who knows the . . . academic standards and the achievements of BJU knows that this institution could qualify for membership in the Southern Association of Colleges." According to Jones, the college did not apply for membership because "we do not wish to take any chance of having our administrative policies controlled or even influenced by any educational association." Specifically, Jones mentioned his unusual method of compensating faculty. At BJU, faculty were paid according to their personal needs, not on the basis of degree, experience, or accomplishments. Revision of this policy would be mandatory if the school joined an association. This notwithstanding, Jones assured his readers that "any young person who makes a satisfactory academic record in BJU" could easily transfer to a state university or enter a secular graduate school. In any case, BJU would not join the Southern Association because it would "take out of this Christian institution the spirit that has made the school what it is. We dare not take any such chances."[48]

Theodore Mercer, the registrar fired in 1953, challenged Jones Sr.'s explanation for the school's lack of accreditation. According to Mercer, "I spent a tremendous portion of our time and energies in writing letters, getting up reports, explaining and battling orally against the stigma of being unaccreditated." Mercer argued that the real reason BJU did not seek membership in an association was because "Dr. Jones could not run the school in the same ironhanded manner if the university were in an association, to wit, he could not summarily fire an employee." Mercer also questioned whether or not BJU could have received accreditation, even if it pursued the matter. He recounted that the dean of Gordon College, an evangelical college in Massachusetts, wrote Bob Jones Jr. a letter asserting that if the information in the BJU catalog were true, BJU could not have gained membership in the New England association. The dean, Carl Amerding, pointed out that the student/faculty ratio at BJU, 30:1, far exceeded the New England standard of 15:1, and he also called attention to the small number of Ph.D.'s on the faculty. According to Mercer, committees from the University of South Carolina came to Greenville and questioned "faculty stability, training and degrees of the faculty, faculty loads, and certain aspects of the instructional program including parts of the library collection." All of the qualities found wanting at BJU, Mercer asserted, were "matters over which Dr. Jones exercised a personal control."[49]

The Joneses steadfastly justify their position on separatist grounds. Bob Jones III wrote in 1983 that "independence from regional accrediting associations was a guiding philosophy at the inception of BJU." Jones III acknowledged that accreditation would enable BJU to gain "respect from its institutional peers." To do so, however, would mean "an unequal yoking with unbelievers, which is scripturally forbidden. Freedom to develop a student's right philosophy of life is more important than giving them a 'right pedigree.'"[50] In 1975 Cedarville College, a separatist Baptist institution in Ohio, received accreditation from the North Central Association of Colleges. In an editorial in the magazine *Faith for the Family,* Bob Jones Jr. wrote that since the leaders of Cedarville had "no real Christian convictions and have sacrificed scriptural conduct and Christian standards, they might as well sacrifice their Christian integrity" by joining the North Central Association. Jones flatly stated that "no institution can be a member of a national or regional educational association without sacrificing scriptural conviction." According to Jones, any Christian college seeking accreditation "immediately loses any right to call itself Christian or to seek the support of fundamental believers."[51]

Bob Jones III explained to an interviewer that educational associations were really "unions. . . . They control their members. They dictate philosophy that we could not adhere to and be true to the Bible." Jones III argued that if BJU adopted the standard faculty tenure system, for example, they could not fire a professor who taught evolution. In essence, according to Jones III, "we wouldn't have a Christian school anymore." Jones asserted that the school's lack of accreditation actually boosted its standards. "We have to keep our standards at the maximum," Jones said, "because we are accreditated by our product and we can't take the chance on the product slipping."[52] The university requires every graduate to take the Graduate Record Examination (GRE), whether or not the student intends to enter graduate school. The GREs are then used as proof that the school's academic standards are high. Still, refusing accreditation is a strange course for a school that has gone to such lengths to standardize its curriculum and which has not shunned state approval for major programs such as teacher education and nursing. The refusal to apply for accreditation is a way, however, for the Joneses to continue to assert not only their personal authority, but their separation from the world. It is a way to reassure themselves that while they are emulating secular education, they are different and more pure. Their distinctiveness is preserved.

The Bob Joneses also continue to assert their separatism with a rigid student rule structure that governs literally every aspect of a student's life. From its inception, Bob Jones College imposed a strictly regulated lifestyle upon its students. The earliest available rules for the students banned dancing, "jazz" music, profanity, and hazing. Students could not leave campus without a chaperon and could not visit home unless parents sent the dean a written request. The rules also required the students to report one another when rules were violated.[53] These stringent rules earned the Joneses praise within fundamentalist ranks. One minister, after visiting the Cleveland campus in 1940, commented that "the spiritual atmosphere . . . on the campus is the highest I have ever seen. . . . This was the happiest, best behaved, and most responsive group of young people I have ever seen."[54]

Bob Jones Sr. promised his constituency that parents with children enrolled in Bob Jones College could "go to sleep at night in perfect peace knowing that their child is safe physically, mentally and spiritually." The Joneses, like their nineteenth-century Protestant forebears, regarded a truly Christian education as one that shaped mind, soul, and body. Bob Jones Jr. explained that "a student needs to learn manners, good study habits . . . learning how to balance and proportion his daily life so that he doesn't . . . dream away his college hours with idle notions and foolish fancies." Without strict discipline, Jones warned, a college student would one day awake to "a dark reality of wasted years and a degeneracy of character."[55]

Another principle undergirding student rules at BJU is the conviction that Christians are in an armed conflict with evil and need to be trained for battle. Bob Jones III called the university a "training camp for Christian soldiers. . . . We tell our students the war with the devil, with the flesh, with sin is out there." This statement reflects the separatist, premillennial heritage of the Joneses. Believers are locked into mortal combat with the forces of evil, a battle that will not be finished until Christ returns. Because the world was increasingly evil, students at Bob Jones were admonished to "manifest their loyalty to Jesus Christ by separated living."⁵⁶ Bob Jones Jr. once proudly commented that "BJU students have never followed the trends of the day."⁵⁷ For separatists, this was the ultimate accolade. It demonstrated that in a world doomed to destruction, BJU students remained true to God. Bob Jones III observed of his students that "these Christian young people have turned their backs on the world and its values. They are living with eternity in view."⁵⁸

While BJU students may be learning to live "with eternity in view," the university is also trying to utilize the harsh discipline code as a way of preparing them for an active role in the world. Requiring men to wear ties and women to wear skirts to class may keep BJU students from looking "worldly," but it also ostensibly prepares them for a secular business world that will value such habits. In a 1992 interview James Berg, Dean of Students at BJU, characterized the BJU rule structure as providing both "protection and preparation." Asserting that God is a "God of order, not confusion," Berg maintained that the BJU rules reflect this theological principle but that they also teach students how to live obediently under authority, a trait that ostensibly will separate them from their counterparts in a secular setting. Berg stated further that "everything about our discipline system starts with accountability."⁵⁹ Assuming that human nature is corrupt and will naturally gravitate toward the wrong, the student rules are designed to minimize the opportunities corrupt human nature has to assert itself. The conduct regulations for students once again vividly illustrate the paradox of BJU's separatism. To use Bob Jones III's phrase, "these Christian young people have turned their backs on the world and its values," yet they are also in rigid preparation to fit into the secular world.

Accomplishing these twin tasks is a continuous, four-year process. First-year students are required to enroll in a year-long orientation class that meets twice weekly. University officials use this class to explain the rules and what is expected of the students. Two recent BJU students indicated that the student orientation covered such diverse topics as rock music, dress, dating, how to study, even table manners. One of the students commented that many of the rules are justified on the basis of the university's size. "They [rules] were needed," this student wrote, "to maintain order and consistency for all students." Another student, a 1985 graduate, remembered that two other principles also buttressed the rule structure. "Never do anything 'ever questionable,'" she wrote, "and never do anything to be a stumbling block to other Christians."[60]

The university ensures that students do not soon forget what they learn in orientation. For example, even in the residence halls, where one might expect students to let down their guard, conduct and attitude are constantly monitored. One BJU graduate described this system. Serving as a hall leader (the functional equivalent of a resident assistant in most other universities), this student was responsible for ensuring that by 7:00 A.M. the residents on his floor were out of bed, had made their beds, emptied the trash, and cleaned the sink in the room. Twice a week he checked each room to see that the floors were vacuumed, and he gave demerits to students for not attending class. Students are assigned three and four to a room at BJU, and a sign on the back of each residence room door reminds the students that "No Griping Is Allowed." Every evening from 10:15 to 10:45 mandatory prayer meetings are held throughout the hall, usually conducted by an upperclass student dubbed a "prayer captain." A "lights out" policy is then enforced beginning at 11:00 P.M. although seniors may study until midnight.[61]

The leader of the evening prayer meetings, the "prayer captain," also, according to a 1991 BJU student, acts as the "spiritual leader, helper, and friend to the others. . . . Each prayer captain also has the responsibility of reporting breaches in the rules to those in authority."[62] If the prayer captain does not catch every offense, the other students should. "Any student," the rule handbook states, "who knows or suspects that another student intends to violate any rule of the school and does not attempt to check the violation or . . . fails to [report] to . . . the proper authority will be considered disloyal and will be dealt with by the Discipline Committee."[63] This closely resembles the honor code used by schools such as the University of Virginia, but at BJU this tradition is used for much broader purposes. Traditional honor codes cover only the offenses of lying, cheating, and stealing. However, at BJU a questioning, critical attitude could easily be added to the list. Any student with a perceived attitude problem or who accumulates too many demerits is assigned to "spiritual probation" status. Described as a "tentative status" by Dean of Students James Berg, spiritual probation "says you have this semester to shape up." During that semester the student may not hold any leadership position, and the student must meet with a counselor once a week. At the end of the semester the administration determines whether or not the student may continue at BJU.[64]

The rules at BJU cover nearly every conceivable situation a college student might encounter. The most obvious offenses, which according to the handbook are "fleshly living, adultery, homosexuality, sexual perversions of any kind, dishonesty, drugs, drinking, gambling, profanity, obscenity, dancing, card-playing, movie-going and pornography," are strictly prohibited. Two of the most common activities for college students, attending movies and listening to rock music, are not tolerated at BJU. As Bob Jones III explained, "The movies today . . . appeal to sex, to licentiousness, to drunkenness. It is not fit material for a Christian to feed his soul upon." Rock music is banned because, again as Jones III explains, "the very beat of it is sensual. It makes animals out of the hearers, to appeal to their passions." Rock is not the only music banned at BJU. According to the handbook, "jazz, folk-rock, country and western, and 'so-called religious music that is performed in folkstyle, country-western style, Southern gospel style or nightclub style'" is also prohibited.[65]

Probably the most distinctive feature of the BJU rule structure is the dating regulations. The late evangelist John R. Rice, visiting BJU in 1945, wrote that after learning of the carefully chaperoned dating life of BJU, "I felt like thanking God that young love could bloom in a Christian atmosphere without the tawdry license . . . and looseness so customary among worldly young people."[66] If Rice could return to the BJU campus of the 1990s, he would no doubt be just as pleased as he was in 1945. No "tawdry license or looseness" is tolerated at BJU. Off-campus dating for all students is not allowed unless the couple is accompanied by a faculty member or a married couple. For on-campus dating, the "dating parlor" is available. The dating parlor is a huge room in the Student Center complete with sofas and love seats where students may talk with, but not touch, one another. Even if engaged to be married, couples may not kiss or hold hands, and in the dating parlor only one partner at a time can have an arm on the back of the sofa. A large desk sits at the entrance to the dating parlor where a monitor enforces the "no-touching" rule. If, for example, a couple were to be caught holding hands, they would be "socialed," that is, they may not see or speak to each other for a week. The crime of kissing carries a penalty of ten demerits plus being "socialed" for a month.[67]

Other on-campus contact between the sexes is also regulated. While students may go to classes and meals together, males and females may not speak to each other after 7:00 P.M. This "no-talking" rule extends even to the library. Since, as Dean James Berg explains it, "the library is not a social place," talking or visiting between the sexes after seven o'clock is not allowed in the library. Certain sidewalks on campus are also off-limits after five o'clock because students may not be as readily observed.[68] Calling a girlfriend or boyfriend after seven may also bring a penalty of ten demerits. Since verbal communication is not allowed in the evenings, an elaborate "note system" is maintained between residence halls. A box in the lobby is available for notes, and every evening the notes are delivered to the appropriate residence hall.[69]

The dating regulations also discriminate between men and women. A man, for example, may date an off-campus student by visiting her home, but a woman could not without a faculty chaperon. This may have to do with the fact that at BJU a woman, in the words of a 1992 female graduate, "is always on display." According to this graduate, the ideal social situation at BJU for a woman is to be dating a future pastor. Women who serve as hall leaders are required to take a class for pastors' wives (taught by Beneth Jones, wife of Bob Jones III), and women who show a greater interest in an independent career rather than marriage risk a spartan social life.[70] Perhaps the most well-known dating rule at BJU is the prohibition on interracial dating. The Bob Joneses' devotion to this principle cost them their tax exemption and landed them in the Supreme Court in 1983 (for full treatment of this case, see chapter 5). One BJU student told an interviewer that the dating regulations "force you to build a mental relationship with one another where you get to really know one another." Another student, commenting upon the entire rule structure, observed that "a person without self-discipline can never achieve anything. For us, it's a privilege to live and act as we feel is in keeping with the Lord."[71]

Learning to live "in keeping with the Lord" includes much more than simply following all of BJU's rules. Walter G. Fremont, former dean of the School of Education at BJU, compiled a "checklist" entitled "Evidences of Spiritual Growth and a Good Christian Testimony." Fremont's list provides further insight into what BJU considers a "separated lifestyle." A sampling of the characteristics that a separated life should encompass include the following:

(1) Do you have a daily devotional time reading God's Word?

(2) Do you have good music standards, and have you eliminated rock music?

(3) Are you getting victory over sinful habits?

(4) Are you submissive to authority and responsive to correction?

(5) Do you take part in a local, fundamental, Bible-believing church?

(6) Do you consistently tithe your income?

(7) Do you invite others to church and gospel services?

(8) Do you have some sort of gospel work going, for example, teaching Sunday School, Bible club, bus ministry?[72]

The Bob Joneses have erected a rule structure, justified it on the basis of biblical authority, and in so doing have given their constituency concrete direction for their lives. Members know what it takes to please God. Uncertainty is eliminated. Decision making and critical thinking are kept to a minimum. This is why the administration requires signs posted on residence-hall doors reading "No Griping." "Griping," or questioning, would threaten the entire structure. Those who transgress are dealt with swiftly. The handbook plainly states that any student "who in the opinion of the university does not fit into the spirit of the institution" will be asked to leave. Thus it is possible to keep the letter of the law at BJU and still be dismissed if the authorities detect a critical or questioning attitude. Bob Jones III once wrote that if a Christian school retained any unsavory elements among the students, the school would soon become a "hellish place." Jones cited biblical authority for expelling students who did not fit into the separatist subculture. He quoted Numbers 5:1–3, a scriptural passage in which God commanded the nation of Israel to "put out of the camp every leper. . . . Both male and female shall ye put out . . . that they defile not the camp, in the midst whereof I dwell."[73]

For those who choose to attend and graduate from BJU, however, the evidence suggests that the strict lifestyle and attitude rules work rather well. Bob Jones III once commented that BJU "students are happiest and most secure when they know what is expected of them." A 1978 BJU graduate observed that "outsiders consider this university to be a curiosity—they can't believe it exists. . . . Many of them also have a misunderstanding about it. It's not a military school—nobody forces us to come here." Another BJU graduate noted that "we leave [BJU] knowing the truth, knowing that we have the answer."[74] One of the students interviewed for this study indicated much the same. "BJU," she wrote, "adequately prepared us to be shining stars and have good testimonies." Even the disgraced Theodore Mercer could write, after his dismissal in 1953, "I love the BJU of teaching in a classroom atmosphere of consecration of students and teachers; I love the BJU of Christian friendships and Christian philosophy and discipline. . . . The years of my association with the university were in the plan of God for me."[75]

The separated, disciplined life also provides a powerful source of identity. Bob Jones III observed in 1981 that the unconverted "don't understand how [BJU students] could enjoy life without cocktails and sexual dalliances. To them we're freaks. We don't expect the unconverted to understand." The students at BJU, he also noted later, "chose to attend the world's most unusual university because they are the world's most unusual people—redeemed Christians. . . . [They] are the people of God, strangers and pilgrims in the earth." Lifestyle separatism took the distinction between the converted and unconverted and sharpened it. A properly separated life should elicit ridicule from the unconverted and unseparated Christians. As Bob Jones III described it in 1965, "There would be something wrong with our testimony if all people thought well of us. We don't ask the ungodly to think well of us. We don't ask the church people to think well of us."[76]

Even though the Bob Joneses actively cultivate an unusual reputation, from their refusal of accreditation to their strict, paternalistic rules, they still retain a desire to fit into the world. While they forbid their students the usual activities of other college students, the Joneses still want their graduates to assume conventional roles in American society as business leaders, doctors, lawyers, teachers. Toward this end, the curriculum and the philosophy behind it stress traditional values and submission to authority. The Joneses want graduates who will become, in Jones III's words, the "hope of America." Simultaneously, and conversely, they want graduates who have, again in Jones III's words, "turned their backs on the world and its values."[77]

The Joneses have, to borrow one writer's phrase, "shaken the dust of a doomed civilization off their feet" while endeavoring to erect a school that, in Jones Sr.'s words, will "save the individual and make the type of character that will save our civilization."[78] Much like the theological separatism that made the Joneses major players in various fundamentalist schisms ranging over the last thirty-five years, paradox and irony characterize their cultural and educational separatism as well.

CHAPTER FIVE

Rapprochement

Throughout its history, Bob Jones University has attracted its fair share of distortions and generalizations. Given the university's theology and rules, this is not surprising. One journalist, researching an article on BJU, found individuals who had heard that the school not only had separate sidewalks for men and women, but also had put bars on dormitory windows to keep students from escaping. John Shelton Reed, a sociologist from the University of North Carolina, wrote after visiting BJU in 1986 that "across town, at Southern Baptist Furman University, the folklore . . . has it that BJU is stockpiling arms."[1] While these assertions border on the ridiculous, other more serious and misleading statements have been made. Of all the generalizations about BJU, the one most repeated with the least justification is that BJU is a "southern" school. Larry King, for example, in his 1966 portrait of BJU, stated unequivocally that "the student body is predominantly Southern."[2]

The first student body was certainly southern; Jones drew recruits locally, from northern Florida and southeastern Alabama.[3] Within a year, however, the college included students from California, Ohio, and Indiana. Enrollment figures obtained from the BJU registrar's office and university archives conclusively demonstrate that, except for the first year, at no time in the school's history could BJU have been considered a "southern" school. From 1928 to 1944, for example, BJU matriculated students from every state except Nevada and New Mexico. During those years Michigan sent 190 students to BJU, Pennsylvania 122, and Ohio 108. Conversely, for the same period, Louisiana sent only 14, Arkansas 2, and South Carolina 73.[4] Then, beginning with the 1945–46 school year, the top five states represented at BJU were Michigan (123), Tennessee (100), North Carolina (82), Pennsylvania (75), and Illinois (73). The next year, 1946–47, the top states at BJU were Michigan (199), Pennsylvania (161), Illinois (124), and New York (102). For this same year, Alabama sent only 71, Georgia 76, and North Carolina 85.[5] By 1949–50, Pennsylvania, Michigan, and Illinois were the most heavily represented states at BJU. For that year, Georgia, Tennessee, Alabama, and Mississippi ranked 12th, 14th, 15th, and 17th, respectively.[6] Ten years later, in 1960, South Carolina sent the most students to BJU with 339, followed by Pennsylvania (190), Michigan (188), Florida (176), Ohio (165), New York (159), and California (151). For 1960, Alabama sent only 33 students, Tennessee 45, and Mississippi 29.[7] The most recent data, for the 1988–89 school year, demonstrated again that BJU continued to draw the majority of its students from outside the South; the top states represented were, in order, South Carolina, Pennsylvania, Michigan, and Illinois.[8]

For more than forty years, then, BJU has drawn its largest delegations from midwestern and northeastern states. The numbers indicate that BJU, while administered by southerners, has a strong appeal to students outside the South.

The fact that since its inception BJU has been located in the South but has never had a predominantly southern constituency is one more factor contributing to its unique status. From the beginning the Bob Joneses, as we saw in chapter 1, never targeted a regional constituency. Within a year of the school's founding, students from as far away as Massachusetts and Indiana matriculated at BJU. The school advertised in religious periodicals with national circulation, including *The Sunday School Times* and *The King's Business,* and it relied on the nationwide contacts established by Bob Jones Sr. in his evangelistic travels. The Bob Joneses were also never key players in the 1920s and 1930s fundamentalist-modernist

Table 1
Religious Employment of Bob Jones University Alumni, 1995

	As Pastors	As Christian School Administrators	As Christian School Teachers
Alabama	16	6	45
Alaska	6	1	3
Arizona	17	2	25
Arkansas	2	0	9
California	32	15	84
Colorado	25	4	57
Connecticut	5	4	24
Delaware	4	2	29
District of Columbia	0	0	0
Florida	44	24	178
Georgia	38	17	147
Guam	0	2	7
Hawaii	4	5	21
Idaho	5	0	7
Illinois	41	12	118
Indiana	51	12	133
Iowa	12	0	32
Kansas	16	2	27
Kentucky	4	1	14
Louisiana	3	0	6
Maine	11	2	15
Maryland	15	7	67
Massachusetts	5	4	16
Michigan	57	15	218
Minnesota	7	1	16
Mississippi	1	1	10
Missouri	7	3	34
Montana	1	0	8
Nebraska	7	3	11
Nevada	3	0	3
New Hampshire	13	3	37
New Jersey	18	3	30
New Mexico	2	1	4
New York	24	1	39
North Carolina	75	34	261
North Dakota	0	0	0
Ohio	51	16	143
Oklahoma	5	2	8
Oregon	8	4	8

Continued on next page

Table 1—*Continued*

Pennsylvania	83	29	275
Puerto Rico	4	2	8
Rhode Island	2	0	3
South Carolina	74	24	357
South Dakota	2	1	5
Tennessee	17	11	77
Texas	11	6	51
Utah	8	2	2
Vermont	6	2	6
Virginia	46	19	133
Washington	11	4	17
West Virginia	33	6	60
Wisconsin	14	5	66
Wyoming	7	0	2
Foreign Countries	68	6	74

controversies that split Southern denominations. While they left the Broad Street Methodist Church in Cleveland, Tennessee, in 1939 because of the infiltration of liberalism, the Joneses preferred to be voices for separatism in national organizations with little grounding in the South at the time, notably the National Association of Evangelicals. Indeed, it would appear that the South became home for BJU because Bob Jones Sr., in his effort to locate the financial and educational resources necessary to start a college, could turn most easily to local leaders in Alabama and Florida whom he had known and cultivated for years.[9]

BJU's ability to market that appeal has been facilitated in a variety of ways. The school's best advertisement has been its graduates, a cadre of loyalists built up over the years into a formidable force of BJU advocates. Graduates pastoring churches, administering and teaching in Christian day schools, and staffing an aggressive outreach ministry have enabled BJU to establish a national network of fundamentalists who in turn support Greenville with both students and money. According to data obtained in 1995 from Bob Jones Jr.'s office, there were 1035 BJU graduates serving as full-time pastors in fundamentalist churches across the nation and abroad (see table 1). In addition, there were 323 graduates serving as associate pastors or youth pastors. In 1995 there were also 89 BJU alumni traveling the nation as full-time evangelists.[10] This exposure in over a thousand pulpits every Sunday is a powerful advertisement for BJU.

Another powerful networking tool for BJU is the burgeoning Christian day-school movement. According to the Council for American Private Education, in 1988 there were 700,000 to one million children enrolled in Protestant day schools. On the average, two such schools per day have been established since 1960.[11] While the Christian school movement did not begin in earnest until after World War II, the Bob Joneses had erected Bob Jones Academy in 1928 to provide secondary instruction. Under the leadership of Walter A. Fremont, dean of education from 1953 to 1991, and James Deuink, dean from 1991 to the present, BJU has produced numerous teachers and administrators for Christian day schools. By the mid-1990s there were 328 BJU alumni administrating Christian day schools throughout the nation and the world (see table 1). In addition, more than 3,000 BJU alumni taught full-time in those schools (see table 1).

Christian day schools have proven to be fertile ground for BJU recruiting. In addition to having its alumni serve as principals and teachers throughout the nation, BJU actively courts the students in these schools. According to the BJU Admissions Office, the university sponsors three regional representatives who visit Christian schools and present a video on BJU. The school also hosts an invitational basketball tournament every January for Christian schools, holds "Let's Get Acquainted Days" for prospective students each Thanksgiving and spring, and sponsors an annual Five Acts Festival for Christian schools. Posters with request cards are sent to these schools, and an annual mailing is sent to pastors and principals requesting the names of prospective students. BJU often enlists its own students to then phone prospects.[12]

Two other important networking resources for BJU are its annual summer camps and its textbook publishing. Every summer, students from fundamentalist churches and schools journey to Greenville for "camp." In the summer of 1992, for example, camps were offered in sports, journalism, music, business, criminal justice, nursing, speech and drama, and science. These camps are run by

BJU graduates, and the students live and eat on campus for a week. The camps supplement the work of Christian day schools, and they obviously give the university invaluable exposure.[13] BJU also offers summer management seminars for Christian school administrators and teachers. Sections are offered for administration, preschool/ kindergarten, elementary, junior high / senior high, and special education. While there are over 282 seminars on Christian schools offered, the following is a representative sample:

Developing higher order thinking and comprehension skills.

The Christian Teacher's Obligation to Excellence.

Science Activities for Young Children.

Ten Ways to Improve Your Teaching.

Biblical and Secular History.

Establishing a Library.

Science Fairs in the Christian School.

The Computer and Your High School Newspaper.

Using Educational Psychology in Junior and Senior High.

Appropriate Identification of Learning Disabled.

Introduction to School Finance.[14]

Another service and a networking resource for BJU are the textbooks published by Bob Jones University Press. In existence since 1972, the Press publishes textbooks in Bible, English (reading, literature, writing, and grammar), social studies, math, computer science, science, and music. In addition, the Press publishes an academic skills evaluation program. Field representatives visit most schools with the textbook offerings. The options for a Christian school curriculum are quite diverse. In 1992, for example, BJU published Bible textbooks for secondary instruction on topics ranging from *Learning from the Life of Christ* to *Patterns for Christian Living*. For secondary math instruction, for example, the Press offers *Consumer Math for Christian Schools* to *Advanced Math*. In literature, a principal may choose texts in American and British literature or a set of videotapes in which Bob Jones Jr. interprets Shakespeare and his daughter-in-law discusses *Cyrano de Bergerac*. For the Christian school science lab, the Press also advertises teaching aids including fossil and rock collections and even weather chart kits. The Press advertises its science curriculum as "free of distortions of truth such as evolution and humanism."

The Heritage Studies offering includes American and world history texts, geography and economics, and government. Also offered in the Heritage Studies series is *Family Living,* a text for grades 11–12. This text "teaches God's pattern for the home and points out where current secular theories conflict with God's Word." For administrators, the Press offers publications ranging from *The Proper Use of Standardized Tests* to *Preparing Schools for the 21st Century.* A full line of videos is also offered for Christian school teachers, including such topics as *Producing Parent Programs* and *Characteristics of a Successful Christian School Teacher.*[15] According to the Press, the university markets to thirteen thousand Christian schools worldwide. In addition, the Press is also the leading supplier of Christian educational materials to home-school families.[16]

BJU also invests a great deal of time and effort in staying in touch with its graduates. *The Voice of the Alumni* is published six times a year and the director of alumni affairs, Bud Bierman, spends approximately twenty-six weeks a year visiting alumni and preaching in BJU-pastored churches. Dr. Bob Jones III also holds "Friendship Banquets" throughout the year in various locations so that alumni may stay in touch. Any graduate may call campus for a recorded message updating them on campus news.[17]

These efforts, both to attract new students and to keep in touch with graduates, have paid dividends for BJU. The university has national exposure in over a thousand churches every Sunday and daily publicity in numerous Christian schools throughout the United States. According to Dean James Berg, a majority of students who matriculate at BJU are graduates of Christian day schools.[18] As these students prepare for careers in the pastorate or as teachers, they return to churches and schools encouraging a new generation of students to attend BJU. While data is not available, this no doubt is the case for BJU graduates in other areas and occupations. BJU has become a self-sustaining entity.

Yet, despite the fact that BJU has a national network and attracts students from around the world, many still describe the university as a southern school. Undoubtedly, the main reason for this—aside from its location—is BJU's unusual stance on race relations. John Shelton Reed described the typical reaction of many when they hear about BJU: "Bob Jones University? Isn't that that segregationist place down in South Carolina someplace?"[19]

BJU's history and student rules indeed reflect traditional white southern attitudes toward race relations. This is largely attributable to the influence of the founder. Bob Jones Sr. mandated that no African-Americans be allowed to matriculate at BJU. Years later, Bob Jones Jr. claimed that his father wished to start a separate, fundamentalist school for African-Americans. "He got ready to do it," the younger Jones explained, "and then the civil rights agitation came along and he couldn't, you know. They didn't want a separate school."[20]

In 1960, as the nation stood on the brink of racial crisis, Bob Jones Sr. published a pamphlet entitled *Is Segregation Scriptural?* in which he detailed his racial beliefs. Jones Sr. assured his readers that he was no bigot. "You talk about a superior race and an inferior race," he wrote, "no race is inferior in the will of God." The trouble began when "way back yonder our forefathers went over to Africa and brought the colored people back. . . . That was wrong. But God overruled. When they came over here . . . they [the slaves] got converted." Jones thought African-Americans of the twentieth century should be grateful. If Africans had not been brought to America, they "might still be over there in the jungles of Africa today, unconverted."

Relations between the races were cordial, Jones believed, until the civil rights movement. "Do not let these Satanic propagandists fool you," Jones warned, "this agitation is not of God. It is of the devil." Jones Sr. avowed that he had "planned to build a school, just like BJU, here in the South for the colored people." But now civil rights agitation had begun, and now "we have a mess on our hands."[21]

Apparently, Jones Sr. made a connection between integration, modernist religion, and the coming of a one-world church led by the Antichrist. Theologically liberal preachers spoke of the universal fatherhood of God and the brotherhood of man. "There is not a word about that," Jones said, "in the Bible." These modernists were trying to eradicate racial boundaries God had set, and they were preparing for the time when "the anti-Christ will take over and . . . rule the world." Both Bob Jones Jr. and Bob Jones III have made similar statements.[22]

The exclusion of African-Americans from BJU was justified on the grounds that they might date white students, intermarry with them, and thus help bring about the "one-worldism" of the Antichrist. So the university administration was hostile to the civil rights movement. Jones Jr. refused to sign an act of compliance with the 1964 Civil Rights Act because, as he wrote to the United States Commission on Civil Rights, it "is a subtle and high-handed scheme to force all educational institutions under the control of a federal agency." Later BJU awarded an honorary doctorate to Alabama Governor George C. Wallace, whom Jones Jr. praised as a "David, warring against the giant, Tyranny." The school remained racially segregated.[23]

Then, a 1970 lawsuit brought by African-American parents in Mississippi led the Lawyers Committee for Civil Rights to argue that tax exemptions for private schools practicing racial discrimination undermined integration in the public schools. Integration could not be achieved, they argued, if the government through tax exemptions sanctioned private discriminatory schools. In *Green* v. *Connally* (1971) a three-judge court ruled that private schools in Mississippi that discriminated against African-Americans were not entitled to tax exemption. The court then ordered the Internal Revenue Service to deny exemption to these schools.[24]

While these court-ordered guidelines applied only to Mississippi, the IRS moved quickly to standardize them nationwide. One of the private schools immediately affected by the IRS ruling was Bob Jones University. In November 1970, the IRS notified BJU that proceedings were underway to revoke the tax-exempt status of the school because African-Americans were not admitted. The reaction from Greenville was swift. The executive committee of the university voted to sue the IRS if it proceeded with the revocation. In a letter to BJU alumni, Bob Jones Jr. warned of the coming battle. Declaring "if the income tax exemption can be used to blackmail educational institutions, the next step is to use it to blackmail churches," he vowed "BJU is going to fight for fairness and freedom for all Christian educational institutions and churches in America."[25] The university then went to court to seek an injunction against the IRS.

Filing suit against the IRS in the South Carolina district court, BJU was successful in temporarily stopping the revocation by the IRS. The IRS appealed the injunction and the Court of Appeals reversed the lower court action. BJU appealed that ruling and in the spring of 1974 the case reached the Supreme Court. The Court, in *Bob Jones University* v. *Simon,* ruled that BJU was in violation of the anti-injunction provision of the IRS code. The court, in other words, could not stop an action (the revocation of exemption) that had not yet occurred. The Court ruled that while BJU could not stop the IRS from collecting taxes, it might sue for a refund if it chose to press the case further.[26]

The IRS proceeded with the revocation of BJU's tax exemption in 1976, making it retroactive to 1970. BJU, the IRS declared, now owed the federal government more than $490,000 in taxes. In compliance with the IRS, BJU filed returns for the 1970–1976 period. The university then paid $21.00 in unemployment tax for one employee for 1975 and requested a refund. The IRS refused, and BJU promptly sued for the $21.00 while the IRS countersued for $490,000. Meanwhile, the original reason for the IRS action, the BJU admissions policy, was no longer an issue. In 1975, the university adopted an open admissions policy. BJU continued to enforce its ban on interracial dating, however.

The district court in South Carolina, in 1978, awarded the $21.00 to BJU and dismissed the IRS counterclaim.[27] The IRS appealed the decision and the case once again went to a higher judicial level. The Fourth Circuit Court of Appeals reversed the lower court when it ruled in 1980 that BJU was not eligible for exemption. The court ruled that the IRS code must be interpreted in light of the "clearly defined public policy . . . condemning racial discrimination." The court ruled further that the government interest in fighting racial discrimination was "so compelling that conflicting religious practices must yield in their favor."[28] So while BJU might continue practicing its racial beliefs, it could not enjoy tax exemption. BJU appealed the decision. The Supreme Court in the fall of 1981 agreed to hear the case.

The twelve-year-old battle came to an end on May 24, 1983. In an eight-to-one decision, the Supreme Court upheld the right of the IRS to deny tax exemption to BJU. The university, the Court said, violated public policy with its ban on interracial dating. Despite the BJU argument that the rule applied equally to all races and hence was not discriminatory, the Court said any rule based on "racial affiliation and association" was in fact discrimination.[29] Bob Jones III ordered the flags on campus flown at half-mast to protest what he regarded as a blow to religious liberty. The Court decision, he asserted, meant "churches and Christian schools will be tolerated only if they serve the purposes of the government."[30] Despite its protests, the university settled quickly with the IRS. BJU was able to meet its new obligations thanks to contingency planning, which had set aside money each year since 1970 in the event that the university lost its litigation. Although it no longer enjoyed tax exemption, BJU did not change its dating rule.

Despite the bruising court battle, by 1983 the Bob Joneses, like many Americans, were settling into the contented state of mind induced by Ronald Reagan. Reagan did not, of course, engineer this feat single-handedly, yet he was able to console millions of conservative Americans with his cheerful and simplistic attitude. By the early 1980s, "Reagan" was really a movement. He represented, as Harvard political scientist James Q. Wilson observed, "a counter-revolution against the dominant political, social and governmental trends of the 1960s and 1970s. . . . [He represented] a revolt against . . . feminism, racial preferences in hiring and schooling, tolerance of homosexuality, drugs, abortion, and what can [be] lumped under the heading of 'permissiveness.'"[31] As we saw in chapter 3, the Joneses had been railing against these forces for years. Locked out of national power for so long, conservatives like the Joneses were ecstatic with Reagan's assumption of power in

1981. A small but significant sign that the Bob Joneses were no longer outsiders came when the new Reagan administration tapped BJU faculty member George Youstra to be an undersecretary in the Department of Education.[32]

Examining samples of BJU's advertising from the 1960s to the 1980s, we can chart a progression from a hostile minority determined to preserve their purity to a confident group anxious to acquaint others with the many opportunities of their university. In the 1960s, as society reverberated from the Vietnam War and the civil rights movement and as traditional values were increasingly questioned, BJU projected a defensive attitude. A September 1968 advertisement featured a Civil War battle scene and proclaimed in bold print, "Some things are worth dying for—freedom is one of them." Reflecting BJU's hostility to the liberal Johnson Administration, the notice boasted that BJU "lives without the shame of knowing it lives by Uncle Sam's grace rather than God's grace." "God's people," the copy continued, "demonstrate by their giving their approval of BJU's separation from the state."[33]

This alienated attitude persisted through the 1970s. A July-August 1973 advertisement capitalized on BJU's "minority status." According to the copy, "God has raised up BJU to provide for a minority group the world cares nothing about—born-again Christian young people. . . . They are rejected by the world but welcomed by BJU." Furthermore, "the majority won't come to BJU, but it is not the majority we are here for." The next year another advertisement compared BJU to the Pilgrims, who "loved freedom to worship God more than they loved security and conformity to wrong." BJU existed for "that rare individual who is sold out to the Lord's way. It's not the world's way; it's the way of the Cross."[34] In 1975 another advertisement proclaimed BJU a place where security still existed. "In our nation," it said, "there is no such thing as security. Money loses it value; people break their vows. America is stripped of her defenses through sedition and appeasement." Nonetheless, "there is security in abundance at this Fortress of Faith."[35]

Then in the 1980s, despite their court troubles, BJU's constant references to their "minority" status became less frequent. Finally, in 1987, the school retained a public relations agency, which helped BJU change its motto from the "world's most unusual university" to "the opportunity place." Staff members began wearing buttons bearing a slogan similar to those of auto dealers and dry cleaners, "BJU Cares." In a July 1990 interview, BJU executive vice-president Bob Wood acknowledged that the school was attempting to soften its image.[36] A summer 1989 advertisement proclaimed that "true quality endures. . . . Students who attend BJU allow God to work the canvas of their mind and character into a thing of beauty. We want you to become a masterpiece of God's good workmanship." In 1990, other copy stated, "We promise . . . the highest quality Christian educational experience and we deliver. . . . Visit us and see what we're really like." In the spring of 1991, BJU also offered in an advertisement to refund the first semester's tuition if the student were not "completely satisfied." Calling it their "You've Got to Love It" guarantee, BJU encouraged prospective students to "ask for your free personal opportunity profile outlining your choice of our more than 100 majors."[37]

One of the clearest signs of BJU's departure from the harsh, separatist rhetoric of the past came in an editorial written by Bob Jones III in the spring of 1991. Jones related an experience during a recent plane trip. He encountered a flight attendant who, in the course of a conversation, stated that she was a Christian. "All she wanted to talk about," Jones wrote, "was the Lord and her Bible study." Also, as they talked, Jones learned the woman enjoyed dancing, a "worldly" activity if there ever was one. Yet, rather than criticize her for her worldliness, Jones observed that "there is more hope for her because she searches the Scriptures than for a well-bred, well-taught fundamentalist young person who has 'not the love of God in him.'" Jones lamented that "I see professing Christian young people who are indifferent to the Scriptures . . . devoid of love for Christ, and smug in their separation. If one of those should stand beside that flight attendant in the presence of the Lord, I wonder who would receive his greatest approval."[38]

Finally, in a statement revealing the new direction beginning to appear at BJU, Jones wrote, "it is not worldly practices that separate good Christians from bad ones. It is whether they have the love of God in them."[39] Given the history of the school and the many battles it has fought over separation, Jones III's statement seems epochal. It is unmistakable evidence that the Joneses no longer feel compelled vehemently to assert their purity and their separation from those less pure. It is evidence that they feel more comfortable in a society that, at least in the 1980s and 1990s, pays respect to the values they have championed.

Meanwhile, the saga of BJU continues. Young Bob Jones IV graduated from George Washington University with his masters degree in 1992, and he has expressed an interest in returning to Greenville to assist his father.[40] He will be assuming his responsibilities at one of the most tranquil times in the school's history. As he has already demonstrated, he will also continue a tradition that has carried the school through the fundamentalist-modernist controversy, the Depression, the new evangelical controversy, the cultural alienation of the 1960s and 1970s, and the seemingly more sedate Reagan-Bush years. Writing as a guest columnist in the *Chicago Tribune* in 1992, the youngest Jones lamented the fact that "in a society that takes pride in its tolerance of diverse viewpoints, we fundamentalists have been set aside as a lone exception." That notwithstanding, the founder's great-grandson promised that "as we become ever better educated, as we climb the corporate ladder and win political office, our troubling message of moral accountability will grow harder to ignore."[41]

The Bob Joneses exemplify in their school and their family the ways in which diverse theological traditions have intertwined or merged to produce twentieth-century fundamentalism. With their emphasis on "soul winning" and the numerous evangelists and missionaries they continue to graduate every year, the Bob Joneses show that their connection to nineteenth-century revivalism is alive and well. The urgent need to evangelize also demonstrates the premillennial influence at BJU. God's timetable is winding down, and the Gospel must be given to as many as possible before it is too late. The Joneses also reflect their premillennial heritage with their constant denunciations of society and of organized, mainline religion. Things are worsening constantly; society is becoming more corrupt, and organized religion is heading rapidly toward a one-world church. Yet, despite their apocalyptic rhetoric, the Joneses clearly retain some of the optimism of their nineteenth-century Protestant forebears. Society is not so far gone that they do not want to play an active role in it. Numerous BJU graduates enter the business world, law, medicine, and other graduate schools every year. These graduates are encouraged to make a difference wherever they may be. In recent years many BJU alumni have run for and won elective office. They are eager to correct what they perceive to be the moral ills of society.

Of all the traditions from which the Bob Joneses derive their identity, separatism is clearly the strongest one. As we have seen, that emerged as their defining characteristic in large part due to the personality of the Jones family. Moreover, events throughout the school's history, particularly the breaks with the NAE and Billy Graham, along with the Mercer affair, exacerbated that defensive mentality. Separatism, in addition to being a doctrinal position, also became a way of dealing with the rapidly changing nature of both American religion and American society in the middle of the twentieth century. It enabled the Joneses and their constituency to retain a distinctive identity in an age when identity became easily blurred.

The Jones family, and the institution they created, are a remarkable example of the persistence of religious fundamentalism in a society that, generally speaking, finds much of what they believe and espouse to be archaic and in some cases dangerous.

In addition, the Bob Joneses and BJU are also examples of a religious sect that, while denouncing modern values and praising the virtues of the past, nonetheless have freely adopted the blessings of at least technological modernity in getting out their message. BJU, in other words, becomes increasingly modern even as it bills itself as the incarnation of past virtues.[42]

Yet, perhaps more importantly, the Bob Joneses and their university also bear witness to the fact that very often American fundamentalists have not conformed to the stereotype created for them.

A fundamentalist institution that imports the Metropolitan Opera and houses an internationally acclaimed Baroque art collection does not lend itself to the easy characterizations of an H. L. Mencken or some of the other early chroniclers of fundamentalism. The Bob Joneses are acutely aware of the images often associated in the popular mind with fundamentalism. In a 1992 conversation, Bob Jones III stated that if there had been any changes at all in BJU, it was a "shift in our effort to be perceived as we are, and not as we've been stereotyped."[43]

Perhaps Bob Jones IV summed up the enigma of BJU best when he wrote, "Our hopelessly old-fashioned students consistently score at or near the top of all colleges in the state on standardized tests for teachers, accountants, law students, medical students, etc. Our principles may elicit condescending smiles, but our achievements demand respect."[44]

Notes

Introduction

1. *Bob Jones University Bulletin, 1988–89* (Greenville: Bob Jones University Press), 6.

2. Bob Jones Jr. to the author, 13 May 1992.

3. Chicago Evangelistic Meeting news release, 26 December 1958, Bob Jones University Archives (hereafter BJUA).

4. Undated advertising copy, BJUA.

5. "Bob Jones, Jr. Lashes Out against Jerry Falwell and the Moral Majority," *Moral Majority Report,* 14 July 1980, 6.

6. Marshall Frady, *Billy Graham: A Parable in American Righteousness* (Boston: Little, Brown, 1979), 96.

7. Bob Jones Sr., *The Perils of America* (Chicago: Chicago Gospel Tabernacle, 1934), 43.

8. Robert Sherrill, *Gothic Politics in the Deep South* (New York: Grossman, 1968), 221–22.

9. Bob Jones III, *Taking Higher Ground* (Greenville: Bob Jones University Press, 1991).

10. See George Marsden, *Fundamentalism and American Culture: The Shaping of Twentieth-Century Evangelicalism, 1870–1925* (New York: Oxford University Press, 1980), and Ernest Sandeen, *The Roots of Fundamentalism: British and American Millenarianism, 1800–1930* (Chicago: University of Chicago Press, 1970).

11. Larry L. King, "Bob Jones University: The Buckle on the Bible Belt," *Harper's,* June 1966, 54.

12. Jane O'Hara, "Oasis of Salvation in a World of Sin," *MacLeans,* 11 October 1982, 10, 13.

13. Robert Webber, *Evangelicals on the Canterbury Trail* (Waco, Tex.: Word Books, 1985), 14.

14. Interview with Bob Jones III, 26 June 1992.

15. Ibid.

16. "Dr. Jones: 'God's Wrath Stirred,'" *Greenville Piedmont*, 12 May 1970; "Bob Jones, Jr. Asks God to 'Smite' Haig," *Chicago Tribune*, 3 April 1982.

17. Interview with Bob Jones III, 26 June 1992.

18. Mencken and Shipley quoted in Marsden, *Fundamentalism and American Culture*, 188–89.

19. Kenneth Cauthen, *The Impact of American Religious Liberalism* (New York: Harper and Row, 1962), 7.

20. William Horndern, *A Layman's Guide to Protestant Theology* (New York: Macmillan, 1955), 31.

21. Ibid., 44.

22. See Friedrich Schleiermacher, *On Religion: Speeches Addressed to Its Cultured Despisers,* trans. Terrence N. Tice (Richmond: John Knox Press, 1969) and *The Christian Faith,* trans. H. R. Mackintosh and J. S. Stewart (Edinburgh: T. and T. Clark, 1928).

23. Lloyd Averill, *American Theology in the Liberal Tradition* (Philadelphia: Westminster Press, 1967), 43.

24. Horndern, *Laymen's Guide to Protestant Theology,* 4.

25. Tim Dowley, ed., *Eerdmans Handbook to the History of Christianity* (Grand Rapids: Eerdmans Publishing Company, 1977), 545.

26. Nathan Hatch and Mark Noll, eds., *The Bible in America* (New York: Oxford University Press, 1982), 103.

27. See Gail Kennedy, ed., *Evolution and Religion* (Boston: D. C. Heath, 1987); James R. Moore, *The Post-Darwinian Controversies* (Cambridge: Cambridge University Press, 1979); and Jon H. Roberts, *Darwinism and the Divine in America* (Madison: University of Wisconsin Press, 1988).

28. William McLoughlin, *Revivals, Awakenings, and Reforms.* (Chicago: University of Chicago Press, 1978), 156.

29. Cauthen, *The Impact of American Religious Liberalism,* 23.

30. See Walter Raushenbusch, *Christianity and the Social Crisis* (New York: Macmillan, 1910) and *A Theology for the Social Gospel* (New York: Macmillan, 1922).

31. Marsden, *Fundamentalism and American Culture,* 102–3.

32. Mark Noll, *Between Faith and Criticism* (New York: Harper and Row, 1986), 11.

33. Marsden, *Fundamentalism and American Culture,* 117.

34. Ibid.

35. Sydney Ahlstrom, *A Religious History of the American People* (New Haven: Yale University Press, 1972), 815.

36. Robert Ashworth, "The Fundamentalist Movement among the Baptists," *Journal of Religion* 4 (November 1924): 625.

37. J. Murray Murdoch, *Portrait of Obedience* (Schaumberg, Ill.: Regular Baptist Press, 1979), 65.

38. Curtis L. Laws, quoted in Joseph M. Stowell, *Background and History of the General Association of Regular Baptist Churches* (Haywood, Calif.: J. F. May Press, 1949), 13.

39. Curtis L. Laws, "Convention Side Lights," *The Watchman-Examiner,* 1 July 1920, 834, BJUA.

40. Shailer Mathews, *The Faith of Modernism* (New York: Macmillan, 1924), 35–36.

41. David Beale, *In Pursuit of Purity* (Greenville: Bob Jones University Press, 1986), 273.

42. Robert Ketcham, *Facts for Baptists to Face* (Waterloo, Ia.: Walnut Street Baptist Church, 1936), 4.

43. Nathan Hatch and George Marsden, eds., *Eerdmans Handbook to Christianity in America* (Grand Rapids: Eerdmans, 1983), 378.

Chapter 1: The Patriarch and the Foundation

1. See Wayne Flynt, *Poor but Proud: Alabama's Poor Whites* (Tuscaloosa: University of Alabama Press, 1989), for an excellent treatment of Alabama during this period.

2. R. K. Johnson, *Builder of Bridges* (Greenville: Bob Jones University Press, 1982), 6.

3. See Charles Reagan Wilson, *Baptized in Blood: The Religion of the Lost Cause* (Athens: University of Georgia Press, 1983); Bertram Wyatt-Brown, *Southern Honor: Ethics and Behavior in the Old South* (New York: Oxford University Press, 1982); and Donald G. Mathews, *Religion in the Old South* (Chicago: University of Chicago Press, 1977).

4. Bob Jones Sr. to Melton Wright, 4 December 1957, BJUA.

5. Bob Jones Sr., editorial, *Bob Jones Magazine,* October 1928.

6. Bob Jones Jr., *Cornbread and Caviar* (Greenville: Bob Jones University Press, 1985), 24.

7. Melton Wright, *Fortress of Faith: The Story of Bob Jones University* (Greenville: Bob Jones University Press, 1984), 2.

8. Johnson, *Builder of Bridges,* 4.

9. Sheldon Hackney, *Populism to Progressivism in Alabama* (Princeton: Princeton University Press, 1969), 81.

10. Flynt, *Poor but Proud*, 251.

11. Bob Jones Sr., "The Country Idea or the City Idea?" *Bob Jones Magazine*, November 1928, 1.

12. Wyatt-Brown, *Southern Honor,* 43.

13. Jones Sr. to Melton Wright, 4 December 1957, BJUA.

14. Robert Walker, "He Built a College in One Generation," *Sunday,* November 1945, 14.

15. See John Boles, *The Great Revival, 1787–1805: The Origins of the Southern Evangelical Mind* (Lexington: University of Kentucky Press, 1972), for an excellent treatment of this phenomenon.

16. Samuel S. Hill, *Southern Churches in Crisis* (New York: Holt, Rinehart and Winston, 1967), 64.

17. Boles, *The Great Revival,* 193.

18. Hill, *Southern Churches in Crisis,* 25.

19. Kenneth Bailey, *Southern White Protestantism in the Twentieth Century* (New York: Harper and Row, 1964), 24.

20. C. Vann Woodward, *The Origins of the New South* (Baton Rouge: Louisiana State University Press, 1966), 170.

21. For more on American Methodism, see Emory S. Bucke, ed., *The History of American Methodism,* 3 vols. (New York: Abingdon, 1964); and Richard Cameron, ed., *The Rise of Methodism: A Source Book* (New York: Philosophical Library, 1954).

22. Hill, *Southern Churches in Crisis,* 145.

23. Bob Jones Sr., quoted in John R. Rice and Robert J. Wells, eds., *How to Have a Great Revival* (Mufreesboro, Tenn.: Sword of the Lord Press, 1956), 93.

24. Hill, *Southern Churches in Crisis,* 147.

25. Jones Sr. to Melton Wright, 4 December 1957, BJUA.

26. Ibid.

27. Wright, *Fortress of Faith,* 13.

28. *American Universities and Colleges,* 13th ed. (New York: Walter de Gruyter, Inc., 1987), 117.

29. Wright, *Fortress of Faith,* 11.

30. Jones Sr. to Melton Wright, 4 December 1957, BJUA.

31. See, for example, Bob Jones Sr., "Why Bob Jones University Was Founded," *Christian Life,* June 1950, 28–30.

32. Jones Sr. to Melton Wright, 4 December 1957, BJUA.

33. Johnson, *Builder of Bridges,* 244.

34. See William McLoughlin, ed., *The American Evangelicals, 1800–1900: An Anthology* (New York: Harper and Row, 1968); William McLoughlin, *Modern Revivalism: Charles Grandison Finney to Billy Graham* (New York: Ronald Press, 1959); and Martin Marty, *Righteous Empire: The Protestant Experience in America* (New York: Dial, 1970).

35. For more on Moody, see Richard Curtis, *They Called Him Mister Moody* (Grand Rapids: Eerdmans, 1962); and James Findlay, *Dwight L. Moody: American Evangelist, 1837–1899* (Chicago: University of Chicago Press, 1969).

36. See Winthrop S. Hudson, *Religion in America* (New York: Scribner's, 1973), 233; and for an interesting study on the contributions of hymns to American revivalism, see Sandra Sizer, *Revival Waves and Home Fires: The Rhetoric of Nineteenth-Century Gospel Hymns* (Chicago: University of Chicago Press, 1976).

37. See William McLoughlin, *Billy Sunday Was His Real Name* (Chicago: University of Chicago Press, 1955); and Ray C. Rensi, "The Gospel According to Sam Jones," *Georgia Historical Quarterly* 60 (Fall 1976): 251–63.

38. William Coleman, "Billy Sunday: A Style Meant for His Time and Place," *Christianity Today*, 17 December 1976, 15.

39. See McLoughlin, *Billy Sunday Was His Real Name*, 203; Wright, *Fortress of Faith*, 114; and Bob Jones Jr., *Cornbread and Caviar*, 90.

40. Rice and Wells, eds., *How to Have a Great Revival*, 89.

41. Rensi, "The Gospel According to Sam Jones," 260.

42. McLoughlin, *Billy Sunday Was His Real Name*, 193.

43. Bob Jones Sr., *Chapel Sayings of Doctor Bob Jones* (Greenville: Bob Jones University Press, 1980).

44. Betty Vann, "Dr. Bob Jones—A Bold Preacher," *Dothan Progress*, 29 April 1987, 16.

45. Wright, *Fortress of Faith*, 18.

46. Ibid., 19.

47. Steubenville Ministers Association press release, Steubenville, Ohio, 24 February 1921, BJUA.

48. See Paul Carter, *The Twenties in America* (New York: Corwell, 1975); and Geoffrey Perrett, *America in the 1920s* (New York: Simon and Schuster, 1982), for good analyses of the 1920s.

49. "Reverend Bob Jones Has National Reputation," *Macon News*, 11 May 1911, BJUA clippings file.

50. Vann, "Dr. Bob Jones—A Bold Preacher," 16.

51. Dolly Dalrymple, "Flapper Mother and Evolution Draw Fire from Evangelist Jones," *Birmingham News,* 6 May 1926, BJUA clippings file.

52. See David Chalmers, *Hooded Americanism: The History of the Ku Klux Klan* (New York: F. Watts, 1981); and John Higham, *Strangers in the Land* (New Brunswick: Rutgers University Press, 1988).

53. "Bob Jones Raps Wicked City Life and Candidacy of Governor Al Smith," *Bellingham Herald,* 1 December 1927, BJUA clippings file.

54. Bob Jones Sr., *Two Sermons to Men* (Chicago: Glad Tidings Publishing, 1923), 40.

55. Higham, *Strangers in the Land,* 292.

56. On the 1928 campaign, see Oscar Handlin, *Al Smith and His America* (Boston: Little, Brown, 1955); Allan J. Lichtman, *Prejudice and the Old Politics: The Presidential Election of 1928* (Chapel Hill: University of North Carolina Press, 1979); and Ruth Silva, *Rum, Religion and Votes: 1928 Reexamined* (University Park: Pennsylvania State University Press, 1962).

57. James B. Sellers, *The Prohibition Movement in Alabama: 1702 to 1943* (Chapel Hill: University of North Carolina Press, 1943), 207.

58. Bob Jones Sr., editorial, *Bob Jones Magazine,* October 1928, 2.

59. Bob Jones Sr., *The Perils of America* (Chicago: Chicago Gospel Tabernacle, 1934), 10.

60. Ibid., 9, 8.

61. McLoughlin, *Modern Revivalism,* 365.

62. Johnson, *Builder of Bridges,* 106.

63. Jones, *Perils of America,* 31.

64. Paul Carter, *The Decline and Revival of the Social Gospel* (Ithaca: Cornell University Press, 1954), 34.

65. See Timothy L. Smith, *Revivalism and Social Reform: American Protestantism on the Eve of the Civil War* (New York: Harper and Row, 1965), and *Revivalism and Social Reform in Mid-Nineteenth-Century America* (New York: Abingdon, 1957); David Moberg, *The Great Reversal: Evangelicalism versus Social Concern* (Philadelphia: Lippincott, 1972); Richard V. Pierard, *The Unequal Yoke* (Philadelphia: Lippincott, 1970).

66. Jones, *Perils of America,* 29–31.

67. George Schmidt, "Colleges in Ferment," *American Historical Review,* 59 (October 1953): 20.

68. William Ringenberg, *The Christian College: A History of Protestant Higher Education in America* (Grand Rapids: Eerdmans, 1984), 26.

69. Richard Hofstader, "The Revolution in Higher Education," in Arthur M. Schlesinger Jr., ed., *Paths of American Thought* (Boston: Houghton Mifflin, 1963), 277.

70. Quoted in Ringenberg, *The Christian College*, 30.

71. See Suzanne Linder, *Prophet of Progress* (Chapel Hill: University of North Carolina Press, 1966); and Edwin Mims, *Chancellor Kirkland of Vanderbilt* (Nashville: Vanderbilt University Press, 1940), ix.

72. Mims, *Chancellor Kirkland*, 319.

73. Edwin Mims, *The Advancing South* (Garden City, N.Y.: Doubleday, 1926), 158.

74. William Louis Poteat, *Can a Man Be a Christian Today?* (Chapel Hill: University of North Carolina Press, 1926), 109.

75. Linder, *Prophet of Progress*, 141.

76. See James J. Thompson, *Tried as by Fire* (Macon, Ga.: Mercer University Press, 1982); Willard Gatewood, ed., *Controversy in the Twenties* (Nashville: Vanderbilt University Press, 1969); and Gatewood, *Preachers, Pedagogues and Politicians: The Evolution Controversy in North Carolina* (Chapel Hill: University of North Carolina Press, 1966).

77. Jones, *Perils of America*, 32, 33, 35, 39.

78. Ibid., 13–14, 20–21.

79. See Bob Jones Sr., *Three College Shipwrecks* (Greenville: Bob Jones University Press, 1948), 2.

80. T. T. Martin, editorial, *Baptist Advance*, 25 March 1920, 22.

81. Henry Clay Morrison, *Crossing the Deadline, or the Recrucifixion of the Lord Jesus Christ* (Louisville: Pentecostal Publishing Company, 1924), 8.

82. Edwin Poteat, "Religion in the South," in W. T. Crouch, ed., *The Culture in the South* (Chapel Hill: University of North Carolina Press, 1934), 263.

83. Wright, *Fortress of Faith*, 31.

84. Dolly Dalrymple, "Bob Jones Labors to Give Christian Education to Youth of the Future," *Birmingham News*, 20 June 1928, BJUA clippings file.

85. See Norman Furniss, *The Fundamentalist Controversy: 1918–1931* (New Haven: Yale University Press, 1954); Loetscher Lefferts, *A Brief History of the Presbyterians* (Philadelphia: Westminster, 1978); and George Marsden, *Fundamentalism and American Culture: The Shaping of Twentieth-Century Evangelicalism, 1870–1925* (New York: Oxford University Press, 1980).

86. Joel Carpenter, "Fundamentalist Institutions and the Rise of Evangelical Protestantism," *Church History* 49 (March 1980): 66, 67.

87. George Tindall, *The Emergence of the New South, 1913–1945* (Baton Rouge: Louisiana State University Press, 1967), 227.

88. Philip M. Hosay, "Graves, David Bibb," *Dictionary of American Biography* (New York: Scribner's, 1973), 317–18.

89. Donald Comer to Bob Jones Sr., 8 September 1927, Donald Comer Papers, Birmingham Public Library.

90. Bob Jones Sr. to bondholders, 1 November 1930, Comer Papers; Johnson, *Builder of Bridges,* 187.

91. Willard B. Gatewood Jr., "Upshaw, William David," *Dictionary of American Biography,* 701–2.

92. Sam W. Small, "The Dream of Bob Jones," *Atlanta Constitution,* undated clipping, BJUA.

93. Tindall, *The Emergence of the New South,* 105. See also Charles W. - Tebeau, *A History of Florida* (Coral Gables: University of Miami Press, 1971), 377.

94. Marlene Womack, "Bob Jones Made Dream a Reality," *Panama City News-Herald,* 26 July 1987, 6e.

95. "Florida as It Is Today," *Florida State News,* 3 March 1927, 2; "Panama City Makes Good Progress during the Year," *Dothan Weekly Eagle,* 9 July 1926, 1.

96. Johnson, *Builder of Bridges,* 176.

97. Womack, "Bob Jones Made Dream a Reality," *Panama City News-Herald,* 26 July, 6e.

98. Johnson, *Builder of Bridges,* 176, 77.

99. "Jones Talks to Large Crowd on Vital Subject," *Dothan Weekly Eagle,* 11 February 1927, 1.

100. "Up-to-Minute Facts about College Point and Bob Jones College," news release, 16 March 1927, BJUA.

101. Bob Jones Jr., *Cornbread and Caviar,* 59.

102. "Florida as It Is Today," *Lynn Haven Free Press,* 4 December 1926, 3.

103. "Big Day at College Point," *Lynn Haven Free Press,* 4 December 1926, 3.

104. Marlene Womack, "Bob Jones Rode Crest of Area Boom," *Panama City News-Herald,* 2 August 1987, 6f.

105. "Dormitories Are Overflowing as Bob Jones College Is Opened," *Montgomery Advertiser,* 14 September 1927, BJUA clippings file.

106. *The College Point Development: Site of Bob Jones College,* pamphlet, BJUA.

107. "Bob Jones to Speak in City," *Dothan Weekly Eagle,* 28 January 1927, 1.

108. *Montgomery Advertiser,* 14 September 1927, BJUA clippings file.

109. *An Epoch in Education: Facts about the Bob Jones College* (Lynn Haven, Fla.: Bob Jones College, 1927), 5.

110. Ibid., 4.

111. *Rules of the Bob Jones College,* 1931, BJUA; "Fifty Years of Change," *Voice of the Alumni,* June 1977, 8.

112. Dalrymple, "Bob Jones Labors to Give Christian Education to Youth of the Future."

113. "Testimonies from Two Students," *Bob Jones Magazine,* April 1930, 30.

114. Bob Jones Jr. to the author, 16 November 1989.

115. *An Epoch in Education,* 15.

116. *Bob Jones College Catalog, 1931–32* (Lynn Haven, Fla.: Bob Jones College, 1931), 37, 20–21.

117. Floyd Collins, "Bob Jones College as I Know It," *Bob Jones Magazine,* November 1928, 20.

118. W. S. Cawthon to Dr. Joseph Roemer, 25 April 1929, Cawthon Papers, Florida Department of State, Tallahassee.

119. *An Epoch in Education,* 32.

120. *Bob Jones College Catalog, 1931–32,* 8.

121. Bob Jones Sr., "Why Bob Jones University Was Founded," 29.

122. *Bob Jones Magazine,* June 1928, 6.

123. J. S. Mack to Bob Jones Sr., 9 November 1936, BJUA.

124. Theodore C. Mercer, *An Additional Statement to the Alumni and Board of Trustees of Bob Jones University,* 4 August 1953, Wheaton College Archives, Wheaton, Illinois.

125. *Montgomery Advertiser,* 14 September 1927, BJUA clippings file.

126. Johnson, *Builder of Bridges,* 182.

127. "Campus Briefs of the Bob Jones College," *Lynn Haven Free Press,* 14 January 1933, 3.

128. "The Ministerial Association and Volunteer Band," *Bob Jones Magazine,* April 1929, 7.

129. "You Will Not Fit In," *Child Evangelism,* November 1943, 10.

130. Dalrymple, "Bob Jones Labors to Give Christian Education to Youth of the Future."

131. *Revised and Amended By-Laws of Bob Jones University,* 27 May 1952, BJUA.

132. H. L. Mencken, *Prejudices: Fifth Series* (London: Jonathan Cape, 1926), 114.

133. Johnson, *Builder of Bridges*, 183.

134. Marlene Womack, "Depression Years Threw Bob Jones College into Ruin," *Panama City News-Herald*, 9 August 1987, 4e.

135. "A Touch of Lace," *Voice of the Alumni*, June 1982, 11.

136. Dan Turner, "Personal Refinement and the Arts: The Cultural Philosophy of Dr. Bob Jones, Sr., and Dr. Bob Jones, Jr." (Ed.D. diss., University of Illinois, 1989), 121.

137. Johnson, *Builder of Bridges*, 180.

138. Jones Jr., *Cornbread and Caviar*, 41.

139. Wright, *Fortress of Faith*, 139, 96.

140. Bob Jones Sr., "A Message from the Bob Jones College," *Bob Jones Magazine*, November 1928, 7.

141. Bob Jones Sr. to bondholders, 19 June 1928; summer 1930, Comer Papers, Birmingham Public Library.

142. Jones to bondholders, 24 May 1929, Comer Papers.

143. Jones to bondholders, 15 November 1929, Comer Papers.

144. "Bob Jones College Goes into Hand of Receiver," *Lynn Haven Free Press*, 14 January 1933, 1.

145. Bob Jones Jr. to J. Willett Vess, 5 November 1982, BJUA.

146. "Bob Jones College Goes into Hand of Receiver," *Lynn Haven Free Press*, 14 January 1933, 1.

147. Johnson, *Builder of Bridges*, 187.

148. Interview with Dr. Bob Wood, Bob Jones University, 20 July 1990.

149. Bob Jones Sr. to Milton Winterberg, 28 July 1952, BJUA.

150. Warner Ogden, "Evangelist Bob Jones Operates a School Where Fundamentalism Is Insisted Upon," *Knoxville News Sentinel*, 11 February 1934, 2.

151. Turner, "Personal Refinement and the Arts," 133.

152. Travis Hedrick, "Bob Jones—His College," *Chattanooga Times*, 20 August 1933, 1.

153. Johnson, *Builder of Bridges*, 188.

154. Turner, "Personal Refinement and the Arts," 134.

155. Womack, "Depression Years Threw Bob Jones College into Ruin."

156. R. K. Johnson, *Miracle from the Beginning*, (Greenville: Bob Jones University Press, 1971), 18.

157. Jones Jr. to J. Willett Vess, 5 November 1982, BJUA.

158. *Bob Jones College Catalog, 1945–46* (Cleveland, Tenn.: Bob Jones College, 1945), 15.

159. "Bob Jones Counts More Attendants," *Chattanooga Times*, 15 May 1936, 3.

160. John R. Rice, "Bob Jones College Training Soulwinners," *Sword of the Lord*, 15 March 1946, 2.

161. Wright, *Fortress of Faith*, 426.

162. Johnson, *Miracle from the Beginning*, 18.

163. Johnson, *Builder of Bridges*, 203.

164. "Folks Invited to College Opening," undated clipping, Rachel Ayers scrapbook, BJUA.

165. "Spiritual Revival Near, Says Jones," *Montgomery Advertiser*, 2 July 1939, BJUA clippings file.

166. Johnson, *Builder of Bridges*, 196–209, 201.

167. See chapter 5 for a full treatment of Bob Jones Jr.

168. Jones Jr., *Cornbread and Caviar*, 41, 66.

169. Hedrick, "Bob Jones—His College."

170. "Bob Jones Ready for Big Classes," *Chattanooga Times*, 25 August 1935, BJUA clippings file.

171. Carpenter, "Fundamentalist Institutions and the Rise of Evangelical Protestantism," 33.

172. Joel Carpenter, "From Fundamentalism to the New Evangelical Coalition," in George Marsden, ed., *Evangelicalism and Modern America* (Grand Rapids: Eerdmans, 1984), 5.

173. Bob Jones Sr., quoted in "News Item," *The Baptist Bulletin*, September 1934, 4.

174. Bob Jones Sr. to Rev. M. A. Stephenson, 5 September 1939, BJUA.

175. Ibid.

176. Jones Jr., *Cornbread and Caviar*, 73–74; Jones Sr. to M. A. Stephenson, 5 September 1939, BJUA.

177. *Little Moby's Post*, Spring 1940, BJUA.

178. Jones Sr. to L. E. Hoppe, 26 March 1940, BJUA.

179. See, for example, Bob Jones Jr., *Scriptural Separation: First and Second Degree* (Greenville: Bob Jones University Press, 1971).

Chapter 2: Separatism Unleashed

1. For more on Riley and Machen, see Marie A. Riley, *The Dynamic of a Dream: The Life Story of Dr. William B. Riley* (Grand Rapids: Eerdmans, 1938); and Ned B. Stonehouse, *J. Gresham Machen: A Biographical Memoir* (Grand Rapids: Eerdmans, 1954).

2. Oliver Van Osdel, "Good Soldiers of Jesus Christ," *Baptist Bulletin*, April 1933, 1.

3. Wheaton College advertisement, *Baptist Bulletin*, December 1935, 36.

4. The GARBC is an excellent microcosm of this phenomenon. For more on the GARBC, see Merle R. Hull, *What a Fellowship! The First Fifty Years of the GARBC* (Schaumberg, Ill.: Regular Baptist Press, 1981); Joseph M. Stowell, *Background and History of the General Association of Regular Baptist Churches* (Haywood, Calif: J. F. May Press, 1949); and Calvin Odell, *The GARBC and Its Attendant Movement* (Salem, Ore.: Western Baptist Bible Press, 1975).

5. Ralph Roy, *Apostles of Discord* (Boston: Beacon Press, 1953), 188–89.

6. See Robert T. Ketcham, *The Answer* (Chicago: Regular Baptist Press, 1949).

7. James Morris, *The Preachers* (New York: St. Martin's, 1973), 200–201, 195.

8. Martin Marty, *Pilgrims in Their Own Land* (New York: Penguin, 1984), 352.

9. Sydney Ahlstrom, *A Religious History of the American People* (New Haven: Yale University Press, 1972), 2:270–72.

10. Carl McIntire, *Twentieth-Century Reformation* (Collingswood, N.J.: Christian Beacon Press, 1944), 173–75.

11. *Newsweek*, 29 September 1941, 62.

12. McIntire, *Twentieth-Century Reformation*, 177.

13. Ibid., 179, 186–87.

14. See Joel Carpenter, "Fundamentalist Institutions and the Rise of Evangelical Protestantism," *Church History* 49 (March 1980): 62–75.

15. Robert Handy, *A History of the Churches in the United States and Canada* (New York: Oxford University Press, 1977), 386–87.

16. "Why No Revival?" *Christian Century*, 18 September 1935, 24.

17. Quoted in William Horndern, *A Layman's Guide to Protestant Theology* (New York: Macmillan, 1955), 101–4.

18. Karl Barth, *The Epistle to the Romans*, trans. Edwyn C. Hoskyns (New York: Oxford University Press, 1963).

19. Quoted in Nathan Hatch and George Marsden, eds., *Eerdmans Handbook to Christianity in America* (Grand Rapids: Eerdmans, 1983), 420–21.

20. Reinhold Niebuhr, *Beyond Tragedy* (New York: Scribner's, 1937), x.

21. Horndern, *A Layman's Guide to Protestant Theology*, 98–99.

22. Charles C. Morrison, "The Liberalism of Neo-Orthodoxy," *Christian Century*, 21 June 1950, 763.

23. James Murch, *Cooperation without Compromise: A History of the National Association of Evangelicals* (Grand Rapids: Eerdmans, 1956), 48.

24. Donald Barnhouse, "Personal Feelings," *Revelation*, 7 October 1937, 420; and J. Elwin Wright, "A Few Observations," *New England Fellowship Monthly*, April 1937, 8.

25. J. Elwin Wright, "An Historical Statement of Events Leading to the National Conference at St. Louis," in Wright, *Evangelical Action: An Historical Statement* (Boston: United Action Press, 1942), 5.

26. McIntire, *Twentieth-Century Reformation*, 192.

27. Wright, "An Historical Statement," 9, 11.

28. Ibid., 65.

29. "Conservatives," *Time*, 17 May 1943, 46.

30. Wright, "An Historical Statement," 101.

31. Louis Gasper, *The Fundamentalist Movement* (Paris: Mouton, 1963), 26.

32. Wright, "An Historical Statement," 32–33.

33. Gasper, *The Fundamentalist Movement*, 29.

34. "News of the Christian World," *Christian Century,* 19 May 1943, 614.

35. Murch, *Cooperation without Compromise*, 155, 93, 165, 167.

36. Roy, *Apostles of Discord*, 191–93.

37. Melton Wright, *Fortress of Faith: The Story of Bob Jones University* (Greenville: Bob Jones University Press, 1984), 31.

38. Bob Jones Sr. to Rev. R. A. Stephenson, 5 September 1939, BJUA.

39. Bob Jones Sr. to Rev E. G. Zorn, 23 July 1943, BJUA.

40. Quoted in Joel Carpenter, "From Fundamentalism to the New Evangelicalism," in George Marsden, ed., *Evangelicalism and Modern America* (Grand Rapids: Eerdmans, 1984), 11.

41. Bob Jones Sr., "Dr. Bob Jones Reports on the Recent National Convention of Evangelicals," *Churchill Tabernacle Evangelist*, June 1944, BJUA clippings file.

42. McIntire, *Twentieth-Century Reformation*, 191.

43. Wright, "An Historical Statement," 14–15; and McIntire, *Twentieth-Century Reformation*, 197.

44. Carl McIntire, "The NAE and Separation," *Christian Beacon*, 7 October 1948, 4; Roy, *Apostles of Discord*, 225.

45. Bob Jones Sr. to R. L. Decker, 16 May 1949, BJUA.

46. Gertrude D. Clark to Bob Jones Jr., 29 April 1947, BJUA.

47. Stephen Paine to NAE board members, 14 June 1948, BJUA.

48. R. L. Decker to Bob Jones Jr., 18 November 1947, BJUA; and NAE Board of Administration members list, April 1950 release, BJUA.

49. Bob Jones Sr. to R. L. Decker, 16 May 1949, BJUA.

50. Bob Jones Jr. to R. L. Decker, 10 September 1949, BJUA.

51. A good discussion of this new generation can be found in Rudolph L. Nelson, "Fundamentalism at Harvard: The Case of Edward J. Carnell," *Quarterly Review* 2 (Summer 1982): 79–98.

52. Harold Ockenga, "From Fundamentalism, through New Evangelicalism, to Evangelicalism," in Kenneth Kantzer, ed., *Evangelical Roots* (Nashville: Thomas Nelson, 1978), 38.

53. Harold Ockenga, "The New Evangelicalism," *The Park Street Spire*, February 1958, 3.

54. Quoted in Murch, *Cooperation without Compromise*, 2.

55. See Carl F. H. Henry, *The Uneasy Conscience of Modern Fundamentalism* (Grand Rapids: Eerdmans, 1947).

56. George Marsden, *Reforming Fundamentalism: Fuller Seminary and the New Evangelicalism* (Grand Rapids: Eerdmans, 1987), 122.

57. "Is Evangelical Theology Changing?" *Christian Life*, March 1956, 16–19.

58. Arnold Hearn, "Fundamentalist Renascence," *Christian Century,* 30 April 1958, 528–29.

59. See, for example, Bob Jones Sr., *The Perils of America* (Chicago: Chicago Gospel Tabernacle, 1934), 43; and *An Epoch in Education: Facts about the Bob Jones College* (Lynn Haven, Fla.: Bob Jones College, 1927), 4.

60. "Readers Say," *United Evangelical Action*, 1 August 1947, 2.

61. Bob Jones Sr. to the editor, *United Evangelical Action*, undated letter, BJUA.

62. Kenneth Wilson, "Keeping Up with the Joneses," *Christian Herald*, June 1951, 24.

63. Bob Jones Jr., *Cornbread and Caviar* (Greenville: Bob Jones University Press, 1985), 73.

64. Bob Jones Jr. to Bernie Stanton, 3 July 1940, BJUA.

65. Bob Jones Jr. to author, 20 August 1990.

66. Quoted in Wilson, "Keeping Up with the Joneses."

67. "Preparing for TV," *Christian Life*, August 1949, 35.

68. Bob Jones Jr., *Cornbread and Caviar*, 103–4.

69. Bob Jones Jr. to Gertrude Clark, 13 June 1951, BJUA.

70. Jones Jr. to the editor, *United Evangelical Action*, 1 June 1953, 11; Robert Schuler Jr. to editor, *UEA*, 29 May 1953, 9.

71. Theodore C. Mercer, *A Statement Concerning My Dismissal from Bob Jones University* (1953), Billy Graham Center Archives, Wheaton College, Wheaton, Illinois, 5; interview with Bob Jones Jr., 16 March 1989.

72. Bob Jones Sr. to alumni, 19 June 1953, Wheaton College Archives.

73. Theodore Mercer, *An Additional Statement to the Alumni and Board of Trustees of Bob Jones University,* 4 August 1953, Billy Graham Center Archives, 2.

74. Bob Jones Jr. interview with author, 16 March 1989.

75. Bob Jones Sr. and R. K. Johnson to Bob Jones Jr., 15 June 1953, Wheaton College Archives.

76. Mercer, *An Additional Statement,* 3.

77. Ibid., 4–5, 10.

78. *Revised and Amended By-Laws of BJU,* 27 May 1952, BJUA.

79. Mercer, *An Additional Statement,* 22, 12, 21.

80. Bob Jones Sr. to alumni, 4 September 1953, Wheaton College Archives.

81. Interview with Bob Jones Jr., Greenville, S. C., March 16, 1989.

82. Ibid.

83. Karl Keefer to 1952–53 faculty and staff, Theodore Mercer file, Wheaton College Archives; Mercer, *A Statement,* 17; *An Additional Statement,* 7.

84. "The Statement of the Joint Alumni–Former Student Committee," December 1953, Wheaton College Archives.

85. Theodore Mercer, *To the Board of Trustees of Bob Jones University,* May 1954, Billy Graham Center Archives, 95.

86. Jones Sr. to the alumni, 4 September 1953 and 19 June 1953, Wheaton College Archives.

87. "Graham in Greenville," *Christianity Today,* 1 April 1966, 44.

88. For more on Billy Graham, see W. Glyn Evans, *Profiles of Revival Leaders* (Nashville: Broadman, 1976); Marshall Frady, *Billy Graham, A Parable in American Righteousness* (Boston: Little, Brown, 1979); and John Pollock, *Crusade: Twenty Years with Billy Graham* (Minneapolis: World Wide Publications, 1969).

89. Frady, *Billy Graham,* 96.

90. Bob Jones Jr., *Cornbread and Caviar,* 153; Pollock, *Crusade,* 13.

91. Johnson, *Builder of Bridges,* 274.

92. Pollock, *Crusade,* 37.

93. Ibid., 98.

94. "A New Evangelist Arises," *Life,* 21 November 1949, 97; "Sickle for the Harvest," *Time,* 14 November 1949, 63.

95. Billy Graham, "The Editorial Policy of *The Pilot,*" *The Pilot,* January 1948, 113; *The Pilot,* April 1951, 222.

96. G. Archer Weniger, "The Position of Dr. Graham before He Embraced Ecumenical Evangelism," tract published by Foothill Boulevard Baptist Church, Castro Valley, Calif., 1958.

97. Billy Graham to Bob Jones Sr., 19 February 1949; 29 December 1949; 23 October 1950, BJUA.

98. Bob Jones Jr., *Cornbread and Caviar*, 154.

99. Bob Jones Jr., "The Position of BJU in Regard to the Proposed Billy Graham Crusade in Greenville," 8 February 1965, manuscript, BJUA.

100. "Billy Graham Speaks at BJU in Greenville," *Little Moby's Post*, March-April 1950, BJUA.

101. Bob Jones Jr., *Cornbread and Caviar*, 154.

102. Mercer, *An Additional Statement*, 21.

103. Bob Jones Sr. to friends of BJU, 6 March 1957, BJUA.

104. Johnson, *Builder of Bridges*, 282.

105. Bob Jones Jr. to Ralph W. Mitchell, 7 November 1956, BJUA.

106. John R. Rice, *Come Out or Stay In?* (Nashville: Thomas Nelson, 1974), 175–76; William McLoughlin, *Modern Revivalism: Charles Grandison Finney to Billy Graham* (New York: Ronald Press, 1959), 500; *Look*, 7 February 1956; Billy Graham, "The Lost Chord of Evangelism," *Christianity Today*, 1 April 1957, 26–27.

107. Bob Jones Sr. to alumni, 6 March 1957.

108. Quoted in letter, Bob Jones Jr. to the author, 20 August 1990.

109. For the most thorough treatment of the alienation between Graham and the fundamentalists, see Butler F. Porter Jr., "Billy Graham and the End of Evangelical Unity" (Ph.D. diss., University of Florida, 1976).

110. Ernest Pyles, "Bruised, Bloody, and Broken: Fundamentalism's Internecine Controversy in the 1960s," *Fides et Historia* 18 (October 1986): 50.

111. "Evangelicals and Fundamentals," *Christianity Today*, 16 September 1957, 20.

112. William Culbertson to Bob Jones Jr., 23 June 1959; Bob Jones Jr. to William Culbertson, 24 June 1959, BJUA.

113. Chicago Evangelistic Meeting news release, 26 December 1958, BJUA.

114. Bob Jones Jr. to Brice Fenning and Gene Lasley, 10 February 1960; Bob Jones Jr. to CEF Committee, 25 August 1961, BJUA.

Chapter 3: The Separatist Path

1. Scriptural references taken from *Revised Standard Version* (New York: New American Library, 1974).

2. V. L. Walter, "Donatism," *Evangelical Dictionary of Theology* (Grand Rapids: Baker Book House, 1984), 329.

3. Sydney Ahlstrom, *A Religious History of the American People* (Garden City, N.Y.: Doubleday Image Books, 1975), 1:122.

4. Roland Bainton, *Christendom: A Short History of Christianity* (New York: Harper and Row, 1966), 2:35.

5. "The Schleitheim Confession of Faith," Appendix 3 of *Glimpses of Mennonite History and Doctrine*, ed. John C. Wenger (Scottsdale, Pa.: Herald Press, 1940), 209.

6. Tim Dowley, John H. Y. Briggs, Robert Linder, eds., *The History of Christianity* (Herts, Eng.: Lion, 1977), 388.

7. Hugh Spurgin, *Roger Williams and Puritan Radicalism in the English Separatist Tradition* (Lewiston, Me.: Edwin Mellon Press, 1989), 66–67.

8. Leland H. Carlson, ed., *The Writings of Henry Barrowe, 1587–1590* (London: George Allen and Unwin, 1962), 54, 320, 304.

9. Spurgin, *Roger Williams*, 38.

10. Edmund S. Morgan, *Roger Williams: The Church and the State* (New York: Harcourt, Brace, 1967), 25, 26.

11. Quoted in Richard T. Hughes and C. Leonard Allen, *Illusions of Innocence* (Chicago: University of Chicago Press, 1988), 54.

12. Morgan, *Roger Williams*, 38.

13. G. Archer Weniger, "Separation Systemized," *Faith for the Family*, November-December 1976, 8–9.

14. Bob Jones University Faculty, *Biblical Separation* (Greenville: Bob Jones University Press, 1980), 15.

15. Bob Jones Jr., untitled editorial, *Faith for the Family*, March-April 1975, 1.

16. Bob Jones III, *What is a Fundamentalist?* (Greenville: Bob Jones University Press, 1985), 5–6.

17. Bob Jones Jr., *Cornbread and Caviar* (Greenville: Bob Jones University Press, 1985), 103.

18. Winthrop S. Hudson, *Religion in America* (New York: Scribner's 1973), 71.

19. Clarence Goen, in his *Revivalism and Separatism in New England* (New Haven: Yale University Press, 1962), has argued that the Awakening fit "the classical pattern of religious reform: exaltation of an earlier era as the golden age . . . belief in the decline or fall from that period of pristine purity . . . and a striving to reproduce . . . the pattern of the golden age" (159). Goen's characterization would easily apply to the Bob Joneses and their quest, both in their associations and their administrative policies, to restore "pristine purity." For more on the Great Awakening, see David Harlan, *The Clergy and the Great Awakening in New England* (Ann Arbor:

University of Michigan Research Press, 1980); Richard L. Bushman, ed., *The Great Awakening: Documents on the Revival of Religion, 1740–1745* (New York: Institute of Early American History and Culture, 1970); and Darrett Rutman, ed., *The Great Awakening: Event and Exegesis* (New York: Wiley, 1970).

20. See Nathan Hatch, Mark Noll, and John Woodbridge, *The Gospel in America* (Grand Rapids: Zondervan, 1979), 183, 193–96.

21. Bob Jones Jr., to author, 30 April 1990.

22. Bob Jones faculty member Daniel Turner provides a different perspective on premillennialism at BJU. In the summer of 1992 Turner wrote,

> In my experience here for twenty years as a faculty member the premillenial position has always been presented in a way similar to the position on predestination—i.e., both sides of these issues appear to be taught in scripture, but "good men disagree" about which is correct. The focus from the chapel platform was, believe either way—premil, postmil—just live like you really believe it. To paraphrase BJsr, "If Jesus is coming today, live a pure, holy life now so you are ready. If Jesus is coming after society has been reformed, then live a pure, holy life to help prepare civilization for His rule. We are not going to go to seed on something on which good men disagree." In one sermon included in the small book *Things I Have Learned*, BJsr said something like, "Jesus might come soon. If you believe that you'll learn patience." This is not the hard premil line one would expect. Both Jr. and BJIII have publicly taken premil positions, but not dogmatically. The creed of the college and the university does not contain any statement relative to the return of the Lord. (Daniel Turner to the author, 20 July 1992).

23. Robert Sherrill, *Gothic Politics in the Deep South* (New York: Grossman, 1968), 229; "Bob Jones, Jr. Lashes Out against Jerry Falwell and the Moral Majority," *Moral Majority Report*, 14 July 1980, 6.

24. "Bob Jones, Jr. Lashes Out Against Jerry Falwell and the Moral Majority," *Moral Majority Report*, 14 July 1980, 2.

25. John R. Rice, *Come Out or Stay In?* (Nashville: Thomas Nelson, 1974), 171.

26. Chicago Evangelistic Meeting news release, December 1958, Bob Jones University Archives.

27. John R. Rice, "Our Beloved 'Intellectuals' Again," *Sword of the Lord*, 18 May 1956, 12.

28. John R. Rice, "Editor Visits Bob Jones College," *Sword of the Lord*, 8 June 1945, 1.

29. John R. Rice, "Dr. J. Oliver Buswell's Charges against Bob Jones U. Answered," *Sword of the Lord*, 8 June 1948, 2.

30. Rice, *Come Out or Stay In?*, 177.

31. Professor Jacob Dorn, remarks delivered at the Ohio Academy of History, Denison University, 21 April 1990, author's personal files.

32. John R. Rice, "Here is Historic Fundamentalism," *Sword of the Lord*, 22 September 1978, 7.

33. Bob Jones Jr., *Scriptural Separation: First and Second Degree* (Greenville: Bob Jones University Press, 1971), 3.

34. Rice, *Come Out or Stay In?*, 196; John R. Rice, "Why Divide Good Fundamentalists?" *Sword of the Lord*, 17 December 1976, 1.

35. George Dollar, *A History of Fundamentalism in America* (Greenville: Bob Jones University Press, 1973), 253–54.

36. Bob Jones Jr., *Facts John R. Rice Will Not Face* (Greenville: Bob Jones University Press, 1977), 15; Jones Jr., *Scriptural Separation*, 1.

37. John R. Rice, "They Did Not Hold to Secondary Separation," *Sword of the Lord*, 1 February 1974, 1; Rice, "Why Divide Good Fundamentalists?" 8.

38. Bob Jones Jr., *Facts John R. Rice Will Not Face*, 4, 11, 21, 12, 25, 24.

39. In 1992 Bob Jones Jr. asserted that the issue with Rice was less doctrinal than it was personal. He wrote to the author that

We never separated from Dr. John Rice. He got upset, broke fellowship with us, and did all he could to hurt the University.

He wrote a book on the inspiration of Scripture. Our Bible faculty came to me saying, "What should we do? Dr. Rice has asked almost everyone of us to review this book because he would like some quotes for advertising it, but it seems to all of us that the position he takes is what we call 'mechanical inspiration.'" (That is, God uses a man like a typewriter rather than letting the Spirit of God move upon a man using his personality, his vocabulary, and choosing out of his experience and his resources the correct words.) "We do not think it is a good book. We do not agree with it, and we cannot endorse it. However, if we do not, Dr. Rice is going to attack us for not believing in the full inspiration of the Word of God."

I told them he had also asked me for a review of it, and I just told him I did not agree with the method of inspiration which he teaches;

and since I do not want people to think there is any difference between us, I would appreciate his excusing me from reviewing the book. Dr. Rice's feeling was, I am afraid, that anybody who did not agree with him in every little point was his enemy. He was already upset with us because we had brought Charles Woodbridge here as a visiting professor for a month. Apparently he and Woodbridge were long-time enemies—something of which we were totally unaware. Anyway, these two things together caused Dr. Rice to break with us. We tried as hard as we could to say nothing about it and certainly made no attack upon him, but he became so vehement in his opposition to us and attacked us so largely that we had to point out in defense of the Univesity some of Dr. Rice's misrepresentations.

40. Bob Jones Jr., *Facts John R. Rice Will Not Face*, 1, 15, 21, 26; and John R. Rice, "Why Divide Good Fundamentalists?" 9.

41. Bob Jones III, "From the University President," *Voice of the Alumni*, February 1977, 6.

42. Jones Jr., *Facts John R. Rice Will Not Face*, 14.

43. Dollar, *A History of Fundamentalism in America*, 283–85.

44. Jack Van Impe, *Heart Disease in Christ's Body* (Royal Oak, Mich.: Jack Van Impe Ministries, 1984), 214, 239.

45. Jerry Falwell, "Falwell Defends against Bob Jones Assault," *Moral Majority Report*, 14 July 1980, 1.

46. Dinesh D'Souza, *Falwell: Before the Millennium* (Chicago: Regnery Gateway, 1984), 97, 144, 130.

47. Ibid., 81, 149, 115.

48. "Mid-Century World Outlook Conference at BJU," *Little Moby's Post*, February 1951, 6; "Americanism Conference," *Little Moby's Post*, January 1952, 2, BJUA.

49. BJU press release, 27 January 1962, BJUA.

50. Robert Sherrill, *Gothic Politics in the Deep South*, (New York: Grossman, 1968), 225; and sermon preached by Bob Jones Jr., 8 December 1963, BJUA.

51. "BJU Stages Write-In," *BJU Bulletin*, May 1966, 15; "BJU Student Leaders Protest Anarchy," *Voice of the Alumni*, June 1970, 2; "Dr. Bob Jones Raps Mob Dissent," unidentified clipping, BJUA.

52. Bob Jones III, "From the University President," *Voice of the Alumni*, October 1979, 6.

53. Elmer Rumminger, "Christians in Politics," *Voice of the Alumni*, April 1979, 6; Rick Rigdon, "The Christian in Politics," *Voice of the Alumni*, April 1979, 11; Michael Ginsburg, "Fundamentalists Exercise Political Muscles," *Greenville Piedmont*, 3 November 1980, 2.

54. Jones Jr., *Cornbread and Caviar*, 172.

55. "Bob Jones, Jr. Lashes Out Against Jerry Falwell and the Moral Majority," *Moral Majority Report*, 14 July 1980, 6.

56. Bob Jones III, *The Moral Majority* (Greenville: Bob Jones University Press, 1980), 2–3.

57. George Marsden has written that, "from the time of the Puritans until about the middle of the nineteenth century, American evangelicalism was dominated by a Calvinistic vision of a Christian culture." That vision specifically called for Christians to "introduce God's kingdom, not only in the lives of the elect, but also by means of civil laws that would . . . transform culture according to God's will." Marsden cites the examples of Charles Finney, who called for the "Christian Church . . . to reform individuals, communities, and governments," and Jonathan Blanchard, who asserted that "the law of God is the law of the land." Later, with the rise of premillennialism, the focus shifted. Now, rather than using civil laws to usher in God's kingdom, premillennial Protestants advocated laws and reform as a means of simply restraining evil, such as liquor. Until Christ returned to earth, evil would never be completely eradicated.

Marsden posits that evangelical social concern lessened significantly between 1900 and 1930. This decline was due in large measure to the fundamentalist reaction to theological liberalism, which championed social reform as its own. This notwithstanding, twentieth-century fundamentalists continued to be politically involved, although, as Marsden points out, their activism tended to be more selective and dealt mainly with issues that touched them directly, such as antievolution and anticommunism. See his "The Great Reversal," *Journal of Christian Reconstruction* 8 (Summer 1981): 182, 187.

58. Jones III, *The Moral Majority*, 5.

59. "Falwell Defends Against Assault by Bob Jones," *Moral Majority Report*, 14 July 1980, 4–5.

60. D'Souza, *Falwell: Before the Millennium*, 177.

61. Jerry Falwell, ed., with Ed Dobson and Ed Hinson, *The Fundamentalist Phenomenon* (Garden City, N.Y.: Doubleday, 1981), 183.

62. Ibid., 163.

63. Edward Dobson, "Does the Bible Really Teach Separation?" *Fundamentalist Journal*, March 1984, 12–13.

64. Edward Dobson, "Casting Off the Shackles of Prejudice," *Fundamentalist Journal*, May 1985, 12–13.

65. D'Souza, *Falwell: Before the Millennium*, 167–68.

66. Nelson Keener, "What Did Baptist Fundamentalism '84 Accomplish?" *Fundamentalist Journal*, June 1984, 59.

67. *World Congress of Fundamentalists Resolution 1980*, (Dunn, N.C.: Anvil Press, 1980), 3, 7.

68. Bob Jones Jr., "Editorial," *Faith for the Family*, July-August 1984, 19; William Simbro, "Battlin' Bob Jones Wages Holy War," *Des Moines Tribune*, 27 March 1982, 10.

69. *World Congress of Fundamentalists Resolutions 1980*, 3; Bob Jones III, "What Is a Fundamentalist?" *Faith for the Family*, October 1985, 6, 2.

70. Robert Jordan, "New Evangelicalism Restated," *FBF News Bulletin*, November-December 1981, 1–3; Homer Massey, "Pseudo-Fundamentalism '84," *FBF News Bulletin*, May-June 1984, 3.

71. *World Congress of Fundamentalists Resolutions 1980*, 7; and *World Congress of Fundamentalists Resolutions 1983*.

Chapter 4: The World's Most Unusual University

1. Jane O'Hara, "Oasis of Salvation in a World of Sin," *MacLeans*, 11 October 1982, 10; and Virginia Brereton, "Examining the Christian College," *History of Education Quarterly* 26 (Summer 1986): 325.

2. See for example Richard Hughes, ed., *The American Quest for the Primitive Church* (Urbana: University of Illinois Press, 1988); and Hughes and C. Leonard Allen, *Illusions of Innocence* (Chicago: University of Chicago Press, 1988).

3. David Beale, *In Pursuit of Purity* (Greenville: Bob Jones University Press, 1986).

4. For an excellent discussion of the cross-cultural context of fundamentalism, see Martin Marty and R. Scott Appleby, eds., *Fundamentalisms Observed* (Chicago: University of Chicago Press, 1991).

5. George Marsden, *Fundamentalism and American Culture: The Shaping of Twentieth-Century Evangelicalism, 1870–1925* (New York: Oxford University Press, 1980), 6–7.

6. Ibid., 7, 200.

7. Quoted in Melton Wright, *Fortress of Faith: The Story of Bob Jones University* (Greenville: Bob Jones University Press, 1984), 31.

8. Bob Jones Sr., "Why Bob Jones University was Founded," *Christian Life*, June 1950, 28.

9. Robert Sherrill, *Gothic Politics in the Deep South* (New York: Grossman, 1968), 221–22.

10. Virginia Brereton, "Examining the Christian College," *History of Education Quarterly* 26 (Summer 1986): 322.

11. Bob Jones Sr., *The Perils of America* (Chicago: Chicago Gospel Tabernacle, 1934), 19, 39.

12. *An Epoch in Education: Facts about the Bob Jones College* (Lynn Haven, Fla: Bob Jones College, 1927), 4.

13. Laurence R. Vesey, *The Emergence of the American University* (Chicago: University of Chicago Press, 1970), 25.

14. Albea Godbold, *The Church College of the Old South* (Durham: Duke University Press, 1944), 52.

15. Mark Noll, quoted in Joel Carpenter and Kenneth Shipps, eds., *Making Higher Education Christian: The History and Mission of Evangelical Colleges in America* (Grand Rapids: Eerdmans, 1987), 69, 104.

16. Godbold, *Church Colleges of the Old South*, 109.

17. Ibid., 71.

18. Clifford Lewis, "To the Youth of America," *Bob Jones Magazine*, April 1929, 14; Bob Jones College advertisement, unidentified periodical clipping, August 1945, BJUA.

19. Bob Jones University Faculty, *The Christian Philosophy of Education* (Greenville: Bob Jones University Press, 1978); and *The Christian Teaching of History* (Greenville: Bob Jones University Press, 1978).

20. BJU Faculty, *The Christian Philosophy of Education*, 1–7.

21. BJU Faculty, *The Christian Teaching of History*, 2–11.

22. BJU Faculty, *The Christian Philosophy of Education*, 2, 4, 3.

23. Guenter Salter, "The Value of a Christian Liberal Arts Education," *Balance*, January 1983, 1–2.

24. Guenter Salter, "The Inconsistencies of Humanism," *Balance*, October 1984, 1–3.

25. Daniel Turner, "Personal Refinement and the Arts: The Cultural Philosophy of Dr. Bob Jones, Sr. and Dr. Bob Jones, Jr." (Ed.D. diss., University of Illinois, 1989), 249; and *What's So Unusual about BJU?*, 1989 promotional flyer.

26. Christopher Connell, "Bob Jones University: Doing Battle in the Name of Religion and Freedom," *Change*, May-June 1983, 41.

27. Turner, "Personal Refinement and the Arts," 108.

28. *Bob Jones College Catalog, 1933–34*, 8; Turner, "Personal Refinement and the Arts," 146.

29. *Bob Jones College Catalog 1947–48*, 29.

30. Turner, "Personal Refinement and the Arts," 237.

31. Ibid., 168.

32. Wright, *Fortress of Faith*, 369.

33. Ibid., 367.

34. *Peterson's Guide to Four-Year Colleges, 1990–1991*. 21st ed. (Princeton, N.J.: Peterson's Guides, 1990).

35. *Bob Jones University Undergraduate Bulletin, 1991–92*, 48.

36. Donald Hoke, "The Unusual Dr. Bob," *Christian Life*, 23; Kenneth Wilson, "Keeping Up with the Joneses," *Christian Herald*, June 1951, 24.

37. Wilson, "Keeping Up with the Joneses," 23; Tina Crawford, "Dr. Katherine Stenholm," *The Collegian*, 9 November 1989, 6.

38. *Bob Jones University Undergraduate Bulletin, 1991–92*, 246.

39. Turner, "Personal Refinement and the Arts," 269–70.

40. *Bob Jones University Fine Arts Calendar, 1992–93* (Greenville: Bob Jones University Press, 1992).

41. Turner, "Personal Refinement and the Arts," 277.

42. Ibid., 165–66; *Bob Jones University Art Collections*, promotional flyer.

43. Interview with Dr. Dan Brown, Dayton, Tenn., 20 July 1992.

44. Monroe Parker, *Through Sunshine and Shadows* (Murfreesboro, Tenn.: Sword of the Lord Publishers, 1987), 66.

45. John Allison, "Athletics at Bob Jones College," *Bob Jones Magazine*, April 1929, 8.

46. Turner, "Personal Refinement and the Arts," 118; Connell, "Bob Jones University: Doing Battle in the Name of Religion and Freedom," 47.

47. *Bob Jones University Undergraduate Bulletin, 1991–92*, 251–59.

48. Bob Jones Sr., "Why Bob Jones University was Founded," *Christian Life*, June 1950, 28, 30.

49. Theodore Mercer, *An Additional Statement to the Alumni and Board of Trustees of Bob Jones University*, 4 August 1953, Billy Graham Center Archives, Wheaton College, Wheaton, Illinois, 8–10.

50. Bob Jones III, "Bob Jones Sr.'s Educational Philosophy," *Balance*, March 1983, 1–2.

51. Bob Jones Jr., editorial, *Faith for the Family*, September-October 1975, 1.

52. Connell, "Bob Jones University: Doing Battle in the Name of Religion and Freedom," 47.

53. *Bob Jones College Rules of Conduct, 1931*, BJUA.

54. William Bruner, "Is a Christian College Possible?" *Western Recorder*, 22 February 1940; John R. Rice, "Editor Visits Bob Jones College," *Sword of the Lord*, 23 June 1945, 2.

55. Bob Jones Sr., *The Perils of America*, 43; Bob Jones Jr., *Design for Culture*, undated manuscript, BJUA.

56. Lyn Riddle, "Bob Jones: A Mystery to Outsiders," *Greenville Piedmont*, 23 February 1981, 1; *Bob Jones University Handbook*, 1989, 6.

57. "World's Most Unusual," *Time*, 14 June 1950, 74.

58. *What's So Unusual About BJU?*

59. Interview with James Berg, BJU, 26 June 1992.

60. Responses of BJU graduates to author's questionnaire, spring 1991.

61. Interview with Tim Barnard, Raleigh, N.C., 19 June 1992.

62. Author's questionnaire.

63. *Bob Jones University Handbook*, 6.

64. Interview with James Berg, 26 June 1992.

65. Riddle, "Bob Jones: A Mystery to Outsiders," 1.

66. John R. Rice, "Editor Visits Bob Jones College," *Sword of the Lord*, 23 June 1945, 2.

67. Interview with Tim and Bonnie Barnard, Raleigh, N.C., 19 June 1992.

68. Interview with James Berg, 26 June 1992.

69. Interview with Tim and Bonnie Barnard, 19 June 1992.

70. Ibid.

71. Connell, "Bob Jones University: Doing Battle in the Name of Religion and Freedom," 42; William Hart, "Christ on Campus," *Detroit Free Press*, 14 May 1978, 25.

72. Walter G. Fremont, "Evidences of Spiritual Growth and a Good Christian Testimony," author's personal files.

73. *Bob Jones University Handbook*, 5; Bob Jones III, "Bob Jones Sr.'s Educational Philosophy," 2.

74. Riddle, "Bob Jones: A Mystery to Outsiders," 1; and Hart, "Christ on Campus," 25.

75. Author's questionnaire; Theodore Mercer, *To the Board of Trustees of Bob Jones University*, May 1954, Billy Graham Center Archives, 22.

76. Riddle, "Bob Jones: A Mystery to Outsiders," 23; *What's So Unusual About BJU?*; Sherrill, *Gothic Politics in the Deep South*, 233.

77. *What's So Unusual About BJU?*

78. Marsden, *Fundamentalism and American Culture*, 213; "Dormitories Are Overflowing as Bob Jones College Is Opened," *Montgomery Advertiser*, 14 September 1927, BJUA.

Chapter 5: Rapprochement

1. Lyn Riddle, "Bob Jones: A Mystery to Outsiders," *Greenville Piedmont* 23 February 1981, 1; John Shelton Reed, *Whistling Dixie* (Columbia: University of Missouri Press, 1990), 213.

2. Larry King, "Bob Jones University: The Buckle on the Bible Belt," *Harper's*, June 1966, 54.

3. *An Epoch in Education: Facts about the Bob Jones College* (Lynn Haven, Fla.: Bob Jones College, 1927), 30–31.

4. *Total Enrollment for Bob Jones College by States, 1928–1944*, undated typescript, Bob Jones University Archives (hereafter BJUA).

5. *Geographic Distribution of Bob Jones College for 1945–46*, undated typescript, BJUA; and *Geographic Distribution, 1946–47 School Year*, undated typescript, BJUA.

6. *States in Order of the Number of Students, 1949–50*, undated typescript, BJUA.

7. *Geographic Distribution 1960–61*, undated typescript, BJUA.

8. *Distribution for Fall Semester 1988*, undated typescript, Bob Jones University Registrar's Office.

9. For an excellent study of the relationship of southern regional identity to religious fundamentalism, see William Glass, "The Development of Northern Patterns of Fundamentalism in the South, 1900–1950" (Ph.D. diss., Emory University, 1991). According to Glass, fundamentalism emerged in the South during the 1920s and 1930s as southern denominations split over theological liberalism, paralleling the earlier development of fundamentalism in the urban North. Northern evangelists and itinerant preachers helped transplant fundamentalist doctrine into the South through their travels throughout the region and through local Bible conferences and revivals. Many of these same northerners were instrumental in helping create southern fundamentalist schools, including Columbia Bible College, Bryan College, and Dallas Theological Seminary, as a means of anchoring fundamentalism in the South. Again, Bob Jones Uni-

versity appears to be an exception to much of this. While northern evangelists were touring the South in the early twentieth century preaching fundamentalist doctrine, Bob Jones Sr. was traveling not only in the South but throughout much of the nation preaching and creating a fundamentalist constituency that would later flock to his school. Jones, in other words, was not so much interested in anchoring fundamentalism among Southern believers as he was in building a school to which fundamentalists from all over America would come.

10. Bob Jones Jr. to the author, 16 August 1995.

11. Susan D. Rose, *Keeping Them out of the Hands of Satan* (New York: Routledge, Chapman and Hall, 1988), 34–35. For more on the Christian day-school movement, also see Alan Peshkin, *God's Choice: The Total World of a Fundamentalist Christian School* (Chicago: University of Chicago Press, 1986); and Paul F. Parsons, *Inside America's Christian Schools* (Macon, Ga.: Mercer University Press, 1987).

12. Student recruitment information obtained from BJU Admissions Office, June 1992.

13. *Summer Camps 1992*, informational brochure.

14. *New Beginnings and Christian Education Workshops*, informational brochure.

15. *Textbooks for Christian Schools: 1992 Catalog* (Greenville: Bob Jones University Press, 1992), 8, 43, 23, 46, 37, 63–64.

16. Fact sheet obtained from Bob Jones University Press, summer 1992. Also in 1992 BJU launched the Academy of Home Education, a program that enables home-educated high school students to earn a diploma.

17. Bud Bierman to Dr. Bob Jones Jr., 22 June 1992, in possession of the author.

18. Interview with James Berg, BJU, 26 June 1992.

19. Reed, *Whistling Dixie*, 210.

20. Jones Jr., quoted in Christopher Connell, "Bob Jones University: Doing Battle in the Name of Religion and Freedom," *Change*, May-June 1983, 39.

21. Bob Jones Sr., *Is Segregation Scriptural?* (Greenville: Bob Jones University Press, 1960), 9, 22, 13, 25.

22. Ibid., 11, 31; Robert Campbell, ed., *Spectrum of Protestant Belief* (Milwaukee: Bruce, 1968), 68; Robert Sherrill, *Gothic Politics in the Deep South* (New York: Grossman, 1968), 229.

23. "Curtained Control," *Dothan Eagle*, 24 June 1965, 6; Sherrill, *Gothic Politics in the Deep South*, 225.

24. *Green* v. *Connally*, 330 F. Supp. 1150 (1971).

25. Bob Jones Jr. to alumni, 9 December 1970, BJUA.

26. *Bob Jones University* v. *Simon*, 94 S. Ct., 2038 (1974).

27. *Bob Jones University* v. *United States*, 468 F. Supp. (1978).

28. *Bob Jones University* v. *United States*, 639 F. 2d 147, 154 (1980).

29. *Bob Jones University* v. *United States*, 103 S. Ct. 2017 (1983).

30. Bob Jones III, "The Initial Reaction of BJU to the Supreme Court Decision," *Faith for the Family*, July-August 1983, 1a.

31. Wilson, quoted in David Broder and Haynes Johnson, eds., *The Pursuit of the Presidency, 1980* (New York: Berkley Books, 1980), 308–9.

32. Interview with Dr. Daniel Turner, BJU, 18 July 1990.

33. Advertisement, *Voice of the Alumni*, September 1968, 26.

34. Advertisement, *Faith for the Family*, July-August 1973, 24; advertisement, *Faith for the Family*, March-April 1974, 25.

35. Advertisement, *Faith for the Family*, September-October 1975, 27.

36. Interview with Dr. Bob Wood, Greenville, S.C., 20 July 1990.

37. Advertisement, *BJU Review*, summer 1989, 20; advertisement, *BJU Review*, summer 1990, 20; advertisement, *BJU Review*, spring 1991, 20.

38. Bob Jones III, "The President's Corner," ibid., spring 1991, 11.

39. Ibid.

40. Interview with Dr. Bob Jones III, BJU, 26 June 1992.

41. Bob Jones IV, "Is the Religious Right So Wrong?" *Chicago Tribune*, 15 June 1992, 19.

42. See Martin Marty and R. Scott Appleby, eds., *Fundamentalisms Observed* (Chicago: University of Chicago Press, 1991), for a discussion of this phenomenon among conservative religious sects.

43. Interview with Dr. Bob Jones III, 26 June 1992.

44. Bob Jones IV, "Is the Religious Right So Wrong?" 19.

Bibliography

Primary Materials:

ARCHIVES

Bob Jones University, Greenville, South Carolina.
    Bob Jones University Archives (BJUA) (The Bob Jones University Archives have not yet been divided into collections. They contain an assortment of the personal correspondence of Bob Jones Sr., Jr., and III and other administrators and faculty. The archives also contain official university records, college catalogs, multiple copies of brochures and flyers, and newspaper and article clippings.)
    Bob Jones University Chancellor's Office Files
    Bob Jones University Registrar's Office Enrollment Records Fundamentalism File (Located next to the archives, the Fundamentalism File contains clippings and articles pertinent to issues in contemporary fundamentalism.)
Billy Graham Center Archives, Wheaton College, Wheaton, Illinois. Theodore Mercer file.
Donald Comer Collection, Birmingham Public Library, Birmingham, Alabama.
W. S. Cawthon Papers, Florida State Archives, Tallahassee, Florida.

PERSONAL INTERVIEWS

Berg, James, Dean of Students, Bob Jones University. Interview by author, 26 June 1992, Greenville, South Carolina.
Jones, Bob, Jr., Chancellor of Bob Jones University. Interview by author, 14 August 1988, Greenville, South Carolina.
———. Interview by author. 16 March 1989, Greenville, South Carolina.
———. Interview by author. 13 June 1989, Greenville, South Carolina.
Jones, Bob, III. President of Bob Jones University. Interview by author, 26 June 1992, Greenville, South Carolina.
Turner, Daniel, Professor, Bob Jones University. Interview by author, 18 July 1990, Greenville, South Carolina.

Wood, Bob, Executive Vice-President, Bob Jones University. Interview by author, 20 July 1990.

AUTHOR'S CORRESPONDENCE

Barnard, Sharon, to author, 10 May 1991.
Jones, Bob, Jr., to author, 16 November 1989.
Jones, Bob, Jr., to author, 4 May 1990.
Jones, Bob, Jr., to author, 30 April 1990.
Jones, Bob, Jr., to author, 20 August 1990.
Jones, Bob, III, to author, 16 May 1989.
Jones, Bob, III, to author, 21 June 1989.
Sparkman, Rachel, to author, 25 May 1991.

ARTICLES

"A New Evangelist Arises." *Life*, 21 November 1949, 44.
"Americanism Conference." *Little Moby's Post*, January 1952, 1, BJUA.
Ashworth, Robert. "The Fundamentalist Movement among the Baptists." *Journal of Religion* 4 (November 1924): 625–27.
Barnhouse, Donald. "Personal Feelings." *Revelation*, 7 October 1937, 420.
"Big Day at College Point." *Lynn Haven Free Press*, 4 December 1926, BJUA.
"Billy Graham Speaks at BJU in Greenville." *Little Moby's Post*, April 1950, BJUA.
"Bob Jones College Goes into Hands of Receiver." *Lynn Haven Free Press*, 14 January 1933, BJUA.
"Bob Jones Counts More Attendants." *Chattanooga Times*, 20 August 1933, BJUA.
"Bob Jones, Jr. Lashes Out against Jerry Falwell and the Moral Majority." *Moral Majority Report*, 14 July 1980, 1.
"Bob Jones Raps Wicked City Life and Candidacy of Governor Al Smith." *Bellingham Herald*, 1 December 1927, BJUA.
"Bob Jones Ready for Big Classes." *Chattanooga Times*, 25 August 1935, BJUA.
"Bob Jones to Speak in City." *Dothan Weekly Eagle*, 28 January 1927, BJUA.
"Bob Jones University Stages Write-In." *BJU Bulletin*, May 1966, BJUA.
"Bob Jones University Student Leaders Protest Anarchy." *Voice of the Alumni*, June 1970, BJUA.
"Campus Briefs of the Bob Jones College." *Lynn Haven Free Press*, 14 January 1933, BJUA.

Collins, Floyd. "Bob Jones College as I Know It." *Bob Jones Magazine*, November 1928, 20.

"Conservatives." *Time*, 17 May 1943, 46.

"Curtained Control." *Dothan Eagle*, 24 June 1965, BJUA.

Dalrymple, Dolly. "Bob Jones Labors to Give Christian Education to Youth of the Future." *Birmingham News*, 20 June 1928, BJUA.

———. "Flapper Moms and Evolution Draw Fire from Evangelist Jones." *Birmingham News*, 6 May 1926, BJUA.

Dobson, Edward. "Casting Off the Shackles of Prejudice." *Fundamentalist Journal*, May 1985, 12–13.

———. "Does the Bible Really Teach Separation?" *Fundamentalist Journal*, March 1984, 12–13.

"Dormitories Are Overflowing as Bob Jones College Is Opened." *Montgomery Advertiser*, 14 September 1927, BJUA.

"Evangelicals and Fundamentals." *Christianity Today*, 16 September 1957, 20.

Falwell, Jerry. "Falwell Defends against Bob Jones Assault." *Moral Majority Report*, 14 July 1980, 4–5.

"Florida as It Is Today." *Florida State News*, 3 March 1927, 2.

"Graham in Greenville." *Christianity Today*, 1 April 1966, 44.

Graham, Billy. "The Editorial Policy of *The Pilot*." *The Pilot*, January 1948, 113.

———. "The Lost Chord of Evangelism." *Christianity Today*, 4 April 1957, 26–27.

Ginsburg, Michael. "Fundamentalists Exercise Political Muscles." *Greenville Piedmont*, 3 November 1980, 2.

Hearn, Arnold. "Fundamentalist Renascence." *Christian Century*, 30 April 1958, 528–29.

Hedrick, Travis. "Bob Jones—His College." *Chattanooga Times*, 20 August 1933, BJUA.

Hoke, Donald. "The Unusual 'Dr. Bob.'" *Christian Life*, February 1950, 22–25.

"Is Evangelical Theology Changing?" *Christian Life*, March 1956, 16–19.

Jones, Bob, Sr. "A Message from the Bob Jones College." *Bob Jones Magazine*, November 1928, 7.

———. "The Country Idea or the City Idea?" *Bob Jones Magazine*, November 1928, 1.

———. "Dr. Bob Jones Reports on the Recent National Convention of Evangelicals." *Churchill Tabernacle Evangelical*, June 1944, BJUA.

———. "Why Bob Jones University Was Founded." *Christian Life*, June 1950, 28–30.

Jones, Bob, Jr. "The Position of BJU in Regard to the Proposed Billy Graham Crusade in Greenville." Unpublished article, 8 February 1965, BJUA.

———. Editorial. *Faith for the Family*. March-April 1975, 1.

———. Editorial. *Faith for the Family*, July-August 1984, 1.

Jones, Bob, III. "From the University President." *Voice of the Alumni*, October 1976, 6.

———. "From the University President." *Voice of the Alumni*, February 1977, 6.

———. "The Initial Reaction of BJU to the Supreme Court Decision." *Faith for the Family*, July-August 1983, 1a.

———. "The President's Corner." *BJU Review*, Spring 1991, 11.

"Jones Talks to Large Crowd on Vital Subject." *Dothan Weekly Eagle*, 11 February 1927, BJUA.

Jordan, Robert. "New Evangelicalism Restated." *Fundamental Baptist Fellowship News Bulletin*, November-December 1981, 1–3.

Keener, Nelson. "What Did Baptist Fundamentalism '84 Accomplish?" *Fundamentalist Journal*, June 1984, 59.

Laws, Curtis. "Convention Side Lights." *The Watchman-Examiner*, 1 July 1920, 834, BJUA.

Lewis, Clifford. "To the Youth of America." *Bob Jones Magazine*, April 1929, 14, BJUA.

Massey, Homer. "Psuedo-Fundamentalism '84." *Fundamental Baptist Fellowship News Bulletin*, May-June 1984, 3.

McIntire, Carl. "The NAE and Separation." *Christian Beacon*, 7 October 1948, 4, BJUA.

"Mid-Century World Outlook Conference Held at BJU." *Little Moby's Post*, February 1951, BJUA.

Morrison, Charles. "The Liberalism of Neo-Orthodoxy." *Christian Century*, 21 June 1950, 763.

"News of the Christian World." *Christian Century*, 19 May 1943, 614.

Ockenga, Harold. "The New Evangelicalism." *The Park Street Spire*, February 1958, 2–7.

Ogden, Warner. "Evangelist Bob Jones Operates a College Where Fundamentalism Is Insisted Upon." *Knoxville News Sentinel*, 11 February 1934, BJUA.

Osdel, Oliver Van. "Good Soldiers of Jesus Christ." *Baptist Bulletin*, April 1933, 1, BJUA.

"Panama City Makes Good Progress during Year." *Dothan Weekly Eagle*, 9 July 1926, BJUA.

"Preparing for T.V." *Christian Life*, August 1949, 35.

"Readers Say." *United Evangelical Action*, 1 August 1947, 2.

"Reverend Bob Jones Has National Reputation." *Macon News*, 11 May 1911, BJUA.

Rice, John R. "Bob Jones College to become Great University." *Sword of the Lord*, 8 June 1945, 2.

———. "Editor Visits Bob Jones College." *Sword of the Lord*, 8 June 1945, 3.

———. "Bob Jones College Training Soulwinners." *Sword of the Lord*, 15 April 1946, 2.

———. "Dr. J. Oliver Buswell's Charges Against BJU Answered." *Sword of the Lord*, 22 June 1948, 1.

———. "Our Beloved Intellectuals Again." *Sword of the Lord*, 18 May 1956, 12.

———. "They Did Not Hold to Secondary Separation." *Sword of the Lord*, 1 February 1974, 1.

———. "Why Divide Good Fundamentalists?" *Sword of the Lord*, 17 December 1976, 1.

———. "Here is Historic Fundamentalism." *Sword of the Lord*, 22 September 1978, 7.

Riddle, Lyn. "Bob Jones: A Mystery to Outsiders." *Greenville Piedmont*, 23 February 1981, 1.

Rigdon, Rick. "The Christian in Politics." *Voice of the Alumni*, April 1979, 11.

Rumminger, Elmer. "Christians in Politics." *Voice of the Alumni*, April 1979, 6.

Salter, Guenter. "The Value of a Christian Liberal Arts Education." *Balance*, January 1983, 1–2.

———. "The Inconsistencies of Humanism." *Balance*, October 1984, 1–2.

"Sickle for the Harvest." *Time*, 14 November 1949, 63.

Simbro, William. "Battlin' Bob Jones Wages Holy War." *Des Moines Tribune*, 27 March 1982, 10.

Small, Sam. "The Dream of Bob Jones." *Atlanta Constitution*, undated clipping, BJUA.

"Spiritual Revival Near, Jones Says." *Montgomery Advertiser*, 2 July 1939, BJUA.

"Testimonies from Two Students." *Bob Jones Magazine*, April 1930, 30.

"The Ministerial Association and Volunteer Band." *Bob Jones Magazine*, April 1929, 7.

Walker, Robert. "He Built a College in One Generation." *Sunday*, November 1945, 14.

Weniger, Archer. "The Position of Dr. Graham before He Embraced Ecumenical Evangelism." Tract, Foothill Boulevard Baptist Church, San Francisco, Calif., 1958.

————. "Separation Systematized." *Faith for the Family*, November-December 1976, 8–9.

"Why No Revival?" *Christian Century*, 18 September 1935, 101.

Wilson, Kenneth. "Keeping Up with the Joneses." *Christian Herald*, June 1951, 24–26.

Wright, J. Elwin. "A Few Observations." *New England Fellowship Monthly*, April 1937, 8.

"You Will Not Fit In." *Child Evangelism*, November 1943, 10.

BOOKS AND PAMPHLETS

An Epoch in Education: Facts About the Bob Jones College. Lynn Haven, Fla: Bob Jones College, 1927.

Barth, Karl. *The Epistle to the Romans*. Translated by Edwyn C. Hoskins. New York: Oxford University Press, 1963.

Beale, David. *In Pursuit of Purity*. Greenville: Bob Jones University Press, 1986.

Bob Jones College Catalog, 1933–34. Cleveland, Tenn: Bob Jones College, 1933.

Bob Jones College Catalog, 1943–44. Cleveland, Tenn: Bob Jones College, 1943.

Bob Jones College Catalog, 1945–46. Cleveland, Tenn: Bob Jones College, 1945.

Bob Jones University Bulletin, 1988–89. Greenville: Bob Jones University Press, 1988.

Bob Jones University Bulletin, 1991–92. Greenville: Bob Jones University Press, 1991.

Bob Jones University Faculty. *Biblical Separation*. Greenville: Bob Jones University Press, 1980.

————. *The Christian Philosophy of Education*. Greenville: Bob Jones University Press, 1978.

————. *The Christian Teaching of History*. Greenville: Bob Jones University Press, 1978.

Bob Jones University v. *Simon*, 94 S. Ct. 2038 (1974).

Bob Jones University v. *United States*, 468 F. Supp. (1978).

Bob Jones University v. *United States*, 639 F. Supp. (1980).

Bob Jones University v. *United States*, 103 S. Ct. (1983).

Carlson, Leland, ed. *The Writings of Henry Barrowe, 1587–1590*. London: George Allen and Unwin, 1962.

Dollar, George. *A History of Fundamentalism in America*. Greenville: Bob Jones University Press, 1973.

Falwell, Jerry, ed., with Ed Dobson and Ed Hinson. *The Fundamentalist Phenomenon*. Garden City, N.Y.: Doubleday, 1981.

Gaebelein, Arno C., ed. *Christ and Glory: Addresses Delivered at the New York Prophetic Conference*. New York: Our Hope Publication Office, 1918.

Henry, Carl F. H. *The Uneasy Conscience of Modern Fundamentalism*. Grand Rapids: Eerdmans, 1947.

Jones, Bob, Sr. *Two Sermons to Men*. Chicago: Glad Tidings Publishing, 1923.

———. *The Perils of America*. Chicago: Chicago Gospel Tabernacle, 1934.

———. *Three College Shipwrecks*. Greenville: Bob Jones University Press, 1948.

———. *Is Segregation Scriptural?* Greenville: Bob Jones University Press, 1960.

———. *Chapel Sayings of Dr. Bob Jones*. Greenville: Bob Jones University Press, 1980.

Jones, Bob, Jr. *Scriptural Separation: First and Second Degree*. Greenville: Bob Jones University Press, 1971.

———. *Facts John R. Rice Will Not Face*. Greenville: Bob Jones University Press, 1977.

———. *Cornbread and Caviar*. Greenville: Bob Jones University Press, 1985.

Jones, Bob, III. *The Moral Majority*. Greenville: Bob Jones University Press, 1980.

———. *What Is a Fundamentalist?* Greenville: Bob Jones University Press, 1985.

———. *Taking Higher Ground*. Greenville: Bob Jones University Press, 1991.

Ketcham, Robert. *Facts for Baptists to Face*. Waterloo, Ia.: Walnut Street Baptist Church, 1936.

———. *The Answer*. Chicago: Regular Baptist Press, 1949.

McIntire, Carl. *Twentieth-Century Reformation*. Collingswood, N.J.: Christian Beacon Press, 1944.

Mercer, Theodore. *A Statement Concerning My Dismissal from Bob Jones University*. Theodore Mercer: 1953. Billy Graham Center Archives, Wheaton College, Wheaton, Illinois.

――. *An Additional Statement to the Alumni and Board of Trustees*. Theodore Mercer: 4 August 1953. Billy Graham Center Archives, Wheaton College, Wheaton, Illinois.

――. *To the Board of Trustees of Bob Jones University*. Theodore Mercer: May 1954. Billy Graham Center Archives, Wheaton College, Wheaton, Illinois.

Morrison, Henry C. *Crossing the Deadline or the Recrucifixion of the Lord Jesus Christ*. Louisville, Ky.: Pentecostal Publishing Company, 1924.

Murch, James. *Cooperation without Compromise*. Grand Rapids: Eerdmans, 1956.

Niebuhr, Reinhold. *Beyond Tragedy*. New York: Scribner's, 1937.

Poteat, William Louis. *Can a Man Be a Christian Today?* Chapel Hill: University of North Carolina Press, 1926.

Revised and Amended By-Laws of Bob Jones University. Greenville: Bob Jones University Press, 1952.

Rice, John R. *Come Out or Stay In?* Nashville, Tenn.: Thomas Nelson, 1974.

――, and Robert J. Wells, eds. *How To Have a Great Revival*. Murfreesboro, Tenn.: Sword of the Lord Publishers, 1956.

Van Impe, Jack. *Heart Disease in Christ's Body*. Royal Oak, Mich.: Jack Van Impe Ministries, 1984.

Wright, J. Elwin. *Evangelical Action: An Historical Statement*. Boston: United Action Press, 1942.

Wright, Melton. *Fortress of Faith: The Story of Bob Jones University*. Greenville: Bob Jones University Press, 1984.

Secondary Sources

BOOKS AND DISSERTATIONS

Ahlstrom, Sydney. *A Religious History of the American People*. New Haven: Yale University Press, 1972.

American Universities and Colleges. 13th ed. New York: Walter de Gruyter, 1987.

Ammerman, Nancy. *Bible Believers: Fundamentalists in the Modern Age*. New Brunswick: Rutgers University Press, 1987.

Averill, Lloyd. *American Theology in the Liberal Tradition*. Philadelphia: Westminster Press, 1967.

———. *Religious Right, Religious Wrong*. New York: Pilgrim's Press, 1989.

Bailey, Kenneth. *Southern White Protestantism in the Twentieth Century*. New York: Harper and Row, 1964.

Bainton, Roland. *Christendom: A Short History of Christianity*. 2 vols. New York: Harper and Row, 1966.

Boles, John. *The Great Revival, 1787–1805: The Origins of the Southern Evangelical Mind*. Lexington: University of Kentucky Press, 1972.

Boone, Kathleen. *The Bible Tells Them So*. Albany: State University of New York Press, 1989.

Bozeman, Theodore. *Protestants in an Age of Science: The Baconian Ideal and Antebellum American Religious Thought*. Chapel Hill: University of North Carolina Press, 1977.

Bucke, Emory S., ed., *The History of American Methodism*. 3 vols. New York: Abingdon, 1964.

Bushman, Richard L., ed. *The Great Awakening: Documents on the Revival of Religion, 1740–1745*. New York: Institute of Early American History and Culture, 1970.

Cameron, Richard, ed. *The Rise of Methodism: A Source Book*. New York: Philosophical Library, 1954.

Campbell, Robert, ed. *Spectrum of Protestant Belief*. Milwaukee: Bruce, 1968.

Carpenter, Joel, and Kenneth Shipps. *Making Higher Education Christian: The History and Mission of Evangelical Colleges in America*. Grand Rapids: Eerdmans, 1987.

Carter, Paul. *The Decline and Revival of the Social Gospel*. Ithaca: Cornell University Press, 1954.

———. *The Twenties in America*. New York: Corwell, 1975.

Cauthen, Kenneth. *The Impact of American Religious Liberalism*. New York: Harper and Row, 1962.

Chalmers, David. *Hooded Americanism: The History of the Ku Klux Klan*. New York: F. Watts, 1981.

Cole, Stewart. *The History of Fundamentalism*. Westport, Conn.: Greenwood, 1931.

Curtis, Richard. *They Called Him Mister Moody*. Grand Rapids: Eerdmans, 1962.

D'Souza, Dinesh. *Falwell: Before the Millennium*. Chicago: Regnery Gateway, 1984.

Dowley, Tim, ed. *Eerdmans Handbook to the History of Christianity*. Grand Rapids: Eerdmans, 1977.

———, John H. Y. Briggs, and Robert Linder, eds. *The History of Christianity*. Herts, Eng.: Lion, 1977.

Evans, W. Glyn. *Profiles of Revival Leaders*. Nashville: Broadman, 1976.

Findlay, James, *Dwight L. Moody: American Evangelist, 1837–1899*. Chicago: University of Chicago Press, 1969.

Flynt, Wayne. *Poor But Proud: Alabama's Poor Whites*. Tuscaloosa: University of Alabama Press, 1989.

Frady, Marshall. *Billy Graham: A Parable in American Righteousness*. Boston: Little, Brown 1979.

Furniss, Norman. *The Fundamentalist Controversy: 1918–1931*. New Haven: Yale University Press, 1954.

Gasper, Louis. *The Fundamentalist Movement*. Paris: Mouton, 1963.

Gatewood, Willard. *Preachers, Pedagogues and Politicians: The Evolution Controversy in North Carolina*. Chapel Hill: University of North Carolina Press, 1966.

———, ed. *Controversy in the Twenties*. Nashville: Vanderbilt University Press, 1969.

Glass, William. "The Development of Northern Patterns of Fundamentalism in the South, 1900–1950." Ph.D. diss., Emory University, 1991.

Godbold, Albea. *The Church College of the Old South*. Durham: Duke University Press, 1944.

Goen, Clarence. *Revivalism and Separatism in New England*. New Haven: Yale University Press, 1962.

Goodwyn, Lawrence. *Democratic Promise: The Populist Movement in America*. New York: Oxford University Press, 1976.

Hackney, Sheldon. *Populism to Progressivism in Alabama*. Princeton: Princeton University Press, 1969.

Handlin, Oscar. *Al Smith and His America*. Boston: Little, Brown, 1955.

Handy, Robert. *A History of the Churches in the United States and Canada*. New York: Oxford University Press, 1977.

Harlon, David. *The Clergy and the Great Awakening in New England*. Ann Arbor: University of Michigan Research Press, 1980.

Hatch, Nathan, and George Marsden, eds. *Eerdmans Handbook to Christianity in America*. Grand Rapids: Eerdmans, 1983.

Hatch, Nathan, and Mark Noll, eds. *The Bible in America*. New York: Oxford University Press, 1982.

Hatch, Nathan, Mark Noll, and John Woodbridge. *The Gospel in America*. Grand Rapids: Zondervan, 1979.

Higham, John. *Strangers in the Land*. New Brunswick: Rutgers University Press, 1988.

Hill, Samuel S. *Southern Churches in Crisis*. New York: Holt, Rinehart and Winston, 1967.

Hofstadter, Richard. *Anti-Intellectualism in America*. New York: Alfred A. Knopf, 1964.

Horndern, William. *A Layman's Guide to Protestant Theology*. New York: Macmillan, 1955.

Hudson, Winthrop. *American Protestantism*. Chicago: University of Chicago Press, 1961.

———. *Religion in America*. New York: Scribner's 1973.

Hughes, Richard. T., ed. *The American Quest for the Primitive Church*. Urbana: University of Illinois Press, 1988.

———, and C. Leonard Allen. *Illusions of Innocence*. Chicago: University of Chicago Press, 1988.

Hull, Merle R. *What a Fellowship! The First Fifty Years of the GARBC*. Schaumberg: Regular Baptist Press, 1981.

Hunter, James Davidson. *American Evangelicalism: Conservative Religion and the Quandry of Modernity*. New Brunswick: Rutgers University Press, 1983.

———. *Evangelicalism: The Coming Generation*. Chicago: University of Chicago Press, 1987.

Johnson, R. K. *Miracle from the Beginning*. Greenville: Bob Jones University Press, 1971.

———. *Builder of Bridges*. Greenville: Bob Jones University Press, 1982.

Kennedy, Gail, ed., *Evolution and Religion*. Boston: Heath, 1957.

Lake, Kirsopp. *The Religion of Yesterday and Tomorrow*. Boston: Houghton-Mifflin, 1926.

Lefferts, Loetscher, *A Brief History of the Presbyterians*. Philadelphia: Westminster, 1978.

Lichtman, Allan J. *Prejudice and the Old Politics: The Presidential Election of 1928*. Chapel Hill: University of North Carolina Press, 1979.

Linder, Suzanne. *Prophet of Progress*. Chapel Hill: University of North Carolina Press, 1966.

Marsden, George. *Fundamentalism and American Culture: The Shaping of Twentieth-Century Evangelicalism, 1870–1925*. New York: Oxford University Press, 1980.

———. *Reforming Fundamentalism: Fuller Seminary and the New Evangelicalism*. Grand Rapids: Eerdmans, 1987.

Marty, Martin. *Righteous Empire: The Protestant Experience in America*. New York: Dial, 1970.

——. *A Nation of Behavers*. Chicago: University of Chicago Press, 1976.

——. *Pilgrims in Their Own Land*. New York: Penguin, 1984.

——. *Modern American Religion*. Chicago: University of Chicago Press, 1986.

——, and R. Scott Appleby, eds. *Fundamentalisms Observed*. Chicago: University of Chicago Press, 1991.

Mathews, Donald. *Religion in the Old South*. Chicago: University of Chicago Press, 1977.

Mathews, Shailer. *The Faith of Modernism*. New York: Macmillan, 1924.

McLoughlin, William. *Billy Sunday Was His Real Name*. Chicago: University of Chicago Press, 1955.

——. *Modern Revivalism: Charles Grandison Finney to Billy Graham*. New York: Ronald Press, 1959.

——. *Revivals, Awakenings, and Reforms*. Chicago: University of Chicago Press, 1978.

——, ed. *The American Evangelicals, 1800–1900: An Anthology*. New York: Harper and Row, 1968.

Mencken, H. L. *Prejudices: Fifth Series*. London: Jonathan Cape, 1926.

Mims, Edwin. *Chancellor Kirkland of Vanderbilt*. Nashville: Vanderbilt University Press, 1940.

——. *The Advancing South*. Garden City, N.Y.: Doubleday, 1926.

Moberg, David. *The Great Reversal: Evangelicalism versus Social Concern*. Philadelphia: Lippincott, 1972.

Moore, James R. *The Post-Darwinian Controversies*. Cambridge: Cambridge University Press, 1979.

Morgan, Edmund. *Roger Williams: The Church and the State*. New York: Harcourt, Brace, 1967.

Morris, James. *The Preachers*. New York: St. Martin's, 1973.

Mowry, George. *The Urban Nation*. New York: Hill and Wang, 1965.

Murch, James. *Cooperation without Compromise: A History of the National Association of Evangelicals*. Grand Rapids: Eerdmans, 1956.

Murdoch, J. Murray. *Portrait of Obedience*. Schaumberg, Ill.: Regular Baptist Press, 1979.

Noll, Mark. *Between Faith and Criticism*. New York: Harper and Row, 1986.

Odell, Calvin. *The GARBC and Its Attendant Movement*. Salem, Ore.: Western Baptist Bible Press, 1975.

Parsons, Paul F. *Inside America's Christian Schools*. Macon, Ga.: Mercer University Press, 1987.

Patterson, Bob. *Reinhold Niebuhr*. Waco, Tex.: Word Books, 1977.

Perrett, Geoffrey. *America in the 1920s*. New York: Simon and Schuster, 1982.

Peshkin, Alan. *God's Choice: The Total World of a Fundamentalist Christian School*. Chicago: University of Chicago Press, 1986.

Peterson's Guide to Four-Year Colleges, 1990–1991, 21st ed. Princeton, N.J.: Peterson's Guides, 1990.

Pierard, Richard. *The Unequal Yoke*. Philadelphia: Lippincott, 1970.

Pollock, John. *Crusade: Twenty Years with Billy Graham*. Minneapolis: World Wide Publications, 1969.

Porter, Butler. "Billy Graham and the End of Evangelical Unity." Ph.D. diss., University of Florida, 1976.

Ramm, Bernard. *The Evangelical Heritage*. Waco, Tex.: Word Books, 1973.

————. *A Theology for the Social Gospel*. New York: Macmillan, 1922.

Rauschenbusch, Walter. *Christianity and the Social Crisis*. New York: Macmillan, 1910.

Reed, John Shelton. *Whistling Dixie*. Columbia: University of Missouri Press, 1990.

Revised Standard Version of the Bible. New York: New American Library, 1974.

Riley, Marie A. *The Dynamic of a Dream: The Life Story of Dr. William B. Riley*. Grand Rapids: Eerdmans, 1938.

Ringenberg, William. *The Christian College: A History of Protestant Higher Education in America*. Grand Rapids: Eerdmans, 1984.

Roberts, Jon. *Darwinism and the Divine in America*. Madison: University of Wisconsin Press, 1988.

Rose, Susan D. *Keeping Them Out of the Hands of Satan*. New York: Routledge, Chapman and Hall, 1988.

Roy, Ralph. *Apostles of Discord*. Boston: Beacon Press, 1953.

Russell, C. Allyn. *Voices of American Fundmentalism*. Philadelphia: Westminster, 1976.

Rutman, Darrett, ed. *The Great Awakening: Event and Exegesis*. New York: Wiley, 1970.

Sandeen, Ernest. *The Roots of Fundamentalism: British and American Millenarianism, 1800–1930*. Chicago: University of Chicago Press, 1970.

Schleiermacher, Friedrich. *On Religion: Speeches Addressed to Its Cultured Despisers*. Translated by Terence N. Tice. Richmond: John Knox Press, 1969.

Sellars, James B. *The Prohibition Movement in Alabama: 1702 to 1943*. Chapel Hill: University of North Carolina Press, 1943.

Sherrill, Robert. *Gothic Politics in the Deep South*. New York: Grossman, 1968.

Sizer, Suzanne. *Revival Waves and Home Fires: The Rhetoric of Nineteenth-Century Gospel Hymns*. Chicago: University of Chicago Press, 1976.

Smith, Timothy. *Revivalism and Social Reform in Mid-Nineteenth-Century America*. New York: Abingdon, 1957.

———. *Revivalism and Social Reform: American Protestantism on the Eve of the Civil War*. New York: Harper and Row, 1965.

Spurgin, Hugh. *Roger Williams and Puritan Radicalism in the English Separatist Tradition*. Lewiston, Me.: Edwin Mellon Press, 1989.

Stonehouse, Ned B. *J. Gresham Machen: A Biographical Memoir*. Grand Rapids: Eerdmans, 1954.

Stowell, Joseph. *Background and History of the General Association of Regular Baptist Churches*. Haywood,Calif.: J. F. May Press, 1949.

Tebeau, Charles W. *A History of Florida*. Coral Gables: University of Miami Press, 1971.

Tindall, George. *The Emergence of the New South 1913–1945*. Baton Rouge: Louisiana State University, 1967.

Turner, Daniel. "Personal Refinement and the Arts: The Cultural Philosophy of Dr. Bob Jones, Sr. and Dr. Bob Jones, Jr." Ed.D. diss., University of Illinois, 1989.

Vesey, Laurence R. *The Emergence of the American University*. Chicago: University of Chicago Press, 1970.

Wenger, John C., ed. *Glimpses of Mennonite History and Doctrine*. Scottsdale, Pa.: Herald Press, 1940.

Wilson, Charles Reagan. *Baptized in Blood: The Religion of the Lost Cause*. Athens: University of Georgia Press, 1983.

Woodward, C. Vann. *The Origins of the New South*. Baton Rouge: Louisiana State University Press, 1966.

Wyatt-Brown, Bertram. *Southern Honor: Ethics and Behavior in the Old South*. New York: Oxford University Press, 1982.

ARTICLES

Brereton, Virginia. "Examining the Christian College." *History of Education Quarterly* 26 (Summer 1986): 322–26.

Carpenter, Joel. "Fundamentalist Institutions and the Rise of Evangelical Protestantism." *Church History* 49 (March 1980): 62–75.

——. "From Fundamentalism to the New Evangelical Coalition." In *Evangelicalism and Modern America*, edited by George Marsden. Grand Rapids: Eerdmans, 1984.

Carter, Paul. "The Fundamentalist Defense of the Faith." In *Change and Continuity in Twentieth-Century America*, edited by John Braeman. Columbus: Ohio State University Press, 1968.

Coleman, William. "Billy Sunday: A Style Meant for His Time and Place." *Christianity Today*, 17 December 1976, 15.

Connell, Christopher. "Bob Jones University: Doing Battle in the Name of Religion and Freedom." *Change*, May-June 1983, 41.

Harvey, Charlotte. "A World Apart." *Emory Magazine*, June 1987, 18.

Hill, Samuel S. "Fundamentalism and the South." *Perspectives in Religious Studies* 13 (Winter 1986): 47–65.

Hofstadter, Richard. "The Revolution in Higher Education." In *Paths of American Thought*, edited by Arthur M. Schlesinger Jr. Boston: Houghton Mifflin, 1963.

King, Larry. "Bob Jones University: The Buckle on the Bible Belt." *Harper's*, June 1966.

Marsden, George. "Defining Fundamentalism." *Christian Scholar's Review* (Winter 1971): 141–51.

——. "The Great Reversal." *Journal of Christian Reconstruction* 8 (Summer 1981): 182–87.

Marty, Martin. "Fundamentalism Reborn." *Saturday Review*, May 1980, 37–38.

——. "Fundamentalism as a Social Phenomenon." *Review and Expositor* (Winter 1982): 23–30.

——. "Modern Fundamentalism." *America*, 27 September 1986, 133–34.

Moore, Leroy. "Another Look at Fundamentalism: A Response to Ernest R. Sandeen." *Church History* 37 (June 1968): 195–202.

Nelson, Raymond J. "Fundamentalism at Harvard: The Case of Edward J. Carnell." *Quarterly Review* 2 (Summer 1982): 79–98.

Ockenga, Harold. "From Fundamentalism, through New Evangelicalism, to Evangelicalism." In *Evangelical Roots*, edited by Kenneth Kantzer. Nashville: Thomas Nelson, 1978.

O'Hara, Jane. "Oasis of Salvation in a World of Sin." *MacLeans*, 11 October 1982, 10.

Poteat, Edwin. "Religion in the South." In *Culture in the South*, edited by W. T. Couch. Chapel Hill: University of North Carolina Press, 1935.

Pyles, Ernest. "Bruised, Bloody and Broken: Fundamentalism's Internecine Controversy in the 1960s." *Fides Et Historia* 18 (October 1986): 45–55.

Rensi, Ray C. "The Gospel According to Sam Jones." *Georgia Historical Quarterly* 60 (Fall 1976): 255–64.

Sandeen, Ernest R. "Towards A Historical Interpretation of the Origins of Fundamentalism." *Church History* 36 (March 1967): 79–87.

———. "Defining Fundamentalism: A Reply to Professor Marsden." *Christian Scholar's Review* (Spring 1971): 227–33.

Schmidt, George. "Colleges in Ferment." *American Historical Review* 59 (October 1953): 15–25.

Vann, Betty. "Dr. Bob Jones—A Bold Preacher." *Dothan Progress*, 29 April 1987, BJUA.

Womack, Marlene. "Bob Jones Made Dream a Reality." *Panama City News-Herald*, 26 July 1987, 6e.

———. "Bob Jones Rode Crest of Area Boom." *The Panama City News-Herald*, 2 August 1987, 6f.

———. "Depression Years Threw Bob Jones College into Ruin." *The Panama City News-Herald*, 9 August 1987, 4e.

Index

American Council of Christian Churches (ACCC): founding of, 52, 55; relationship with the NAE, 59–62, 64–65

Baptist Fundamentalism, 84, 113
Bob Jones University: academic growth of, 42–43, 47–48, 130–33; and academic inbreeding, 137; advertising of, 9, 84–85, 159–60; alumni of, 6, 132, 150–52; Art Gallery, 135; challenging fundamentalist stereotypes, 44–45, 134–35, 162–63; and Christian Day School movement, 130, 152–53; court case of (1983), 156–58; educational philosophy of, 3, 40, 119–20, 124–31, 140; faculty of, 46, 74, 75, 76, 137, 138; fine arts and drama at, 133–35; founding of, 36–40; intercollegiate sports at, 136; lack of accreditation at, 6, 42–43, 76, 118, 137–40; marketing and national networking of, 151–54; move to Cleveland, Tennessee, 46–48, 193; move to Greenville, South Carolina (1947), 131; political involvement of, 105–7; race relations at, 155–58; separatist critique of other Christian colleges by, 102–3; as a "Southern School," 5, 148–51, 155; and student conduct rules, 41, 140–47; University Press of, 153–54; Unusual Films, 133–34. *See also* Jones, Bob, Sr.; Jones, Bob, Jr.; Jones, Bob, III
Bob Jones University v. Simon (1974), 157
Bob Jones University v. U.S. (1983), 158

Cedarville College (Ohio): BJU's critique of, 103; criticized for accreditation, 139; faculty connection with Bob Jones University, 111

Denominational Colleges (19th century), 121–24

Falwell, Jerry, III: critique of the Bob Joneses, 110–11; as founder of Liberty Baptist University, 107–8; as founder of the Moral Majority, 103–4; labeled "most dangerous man in America" by Bob Jones Jr., 108; as leader of moderate fundamentalism, 111–13; role in Baptist Fundamentalism (1984), 113; role in 1980 election, 104–5; separatist debate with the Joneses, 108–16. *See also* Fundamentalism; Jones, Bob, Jr.